MW01256021

BURDENED
CHILDREN

Theory, Research, and
Treatment of Parentification

Editor

NANCY D. CHASE

SAGE Publications
International Educational and Professional Publisher
Thousand Oaks   London   New Delhi

Copyright © 1999 by Sage Publications, Inc.

All rights reserved. No part of this book may be reproduced or utilized in any form or by any means, electronic or mechanical, including photocopying, recording, or by any information storage and retrieval system, without permission in writing from the publisher.

For information:

SAGE Publications, Inc.
2455 Teller Road
Thousand Oaks, California 91320
E-mail: order@sagepub.com

SAGE Publications Ltd.
6 Bonhill Street
London EC2A 4PU
United Kingdom

SAGE Publications India Pvt. Ltd.
M-32 Market
Greater Kailash I
New Delhi 110 048 India

Printed in the United States of America

Library of Congress Cataloging-in-Publication Data

Main entry under title:
    Burdened children: Theory, research and treatment of parentification /
edited by Nancy D. Chase.
        p. cm.
    Includes bibliographical references and index.
    ISBN 0-7619-0763-7 (cloth: alk. paper)
    ISBN 0-7619-0764-5 (pbk.: alk. paper)
    1. Parental influences.   2. Stress in children.   3. Problem families.
4. Helping behavior in children.   5. Role playing in children.   I. Title.
    RJ507 .P35 C47   1999
    155.4—dc21   99-6009

This book is printed on acid-free paper.

99 00 01 02 03 04 05 7 6 5 4 3 2 1

Acquisition Editor:	Jim Nageotte
Editorial Assistant:	Heidi Van Middlesworth
Production Editor:	Denise Santoyo
Editorial Assistant:	Patricia Zeman
Typesetter.	Lynn Miyata
Cover Designer:	Ravi Balasuriya
Indexer:	Teri Greenberg

For Dixie

This book is dedicated to the intricate, constant,
and profoundly healing nature of friendship.

Contents

Part II: Clinical and Contextual Perspectives 115

Preface

On the cover of an issue of *Time* magazine (April, 1996) is the picture of a seven-year-old girl, Jessica, who died in the crash of her small plane while attempting to set a record as the youngest pilot to fly across the United States. The caption below the young girl's photograph raises questions about who should claim responsibility for her death and for the expectations under which she lived. Implicated in the feature article are her parents, but not because they neglected or abused Jessica in any traditional sense. On the contrary, these parents encouraged Jessica to pursue her dreams and fear nothing. Yet, questions remain about whose dream it really was to fly cross-country. Was this a seven-year-old's dream? Or projections of parental ambition run wild? Is it true, as Jessica's mother claims, that children are fearless unless taught to be afraid? Or is it possible that children silence their fears and push on bravely when no adult is near to comfort them in their childhood anxiety and doubt? The story of Jessica and her parents drew national attention, however superficially and briefly, to fundamental questions about the lengths to which parents will go to promote their kids and the extent to which children comply in meeting needs and wishes of their parents. Jessica's story, no doubt, is extreme. It illustrates, however, a phenomenon that often remains invisible unless manifested in dire and tragic consequences: a parent's needs and narcissism overriding a child's well-being. As a society, we are shocked and disdainful of the gross and overt expressions of parental narcissism and abuse of power. Meanwhile, subtler aspects of such phenomena as they occur in day-to-day interactions and in assumptions transmitted across generations are less understood, even though terms such as *parental child, parentification, hero-child, overachiever, underachiever, hurried child,* and the more popularly used phrase *adult-child* have appeared in academic, professional scholarship and lay literature for many years.

Parentified children, in effect, are parents to their parents, and fulfill this role at the expense of their own developmentally appropriate needs and pursuits. With uncanny sensibilities, these children are attuned to their parents' moods, wishes, vulnerabilities, and nuances. I've heard many children and adolescents say with great yearning and insight, "I just want my mom to be happy," "I worry about my dad—he doesn't take care of himself," "My mom gets a kind of look and I know she's really depressed, she's checking out," and, in the words of one reflective eight-year-old, "I don't think my mom can take it, she's not strong enough—it's embarrassing." Children are aware of their parents' stresses about money, about love, and about health, and these children bear a passionate hope, to the point of being overwhelmed, that they can be of use: saviors, of sorts. Yet, parents often remain blind to their child's efforts. The grief-struck and overworked father of a young adolescent in a family that had suffered multiple losses and changes in a short period of time complained that his son was too stoic, withdrawn, and at times angry. "What's wrong with this boy?," he asked. The boy loved his mother (who had divorced the father, leaving the son in his custody several months prior). "I don't know how we're gonna live. . . . I don't know anything . . .", he said, then began to cry. The father seemed completely baffled when I suggested that perhaps the son was "acting strong to help" while the father fell apart. "Well," said the father, "if he [the son] really wants to reassure me he should. . . ." At this point, I suggested that it was also the father's place to reassure his son, to which the father responded, "Hmmm. . . . I don't know, I'll think about that."

Parentification is more complex than simply the logistical "filling in" in the absence of the parent. When the child is parentified in covert or emotional ways, the long-term effects are considered to be more insidious and of greater threat to a child's well-being and development. A parentified child may present in clinical settings as infantilized, rebellious, or cooperative and highly achieving. The mother of a 10-year-old who behaved very "babyishly" or very oppositionally admitted that her daughter's misbehavior served to distract her (the mother) from her own depression. "When Molly throws a tantrum, I get out of bed and get more organized," the mother stated. A parentified child may also appear as overindulged, overparented, and highly achieving, especially when the child is expected to carry and live out the unfulfilled accomplishments and dreams of the parent, but with little acknowledgment of the child's own inclinations, needs, or wishes. A competent child can be a great comfort to an anxious or overwhelmed parent. According to one father, "After the divorce from her mother I was so devastated I wanted to die. My little girl was the only reason I lived . . . she was always so bright, talkative, and happy. Now that she's 14 she's changed and doesn't want to do things with me. What's wrong with her? Are her peers corrupting her?"

A comprehensive study of parentification in the family must explore the complexity and multifaceted nature of these phenomena as well as immediate and long-term developmental consequences. This volume is a compilation of theoretical and clinical topics, and it represents the wide variety of voice and perspective. Chapters in this book are grouped according to their emphasis into two sections: theory and research, and clinical and broader contextual perspectives. Topics include research related to parentification and gender, work addiction, families with a disabled or chronically ill child, and assessment for clinical or research purposes. Chapters having a more clinical focus address varied interventions and theoretical orientations in working with adults who have a history of childhood parentification, and with children and their parents suffering the immediate stress of such dynamics. Finally, parentification is examined in the context of broader cultural and ethnic considerations, and from a Jungian orientation. The last chapter presents an archetypal understanding of these phenomena with clinical implications.

Each chapter stands on its own as an examination of particular aspects of the parentified child's experience. Although each chapter emphasizes different aspects, orientations, and clinical presentations, the cohesiveness of the book will be ensured if the reader reflects on the following themes or assumptions in addressing this topic, and more generally, in describing effective clinical practice:

1. Parentification is a construct describing behaviors that occur in the context of ever-widening systems of influence and meaning involving individual, interpersonal, family, institutional, cultural, and historical issues.

2. Parentification describes behaviors transmitted across generations and involving assumptions of what children and parents are obliged to give and receive from each other.

3. Parentification disrupts appropriate developmental stages involving early attachment, and later stages of individuation-separation.

4. Parentification functions in a context of cultural and societal determinants (related to assumption 1).

5. There are healthy, as well as unhealthy, dimensions to parentification that require clarification for effective clinical intervention.

6. Parentification has been investigated and documented empirically and qualitatively. This research must be disseminated to inform clinical practice and to determine directions for continued investigation of this topic.

Each chapter included in the volume substantiates and elaborates one or more of the above assumptions. In doing so, this text offer readers the first comprehensive picture, in an accessible format of an edited volume, of what happens to parentified children and how clinicians can treat immediate and long-term problems related to parentification.

Acknowledgments

I owe much appreciation to so many people for the completion of this book. The contributors to this volume worked with great willingness, enthusiasm, and perseverance in conceptualizing and writing their chapters. You each shared with me not only your ideas and the texts you authored, but also your belief that an edited volume on parentified children was an important and timely undertaking. I would especially like to thank Helen W. Coale at Atlanta Area Child Guidance Clinic, Gregory J. Jurkovic at Georgia State University, and Katherine Thompson at The University of Georgia for their encouragement, suggestions, and insights, especially at the early stages of this project, when our conversations truly shaped the direction and content of this book.

Likewise, a very special thank you is owed to Bryan E. Robinson at the University of North Carolina at Charlotte for his insightful inspiration and invaluable practical advice.

I also want to thank the faculty and staff in the Department of Academic Foundations at Georgia State University, and Margaret Zusky and Jim Nageotte of Sage Publications. I am most appreciative of the technical assistance Glenda Haliburton and Jarvis Dixon offered in preparation of this manuscript.

Finally, I will always be grateful for the good humor and loving support of great friends, especially Dixie Card, Linda Melrose, and Mia Mundale—thank you. And to Kalyani Luckhardt—your happy, gentle company is a blessing, and your wisdom keeps me remembering what is really important.

PART I

Theory and Research Perspectives

CHAPTER 1

Parentification

An Overview of Theory, Research, and Societal Issues

Nancy D. Chase

INTRODUCTION

Parentification as a topic of scholarly investigation presents some special challenges in determining scope that, at the outset of this overview, are important to specify. These challenges are themselves factors offering insight into the concept of parentification and its workings in parent-child relations, in families, and in communities and societies across generations.

References to generational boundary transgression appear in a very wide range of clinical descriptions and empirical studies. Parentification, the parental child, role reversal, and generational boundary dissolution are concepts directly mentioned or implicated in literature on children of alcoholics and familial alcoholism, co-dependency, sexual abuse, single-parent families, the impact of parental death or mental illness on the family, marital conflict, divorce, addictive relationships, attachment styles, infant and child development, identity development and adolescent separation, hyperactivity/attention-deficit, depression, and anxiety. In other words, a comprehensive examination of parentification could lead into seemingly inexhaustible sources of relevant information and insight, thus making it difficult to know where to set limits on investigating this topic. With consideration of parentification most often embedded in related topics such as those listed, it is not surprising to find that studies of parentification per se are somewhat limited in number (see also Jurkovic, 1997). Perhaps it is easier to study parentification if the focus is actually directed to more tangible, less covert phenomena.

Determining which of countless theoretical constructs to use in explaining the nature and effects of parentification is another challenge to address in attempting an adequate review of this literature. In understanding the effects of

3

parentification, one might begin with references to fundamental assumptions of psychoanalytic theory regarding "narcissistic injury" and transference (Burt, 1992; Lowen, 1985; Miller, 1981; Searles, 1975). Further understanding may be gained by considering various psychodynamic descriptions of parentification, most often according to its impact on psychosocial development (Erikson, 1959, 1963, 1968) or object-relations development (Mahler, 1968; Masterson & Costello, 1980; Winnicott, 1958, 1965, 1971), attachment (Alexander, 1992; Bowlby, 1980; Jacobvitz & Bush, 1996; Zeanah & Klitze, 1991), and development of self (Kohut, 1971, 1977; Kohut & Wolf, 1978). In addition to psychodynamic constructs for understanding parentification, the literature also includes descriptions that emphasize relational dynamics (Boszormenyi-Nagy & Spark, 1973) and strategic (Madanes, 1981) and structural aspects (Minuchin, Montalvo, Guerney, Rosman, & Schumer, 1967) in families. Various family therapy theories describe relevant concepts such as intergenerational transmission, triangulation, boundaries, and child-focused families. In addition, parentification can be examined from societal, cultural, and historical perspectives that still further broaden the context in which such phenomena are placed (Aries, 1960/1962; Elkind, 1982; Garbarino, 1981; Greenleaf, 1978; Harkness & Super, 1983; Harrison, Wilson, Pine, Chan, & Buriel, 1990; Schneider, 1995). Many believe that greater prevalence of certain social conditions such as one-parent families, financial stress, social isolation, and disintegration of community result in greater demands on children to raise themselves, to become parentified in response to overtaxed adults who are unavailable, or at best are "doing the best they can" in a depleting and confusing postmodern society. Questions about the short- and long-term effects of childhood parentification are poignant when social and cultural circumstances make it increasingly difficult for adults to receive the logistical and emotional supports they need to parent children (Bronfenbrenner, 1977; Edelman, 1987; Pipher, 1994).

Finally, the theoretical and empirical literature on parentification addresses many questions. How is parentification defined? What are its patterns? Is parentification simply parent-child role reversal in the performance of instrumental tasks? Or, more broadly, is parentification characterized as a transgression or breakdown of generational boundaries in emotional as well as functional areas? Is there "normal" or nonpathological parentification, and if so, what distinguishes it from unhealthy parentification? When, and according to what conditions, do parentification patterns become problematic or dysfunctional? What are immediate and long-term effects of childhood parentification? Are descriptions of parentification limited to relationship dynamics between adults (parental figures) and children, or do such descriptions also include adult-to-adult relationships? What interventions are useful in working with parentified children and their families, or with adults who continue to struggle unhappily with the residual patterns of their parentified status from childhood or adolescence? In one of the most recent examinations of parentification, its etiology, and its treatment, Jurkovic (1997) integrates existential, ontological considerations and an ecological framework for understanding human development. Jurkovic, from this perspective, broadens the questions regarding the theoretical construct to include those of an ethical nature about what human beings "owe" each other in a variety of human arrangements—adult to adult, adult to child, child to parent—and involving issues of power, loyalty, responsibility, entitlement, and posterity. "Co-being," he writes, "has ethical implications" (p. 15). To understand most fully a relational dynamic such as parentification, one must contemplate essential qualities of human relating and the functioning of society. Jurkovic continues by saying, "the livelihood of the newborn and ultimately the viability of the human community depend on responsible and ethical intergenerational relating" (p. 15), and by making this assertion he places the study of parentification in a context encompassing, but not limited to, individual developmental issues or isolated family dynamics. Furthermore, Jurkovic makes a substantive argument for analyzing the development and symptomatology of "destructive parentification" as a form of child maltreatment with a mandate of establishing criteria comparable to frameworks used for defining neglect and physical abuse.

Given these factors, it is understandable that a comprehensive review of parentification studies has not been undertaken. On the other hand, these challenges also make this topic compelling simply by virtue of its pervasiveness. The concept of parentification becomes a meeting point for so many varied perspectives and issues (intrapsychic, interpersonal, historical, societal) that, at the risk of becoming diluted because of breadth, it offers rich possibilities for applications to clinical practice, research, and scholarship. The purpose of this chapter is to give readers a sufficiently comprehensive overview of varied theoretical, empirical, sociocultural, and historical approaches to the concept of parentification and to illustrate the breadth and depth of its relevance to clinical practice and ongoing research.

THEORETICAL CONSTRUCTS FOR UNDERSTANDING PARENTIFICATION

Despite numerous descriptions of theories, concepts, and definitions, it is generally believed that parentification in the family entails a functional and/or emotional role reversal in which the child sacrifices his or her own needs for attention, comfort, and guidance in order to accommodate and care for logistical or emotional needs of the parent. Because children need their parents, children learn readily to respond to what their parents need. Responsiveness to parental need is not inherently problematic, and in fact, in a healthy sense, it helps the child develop sensitivities and reciprocity with others. In its worst sense, however, exacting such "responsiveness" from one's children may be gravely exploitive of them. In extreme cases when a parent's dependency is too great and when the parent abdicates parental responsibility for structuring and protecting the child from "doing too much" or "carrying the load," the parentified child may learn in this process that her needs are of less importance than those of others, or may actually become depleted of energy and time for pursuing school, friendships, childhood activities, and, at later stages, exploration of career and relationship possibilities. These pursuits may be postponed or abandoned because of overriding and persistent priorities of parental expectations and demands communicated overtly or covertly in the family. Because the child often complies in meeting the parent's requests, such dynamics in families are confusing and sometimes quite subtle. When adults abdicate parental responsibility, children face abdication, by default, of their childhood status and the range of developmental needs, pleasures, struggles, and opportunities childhood rightly entails. Children thus learn first to give up their childhood, and then, with a cycle of abdicating needs and responsibilities well grooved, they become candidates for later abdicating adult responsibilities, including those involved in raising children.

Generational divisions and boundaries exist in families and societies cross-culturally and serve multiple functions for protecting spousal bonds and ensuring developmentally appropriate separation-individuation of children from their parents (Frances & Frances, 1976; Parsons, 1954). When generational boundaries are altered or confused, parentification may manifest in at least one (or a combination) of three possible forms: child-as-parent, child-as-mate, and spouse-as-parent (Boszormenyi-Nagy & Spark, 1973; Minuchin, 1974; Sroufe & Ward, 1980; Walsh, 1979). Roles of the parentified child as parent and/or surrogate mate to the parent may be further delineated as roles designed to fulfill (a) logistical, instrumental parenting tasks, such as preparing meals, caring for younger children, performing household chores, earning money, or managing the family budget, and (b) emotional, expressive parenting tasks such as providing for or responding to the emotional needs of the parent or family, and serving as parental confidant, peacemaker, or mediator (Jurkovic, Jessee, & Goglia, 1991). Expressive types of parentification are considered to be a greater threat to a child's well-being than parentification through assignment to the more clearly defined and acknowledged instrumental roles (Jurkovic et al., 1991; Minuchin, 1974; Parsons & Bales, 1955). Because all families communicate parentifying messages to some degree to their children, discussions of parentification must distinguish carefully between benign and detrimental types and duration of parentified roles. Clinicians agree that assuming some adult-like responsibilities may actually be beneficial to the child's growth and healthy sense of belonging and usefulness. Similarly, all children to some degree carry their parents' dreams and unfinished struggles forward to a new generation, and certainly as mature adults they contribute to the care of aging parents. Parentification becomes problematic, however, when there is a lack of acknowledgment and reciprocity between adults and children in terms of the nurturance exchanged, or when expectations, emotional or logistical, exceed the child's abilities, damage well-being, and ignore the child's developmentally appropriate needs, thus setting in motion detrimental and interrelated cycles of abdication in both parent and child (Boszormenyi-Nagy & Spark, 1973; Jurkovic, 1997; Minuchin, 1974).

Jurkovic (1997) delineates four categories of roles on a continuum of responsibility according to duration and extensiveness of caretaking. Extreme overfunctioning is labeled "destructive parentification," and extreme under-functioning is "infantilization." In the middle range of this hypothetical contin-uum are "healthy nonparentification" and "adaptive parentification." These two categories entail some appropriate responsibility for the child. In the "adaptive" category, caretaking responsibility may increase or intensify because of crisis or acute stress, but such contribution by the child is recognized and expected for a limited time only. Jurkovic also lists nine criteria used in assessing destructive parentification in families. The varied qualities and pervasiveness of parentification are so great that clearly defined terminology and criteria are necessary to facilitate this concept's usefulness in research and clinical practice (Jurkovic, 1997).

Clinical documentation of parent-child role reversal appeared long before the descriptive labels of "parental child" or "parentification" were assigned to such phenomena. One of the earliest references to the notion of parental role reversal was Schmideberg's (1948) statement that "an infantile level of devel-opment persists actively in all adults" (p. 207) but persists to such an extent in some adults that these adult individuals may unconsciously look to their own children for parental care and nurturance. In the early 1950s, Bateson's studies of paradoxical communication patterns between schizophrenic children and their mothers revealed antecedents to more recent, and less pathological, notions about parentification. Bateson, Jackson, Haley, and Weakland's publi-cation of "Toward a Theory of Schizophrenia" (1956) described the concept of "double-bind" in which the child, who lacks the cognitive capacity and lan-guage skill of the parent, is "caught" in a paradoxical interaction with a mother who "is driven not only to punish the children's demand for love, but also to punish any indication which the child may give that he knows that he is not loved" (Haley, 1976, p. 67). In this reactive bind, predicated on the parent's need and power, the child is never allowed an experience of his or her own feelings or self-experience, a situation that may culminate in the extreme expression of schizophrenic psychosis (Bateson et al., 1956). In the same year, Mahler and Rabinovitch (1956) wrote about "various unnatural roles" assumed by children in families where marital conflict or tension existed, and stated that such "unnatural roles" could have deleterious effects on the child's social and emotional development if not mitigated by an adult's capacity to show "empa-thy for the child as a child" (p. 53).

The decade of the 1960s brought the publication of numerous articles with references, direct and indirect, to what later would be termed parentification. Rosenbaum (1963) presented case studies of preadolescent children "over-burdened" with care of younger siblings, and concluded that, because of "aggressive and murderous impulses [characteristic of sibling rivalries] . . . not tempered by maternal drives," older children, even adolescents, were ill-equipped developmentally to care for younger siblings (p. 517). Morris and Gould (1963) connected parental physical abuse of children to role reversal, and they appealed to social service agencies, courts, mental health workers, and physicians to view role reversal as an antecedent to child abuse and as a useful framework for intervention and prevention. In 1965, Anna Freud expressed concern about the negative effects of a "broken home" resulting from divorce or parental death because of the role vacuum created by such a loss. She maintained that this "vacuum" is often filled by a child who then becomes prematurely responsible for adult functions in the family. Similarly, Tharp (1965) wrote about the delineation of family roles as optimal to the child's growth when such roles allowed for the child's skills and abilities to be challenged, but not "overchallenged." In cases where children were expected to assume parental roles, Tharp maintained that the demands of such roles were excessive and undermined appropriate childhood development. Zuk and Rubenstein (1965), in reviewing studies of families of schizophrenics, described the parental need to establish a relationship with the child that resembled the parent's unfulfilled or problematic relationship with his or her own mother or father. Other early references to parentification, yet unnamed, include Friedman's (1964) discussion of the "well-sibling" role in schizophrenic or neurotic families, Brody and Spark's (1966) concept of the family "burden bearer," and Ackerman's (1966) notion of "the family healer who takes on the role of peacemaker, protector . . . family doctor" (p. 83). In all these constructs, the caretaking role assigned to the child serves the needs of the parents or the family constellation and stabilizes family interactions, but yields damaging effects to the designated child's maturation and development.

It was not until the publication of *Families of the Slums: An Exploration of Their Structure and Treatment* (Minuchin et al., 1967) that the term *parental child* was introduced and that the concept of children assuming parental responsibilities was placed in a larger context of economic class and family size. According to Minuchin and colleagues (1967), it was not uncommon, and even served many practical purposes, for an older child in families of lower economic classes to assume parental responsibilities in the absence of the parent who was the primary wage-earner for the family. To some extent, this description of the parental child de-pathologized this phenomenon, especially compared to previous publications, by pointing out adaptive functions of such role reversal in the light of economic and social conditions. Minuchin clarified that if parental responsibilities were shared by several siblings, if responsibilities did not exceed the children's abilities, and if the child received recognition and support for what he or she gave, then the parental child role was not necessarily problematic. If parental children lacked adequate support from adults in the execution of these responsibilities, however, and if adult-child boundaries and power structure in the family became too blurred, then such role reversal patterns became problematic.

With Minuchin and colleagues' 1967 description of the parental child established in the literature, the early 1970s marked a period of further exploration, refinement, and extension of this concept. Minuchin and colleagues' parental child concept emphasized mostly functional tasks performed by the parental child in the interest of the family's welfare and survival (e.g., child care, meal preparation, household maintenance, worry about money). The parental child represented a structural rearrangement of family subsystems involving who carried responsibilities for certain tasks, and to what degree "power" and "authority" were commensurate with designated responsibilities.

In 1973, Boszormenyi-Nagy and Spark first used the term *parentification* to describe "a ubiquitous and important aspect of most human relationships," and placed this notion in the context of "dialectical relational theory" emphasizing dynamics of reciprocity, justice, fairness, and loyalty characteristic of all significant relationships (p. 151). Thus, whereas Minuchin's concept of the parental child described a functional arrangement of subsystems and task accomplishment, Boszormenyi-Nagy and Spark's concept of parentification described an added dimension of "invisible" aspects of relationship dynamics, or in their words, "relationship patterns which have overt role assignment as well as internalized expectation and commitment characteristics" (p. 154). Boszormenyi-Nagy and Spark's dialectical theory, in which their concept of parentification was embedded, assumed dialectically that individual and relational experience is inseparable, and that the development of the individual self is contingent on its relation to "the other."

Boszormenyi-Nagy and Spark broadly defined parentification—a component of all relationships, even healthy ones—in this existential, dialectical context as "the subjective distortion of a relationship as if one's partner or even children were his parent" (p. 151). Accordingly, their definition of parentification encompassed a dynamic in parent-child, as well as other intimate, relationships. These relationships, because of their intensity, have a "regressive core" in which one member (the parent or partner) desires a childlike union or "possession" of the loved one and fears greatly the "loss of loved ones" (pp. 151-153). Intermingled with desire for possession and fear of loss are also guilt, resentment, obligation, and reciprocal exchange in these relationships.

In this intricate and philosophical theory of the dialectic of human connection and separation, Boszormenyi-Nagy and Spark maintained that parentification is *not* an inherently pathological phenomenon. In fact, in its benign sense, parentification of children "is probably a part of every parent's attitude toward his child" and, in this positive sense, "is an attempt to prevent the parent from being emotionally depleted" (p. 153).

Unhealthy parentification, on the other hand, occurs when reciprocity, "symmetry," or balance of give and take is lost in the parent-child exchange, and results in detrimental effects to the child's development. Such pathological parentification can manifest as infantilization of the child as well as in roles that require premature overfunctioning of the child, emotionally or instrumentally.

Another aspect of Boszormenyi-Nagy and Spark's, and later Boszormenyi-Nagy and Krasner's (1986), concept of parentification is the necessity of viewing such phenomena in the context of three generations. More simply stated, parents may seek to "balance the ledger" of unfulfilling relations with their mother and father by turning to their children (or to other significant relationships) to settle these "debts." Themes of loss and compensation provide contours for tracing parentifying behaviors within and across generations. Karpel (1977) discussed the notion, essential to further understanding this parentification concept, of "loyal object" operating in the pathological parentification process and referring to "the non-reciprocal use of the individual as an object by the other(s) and the loyalty which binds him/her to the exploiter(s)" (p. 166). Again, Boszormenyi-Nagy and Spark's theoretical focus emphasized the parentified child's paradoxical situation as exploited object to parental needs (many unfulfilled from relations with their parents), while at the same time the child willingly cooperates and volunteers for such duties that can be expressed in varied roles.

Bowenian family theory is also useful in elucidating parentification phenomena in ways that relate closely to Boszormenyi-Nagy and Spark's three-generation model and loyal-object concept. Critical to Bowen's (1978) model, like assertions made by Boszormenyi-Nagy and his colleagues, is that emotional health, maturity, and the capacity to function in a nonthreatened manner in close relationships are gauged by an individual's degree of differentiation, or a sense of oneself in relation to others.

Bowen (1978) described the family as an "undifferentiated ego mass" operating in triangular arrangements as an emotional system. Triangles, the smallest relationship unit, function to reduce the anxiety produced in "emotionally fused" relationships when conflict is experienced. The spousal unit is the original source of emotional fusion within the nuclear family and will seek to triangulate a third party—usually a child—to relieve the intensity of undifferentiated closeness between the two partners when conflict arises. Bowen described three ways that fusion (i.e., lack of two "solid selves") in the marriage is expressed "as if there is a quantitative amount of undifferentiation to be absorbed" or directed into some designated area as an outlet for the tension generated by overcloseness (p. 203). Lack of differentiation may be "absorbed" and expressed as conflict between the spouses, may appear as dysfunction in one spouse and overfunction in the other, or may be expressed as problems in a child or children. The family projection process, according to Bowen, is "the basic process by which parental problems are projected to children" (p. 204). In this sense, the child in such an arrangement is so "fused" emotionally with one parent that the child holds and manifests this parent's anxiety, which actually serves to relieve both parents of assuming the burdens of their own undifferentiated anxieties. Again, in Bowenian theory as with other descriptions of similar family patterns, questions are raised about the extent of pathology and mitigating factors in such dynamics.

Bowen maintained that healthy relational functioning is present according to degree of differentiation present; that is, families whose members function at higher ranges of the hypothetical continuum of differentiation, with a greater sense of oneself in relation to other, present less dysfunction than those in lower ranges, who often become confused about "what's me and what's not me" or experience a loss of self in closeness to others. In fact, Bowen's description of parents of schizophrenic children and schizophrenic children themselves provides perspective on the parentification process if the parentified child is assumed to be in service as object to a parent's ego needs. Parents of children with schizophrenia are described as "people with very low levels of differentiation of self who manage to function reasonably well in their life adjustments" (p. 109). Even though as children these individuals did not, as Bowen described, "begin the steady process of growing away from their parents . . . they remain emotionally attached," but at adolescence are able to "tear themselves away to establish pseudo-selfs with a pseudo-separation from their parents" (p. 109). Bowen was quick to clarify that physical distance from parents does not necessarily determine emotional differentiation. People with schizophrenia, in a more extreme version of this pattern, "are never able to tear themselves away to achieve a workable level of pseudo-self" as separate from their parents (p. 110). Parentified children are in an at-risk circumstance to remain forever undifferentiated from the parent or, more generally, from the object-role defined in the parentification process.

To blend these various theoretical assumptions with the language of a structural model, it could be said that the lack of clearly defined generational boundaries or subsystems in a family is, in effect, a lack of differentiation and continues to perpetuate emotional fusion in its members. The parentified child concept can be explained theoretically using a structural model of family dynamics (Minuchin, 1974), or an existential-psychodynamically oriented interpersonal model of family dynamics (Boszormenyi-Nagy & Spark, 1973; Boszormenyi-Nagy & Krasner, 1986; Bowen, 1978). Karpel (1977) asserted that it is important to distinguish between the structural explanation of the "parental child" and the broader concept of parentification as an internal/external process of relational imbalance or emotional fusion. In either case, these approaches emphasize interpersonal family dynamics. They are, thus, based on general or natural systems conceptualizations of behavioral phenomena in the context of a network of relationships operating to influence the individual, and simultaneously, the entire relationship (emotional) system (Boszormenyi-Nagy & Spark, 1973, Boszormenyi-Nagy & Krasner, 1986; Bowen, 1978; Minuchin, 1974).

Although encompassing, relational and structural explanations of parentification would be incomplete without understanding intrapsychic processes explained in several psychosocial or psychodynamic models also used to inform the parentification concept. Models of systemic family dynamics are essential in describing the phenomena of parentification, or what Karpel referred to as "the preconditions," but when consideration is directed to developmental effects of the parentified status on an individual, then intrapsychic and developmental models are useful.

Four developmental models are cited frequently in the literature when effects of parentification are examined: psychosocial theory, object-relations theory, development of self theory, and attachment theory. Erikson's (1959) epigenetic stage model of psychosocial ego development has often been used as the framework for explaining developmental interferences experienced by the parentified child (Evans, 1979; Fullinwider-Bush & Jacobvitz, 1993; Karpel, 1977). Interestingly, Erikson's stages also account for the child's "contribution" to the parentification process in the form of a desire to be useful and functional in his or her family relations, specifically in the initiative versus guilt and the industry versus inferiority stages. At least for a time, the parentified roles complement the child's developmental needs at these stages to exercise purpose and competence in relationship to others. Forms of healthy parentification thus can become the expression of the child's capacity to be helpful to the parent, which is a precursor to adult purposefulness and responsibility. In its negative form, exploitive parentification is overwhelming, leaving the child with feelings of inadequacy (guilt, inferiority) in the face of demands that cannot be met despite his or her desire to do so. Karpel, for instance, described in his case studies of six families the consuming sense of failure the child experiences in trying to comfort a depressed parent or in trying to make a hopeless marriage happy.

Object relations models, specifically Mahler's stages of separation-individuation (Mahler, 1968; Mahler, Pine, & Bergman, 1975) and Winnicott's (1958, 1965) concepts of "holding environment," "transitional objects," and the "development of concern" and guilt in the child, are basic theoretical perspectives that contribute to understanding parentification (Burt, 1992; Karpel, 1977). Again, an examination of the developmental stages in these theories reveals, as in Erikson's model, the child's developing capacity to assist the parent: It is a natural and necessary developmental process for the child to focus on the well-being of the parent and to want to, in Winnicott's terms, "contribute-in" to a relationship with the parent. What this reinforces is that parentification per se is not inherently pathological if placed in the context of appropriate and adequate parental support. When such patterns, however, become pathological and function outside the context of adequate parental nurturance and guidance, then they truly constitute a process of exploitation of the child's natural tendencies. From this perspective, parentification can be understood as a breakdown of safety and containment in the child's holding environment.

From a psychoanalytic tradition, Searles (1973, 1975) described the "symbiotic therapist" concept that elucidated the parentified child role.

> Whenever the child showed any therapeutic concern for the parent, the latter reacted to the child as though the child were the parent's parent. . . . This mode

of relatedness is founded upon a relationship with his mother in which ego-functioning was fixated similarly at a level of relatively infantile fragmentation and non-differentiation, partially because the precarious family-intactness required that he not become a whole person but remain instead available for complementing the ego-incompleteness of the others in the family, individually and collectively. (Searles, 1973, p. 249)

Self-development models also comment on the parentified child (Burt, 1992; Kohut, 1971; Kohut & Wolf, 1978; Lowen, 1985; Miller, 1981). According to Kohut, the parent facilitates the growth of a strong and stable sense of self in the child by serving in relationship to the child as a "self-object" that the child over time internalizes. If the parent, or self-object, does not have a secure or stable enough sense of self, then the parent is unable to be responsive to the child's object-need for "mirroring" and "idealization." For the parent "to repeatedly focus on their [*sic*] own and not the child's accomplishments and/or to withdraw from the child when he or she tries to idealize and adore the parent" ultimately deprives the child of parental comforting and bonding (Burt, 1992, p. 54). Lowen (1985), discussing narcissistic development, stated that "a parent's distress is always too much for a child . . . there is nothing a child can do" (p. 181). The needy parent "seduces the child into a special relationship" that circumvents the child's experience of (in relation to her parents) ego boundaries and prevents subsequent development of her own ego boundaries to contain and express emotions. This is even more problematic, according to Lowen, because the child is "overstimulated" by adult emotions and adult sexuality embedded in those emotions.

> Living with the underlying insanity of a narcissistic parent is more difficult for the child to handle than a parent's outright nervous breakdown. . . . With the narcissistic parent, the facade of sanity confuses the child. . . . For a mother to demand that an undernurtured child respond to the mother's needs is another form of craziness. (Lowen, 1985, p. 144)

Attachment theory (Ainsworth, 1989; Bowlby, 1973, 1979, 1980) provides a frame for understanding parentification as a disruption in the mother-child relationship, and as a reflection of the parent's (usually mother's) attachment pattern with her parent. According to Bowlby, "internal working models" of relationships, formed through early infant-parent interactions, shape the child's understanding of her own worthiness in relation to the attachment figure, and a sense of the other's responsiveness (i.e., fundamental aspects of giving and receiving in relationship). The quality of attachment with the parent and relationship models are delineated as secure or insecure (avoidant, resistant, or disorganized). Investigations of early attachment, role reversal, and boundary dissolution cross-generationally, along with various forms of physical, emotional, and sexual abuse, associate a parentified role with resistant or disorganized attachment (Alexander, 1992; Benoit & Parker, 1994; Cotroneo, 1987; Main & Goldwyn, 1984; Main & Hesse, 1990; Sroufe & Fleeson, 1986).

Each of these four theoretical perspectives assumes that detrimental parentification interferes with the "normal" developmental sequence of attachment, "holding," "mirroring," separation, and identity or self-definition described in respective theories. The psychodynamic, structural, role, and psychosocial literatures all support the distinctions between developmentally detrimental and less harmful parentification: parentification that serves the healthy development of a sense of competence, identity, belonging, and mutuality and trust in relationships versus parentification that overwhelms and exploits, jeopardizing the child's ability to accomplish developmental tasks involving separation and individuation.

EMPIRICAL AND QUALITATIVE STUDIES OF PARENTIFICATION

Efforts have been made to test empirically and document qualitatively many of the parentification theories. Some generalizations can be made about the seeming popularity of different terms used to describe the parentification construct. Especially in the earlier studies, when the focus was on family organization and dynamics, investigations usually labeled such phenomena *parent-child role reversal*. More recently, and perhaps reflecting the influence of extensive publication of studies on incest and sexual abuse, the term *generational boundary dissolution* has been used to describe parentification (Burkett, 1991; Jacobvitz, Morgan, Kretchmar, & Morgan, 1991; Sroufe, Jacobvitz, Mangelsdorf, DeAngelo, & Ward, 1985). Studies that focus on the impact of these phenomena on the individual per se seem to most often use the actual term *parentification*. It is noteworthy, however, that similar behaviors and related emotional aspects of children caretaking their parents in any number of forms are given such a wide variety of labels (see also Jurkovic, 1997). For purposes of reviewing trends and assimilating research findings, studies conducted over the past 25 years of parent-child role reversal, generational boundary distortion or dissolution, and parentification can be organized into three broad categories according to the focus of investigation, regardless of the specific term assigned. The organizational categories are (a) studies investigating aspects of family organization, dynamics, and developmental theory; (b) studies investigating the impact of family alcoholism and substance abuse, parental illness, or death; and (c) studies investigating long-term effects of parentification on the parentified individual.

Family Organization and Dynamics

The earliest studies of parentification phenomena examined family variables, with much of the research being based on studies of families of schizophrenics (Bateson et al., 1956; Bowen, 1960; Haley, 1967; Slipp, 1973; Stierlin,

1974; Zuk & Rubenstein, 1965). Jules Henry (1965), an anthropologist, published an ethnography of a family whose oldest son was institutionalized for schizophrenia. In *Pathways to Madness*, Henry documented the daily lives of the two younger sons and their parents and presented a vivid picture of the distinct and rigid roles assumed by each family member. The youngest son, age 12, served as family nurturer in both instrumental and emotional ways. Karpel (1977) wrote an even more extensive qualitative study of parentification by describing five families undergoing family treatment, and in addition included Henry's data on the Rosenberg family as a sixth case to analyze. Karpel's study was, and possibly still is, one of the most comprehensive and thorough qualitative analyses of parentification processes.

Karpel identified four variables, two characteristic of parents and two characteristic of children, that operate in unhealthy parentification. According to Karpel, the elements contributed by parents to such dynamics either involve "a failure of parenting" (defined as either abdication of responsibility to guide the child or as lack of responsiveness to the child's needs) or involve preoccupation with marital conflict or "disappointment" in the marriage. The child matches these two elements contributed by the parents with his or her own "capacity for concern" and a developmental "readiness for responsibility" (p. 78). In the light of the interaction of these variables, Karpel proposed that "parentification represents a chain of social processes, not the acts or initiative of any one person . . . it persists as a covert organizing structure, shaping more overt family interactions" (p. 181). Karpel concluded that pathological parentification is seriously damaging to the parentified child and summarized discernible themes from the naturalistic data on these six families, including the child's loss of self-trust, autonomy, exploration of and access to involvement beyond the home, and limits on the child to an identity role that is "essentially relational and reactive" (p. 153).

Froma Walsh (1979) published one of the first controlled studies of parentification. Walsh investigated whether parentification, either child-as-mate type or child-as-parent type, was a contributing factor in schizophrenia. She found that parentification according to the child-as-parent type did not discriminate between groups of schizophrenics, hospitalized nonschizophrenics, and normal groups of young adults and their parents. On projective testing, however, the schizophrenic group did show higher numbers of child-as-mate fantasies and "sexualized bonds" between parent-like and child-like figures than the other two groups. Walsh interpreted these findings as supporting Haley's (1967) description of the "perverse triangle" of a child's overinvolvement with one parent, and she concluded that

> the distinguishing feature of intergenerational relations in families of schizo-phrenics may not be parentification, per se, but the blurring of the boundaries in intense eroticized cross-generational attachments . . . transforming the child into the status of mate to the parent, in rivalry with the other parent, and to the extreme of sexual relations. (p. 273)

Walsh also concluded from her study that the overresponsible "parental child" described by Minuchin is not vulnerable to schizophrenia because the child-as-parent construct did not differentiate schizophrenic and nonschizophrenic groups.

Studies also relate child-as-mate parentification to family variables other than schizophrenia. Sroufe and Ward (1980) found an empirically significant predominance of child-as-mate "cross-generation bonds" among young, low socioeconomic status mothers and their toddler children. In addition, these mothers had themselves experienced physical or eroticized-emotional relations with their fathers, lending support to intergenerational hypotheses about such patterns. A further investigation of mothers' seductive behavior with young children found specific patterns according to the child's gender (i.e., seductive with sons and hostile or aloof with daughters) and related these patterns to the mother's relationship history (Sroufe et al., 1985). Still another study found child-as-mate role reversals among parents and young children related to the child's hyperactivity in school (Jacobvitz & Sroufe, 1987). Burkett (1991) found that mothers with their own childhood histories of sexual abuse were more likely to turn to their children for excessive emotional caretaking, and as parents were described as more "self-focused, as opposed to child-focused," exhibiting either overinvolvement or underinvolvement with their children (p. 432). This research and other studies investigating sexual abuse in families and patterns of parentification find role reversal as a possible antecedent to sexual abuse (Alexander, 1992; Cotroneo, 1987; Levang, 1989), whereas other studies find less overt, "milder" parentifying behaviors and expectations as characteristic of mothers with childhood sexual abuse histories and problematic (insecure) relationships with their parents (Burkett, 1991; Fish, Belsky, & Youngblade, 1991; Zeanah & Klitzke, 1991). Burkett observes a distinction, but also notes an important and revealing interconnectedness between overt sexual trespass and "more subtle" boundary transgressions:

> Using a child to meet an adult's sexual needs, as had happened to the mothers in this study, is clearly a grossly inappropriate expression of the lack of generational boundaries. This study indicates that more subtle types of role reversal are likely to be found in such families, and to continue in subsequent generations, even if sexual abuse is curbed. Becoming a child's "best friend" may not appear abusive, but it may have an unwanted impact on the child's emotional development. (p. 433)

These studies allow for generational boundary trespass to be conceptualized on a continuum ranging from most extreme, invasive behaviors involving sexual abuse to less dramatic, but nevertheless excessive, forms of inappropriate caretaking of the parent by the child. Alexander, in fact, maintaining that insecure parental attachments resulting from chronic, problematic family dynamics are more damaging to the child's well-being than an isolated incident of sexual trespass, suggests that research and clinical practice involving sexual abuse emphasize the context and long-standing patterns of relating (e.g., adult-child role reversals) existing in families where severe forms of abuse occur.

Other studies conducted at this time, when empirical investigation of parentification was fairly new, examined generational boundary transgressions and Eriksonian developmental maturation of child-abusing and nonabusing mothers. Abusing mothers showed lower developmental maturity in measures of Eriksonian stages and a greater number of generational boundary transgressions with their children than nonabusing mothers (Evans, 1979; Morris & Gould, 1963).

The parentified child status has also been studied in examining the impact of divorce on families and in single-parent families. Dawson (1980), like Weiss (1979), found that children in single-parent families assumed more parental responsibility than children in two-parent families, and often in roles as surrogate spouse. Using measures of responsibility and sociability/isolation, Dawson found significant negative correlations between responsibility and sociability of children. Dawson used these findings to suggest that increased responsibility assumed by children in one-parent families may have the effect of overinvolving them with their parent and preventing their involvement with peers. The social isolation of these children and adolescents from peers was considered to be a clinical sign of pathological parentification according to Dawson's study. Johnston (1990) found parentification as a significant factor contributing to negative outcomes for children of divorced parents.

Finally, in examination of still another family constellation, Mitchell and Cronson (1987) presented a case study of a family in which one parent was "a celebrity." In this case study, the father was a professional sports figure and the entire family had organized around "enabling" him to put his full energies into his career in exchange for the financial and social rewards it provided the family. The spouse of this "celebrity" benefited from her husband's focus outside the marriage and parenting responsibilities, but in the void of emotional and logistical support looked to her children (or a designated child) for these qualities of involvement. As illustrated in this study, such a dynamic did not become problematic until the "spousified" child reached adolescence and became "increasingly difficult for the mother to control" (p. 238). An added problematic aspect to this arrangement was the confusing nature of the spousified position for the child, a status that was constantly changing according to the comings and goings of the father.

Keele (1984) described a similar pattern in families of highly successful business executives, and later Robinson and Post (1995) documented similar family dynamics in studies on work addiction. Jurkovic and colleagues (1991) emphasized the insidious nature of parentification in such family arrangements as these because the child also experiences "grandiosity" and power that comes with the parentified or spousified status. In fact, such children do not always appear symptomatic as long as the prescribed family "contract" is operating.

The pathological effects of parentification may not appear until the child becomes old enough to face his or her own issues of identity, intimacy, and depression when confronted with developmental tasks of separation from the grandiose role secured in the family.

The point of commonality in all the studies of family arrangements and parentification is the impact of the parent's family relationship history and spousal relationship, or lack thereof, on the adult's relationship with the child (Beavers, 1985; Fish et al., 1991; Gilbert, Christensen, & Margolin, 1984). This feature, as a theme throughout these studies, suggests that a fundamental step in understanding parentification patterns is to examine carefully the sources of support (other than children) available to the parent.

Family Alcoholism and Substance Abuse

Some of the most extensive work, empirical and qualitative, that gives understanding to childhood parentification consists of studies of substance abusing families. In these circumstances, the family organizes around alcohol or other abused substances at the expense of the actual needs of each family member (Black, 1981; Bowen, 1974; Cermak, 1986; Dulfano, 1981). Living in a family where substance abuse is present can be so demanding and threatening that individual members adopt roles (hero, enabler, scapegoat, lost one, mascot, placater) in efforts to protect the family system (Black, 1979; Copans, 1989; Wegscheider, 1981, 1983). As children in these families become adults, they function skillfully, but primarily in ways prescribed by their given family role. Because, the theory holds, the family functioned primarily to fulfill the needs of its system and not the needs of its individual members, these "adult-children," as they are referred to in literature on children of alcoholics (COA), suffer developmental deficits in adulthood, limiting their broader social functioning in relationships or work (Black, 1981; Bowen, 1974; Cermak, 1986; Dulfano, 1981; Latham, 1988; Womack, 1991; Wood, 1987).

Embedded, implicitly or explicitly, in the studies of familial alcoholism are descriptions of the parentified functioning of many, if not all, individuals close to the alcohol or substance abuser. Addictions literature describes these phenomena as "enabling" or "co-dependent" behaviors and functions, but such descriptions are linked closely to parentification behaviors (Olson & Gariti, 1993). The studies of parental alcoholism and substance abuse thus have yielded important insights about parentification. Karpel (1977), drawing from various theoretical descriptions, maintained that the parentified role typically, but not exclusively, refers to overresponsible, nurturing behaviors in the child toward the parent. In serving parental needs at the expense of one's own, the child may express underfunctioning such as symptomatic, infantilized, helpless, rebellious, or self-destructive behaviors, as well as responsible, pseudo-mature overfunctioning behaviors. In this light, all delineated COA roles can be perceived as examples of parentification in that the child is cast into a reactive position in relation to the parent, as acting to protect the parent, or as engaging in rebellious or dependent behaviors to "invite" the parent back into parenting the child (Karpel, 1977; Kerfoot, 1972; Madanes, 1981; Stierlin, 1974).

Burt (1986), using both projective and objective measures of parentification, found higher scores on child-as-parent and child-as-mate statuses for college-age COAs in comparison to their non-COA cohorts. More recently, Goglia, Jurkovic, Burt, and Burge-Callaway (1992) published a study with similar results, with additional findings that gender of the adult-child results in differential effects. Objective measures of parentification revealed higher scores for females, suggesting, on the surface at least, that females are more likely than males to assume caretaking roles. Other studies have reported similar results on objective measures (Burt, 1992; Goglia, 1982). Interestingly, in the study by Goglia and colleagues (1992), results on *projective* measures indicated no differences between males and females on child-as-mate and child-as-parent responses. In other words, males were just as likely on projective measures to report generational boundary distortions in their Thematic Apperception Test (TAT) responses as females. Goglia and colleagues interpreted these results as suggesting a "response bias due to male socialization" (1992, p. 296). They proposed that males may be less likely to admit to caretaking behaviors specified in objective measures, but may be just as engaged in such behaviors, although in expressions considered more "stereotypical" for males (i.e., "misbehavior" or underresponsibility, not overresponsibility).

Bekir, McLellan, Childress, and Gariti (1993) studied families over three generations in which alcohol or drug abuse was present. They found in these families that because of the absence of an important adult, usually the father, at least one of the children was expected to assume adult-like responsibilities. Two parentification roles were proposed by the authors: child-as-rescuer and child-as-rebel. Bekir and colleagues also found that "these previously parentified children often break down when faced with problems of raising their own children and sometimes resort to alcohol or drugs, thereby abandoning parental responsibility in their own homes" (pp. 614-615). The authors concluded that parentified status in one's family of origin contributes to later abusive use of alcohol and/or drugs.

Also noteworthy and relevant to understanding effects of parentification is that deleterious consequences of losing a parent through illness or death may be mitigated by ensuring that children experience ample support in ways that build up and do not tax the child's physical or emotional resources; in other words, supportive aspects contrary to the depleting behaviors associated with adult-child role-reversal (Downey & Coyne, 1990; Rutter, 1987).

Long-term Effects of Parentification

The final group of studies to be considered are those attempting to determine long-term effects of parentification on the parentified individual. What happens when parentified children become adults? Studies grouped in this category cover a wide range of topics investigated as related hypothetically to childhood parentification. These studies have produced mixed results as to the extent of damaging and enduring effects of parentified roles.

Studies of families of adult female incest survivors and female adolescents with anorexia found patterns of the daughters' overinvolvement with either or both parents (Cole & Woolger, 1989; Kalucy, Crisp, & Harding, 1977; Minuchin, Rosman, & Baker, 1978). Campbell, Adams, and Dobson (1984) studied a nonclinical group of families and concluded that in families where there were low levels of independence and high levels of emotional connectedness, young adults (male and female) tended to readily adopt family values with little exploration in career and relationship decisions; they referred to these phenomena as "identity foreclosure" or "premature commitments" (Fullinwider-Bush & Jacobvitz, 1993, p. 90). Fullinwider-Bush and Jacobvitz (1993), in a study of 45 young adult females and their families, hypothesized that "generational boundary dissolution" would have detrimental effects on the identity development of this population of young women. Indeed, when some form of parentification was present, they found that the young women were less likely to diverge from their parents' values and expectations regarding decisions about dating, friendships, and career. In cases where the daughter was overly involved with the father as spouse-substitute (companion, confidante), results showed low commitment by the daughter to any career or relationship path, indicating an even more intense interference with development of an independent identity. In a more recent study, Jacobvitz and Bush (1996) found that inappropriate father-daughter alliances resulted in problems of depression, self-esteem, and anxiety in young adult women, and that mother-daughter alliances resulted in greater anxiety for daughters.

A number of other studies have reported gender effects in parentification (Burt, 1992; Goglia, 1982, 1985; Wolkin, 1984). Burt (1992) found parentified childhood roles especially problematic to young women and, in fact, called parentification "particularly devastating for women's development" (p. 103). Goglia (1982, 1985) and Wolkin (1984) also found differential effects according to gender. Wolkin found that parentification scores for young adult women were negatively correlated to depression scores, and explained this finding by noting that a woman may actually experience a certain degree of satisfaction for fulfilling socially approved caretaking roles even though these roles have also discouraged her individuation. Burt (1992) investigated whether various forms of parentification would result in problematic object-relations development in a population of 113 college students and concluded that "parentified individuals appear to be persons who have sustained serious levels of narcissistic injury," (p. 99) resulting in ego boundaries that are too diffuse or too rigid, low tolerance of separation, and generally low levels of satisfaction in their intimate adult relationships. Studies of college-age males and females show a relationship between a parentified childhood history, academic performance, and poor adjustment to college (Berman & Sperling, 1991; Chase, Deming, & Wells, 1998; Held & Bellows, 1983).

Other studies also have given support to the hypothesis that problematic adult relationships are a legacy of childhood parentification (Betchen, 1996; Olson & Gariti, 1993; West & Keller, 1991). Jones and Wells (1996) found parentification history predictive of certain patterns of masochistic and narcissistic personality styles, with implications for adult relationship difficulty. "Compulsive caregiving" or addictive relationships, also frequently described as codependent patterns of relating in which the individual overfunctions to maintain the approval or connection with others even at the expense of personal well-being, are shown to be long-term results of childhood parentification roles. Olson and Gariti (1993) described members of couples who parentify each other in attempts to seek fulfillment for previous losses or unmet needs endured as parentified children with their parents. Olson and Gariti maintained that "addictive relationships" are actually "symbolic relationships" in that the dynamics of such relationships enable each partner to simultaneously avoid and reexperience childhood disappointments, producing painful cycles of "engagement-disengagement" in the couple's relationship. The authors called interventions with such couples a "de-parentification process" through which each partner addresses historical losses and resentments "in the context to which they properly belong, rather than to continue to displace and project their unresolved emotions within the confines of a present relationship" (p. 205). De-parentification also involves mourning losses that resulted from the restrictiveness and deprivation of childhood parentified roles. The authors cautioned that working with adults who were parentified as children requires an appreciation for slow and gradual change if "de-parentification" is attempted.

Still another group of studies examines effects of parentification in terms of later career choice and functioning in work. Sessions (1986), when comparing graduate psychology and engineering students, found that psychology students produced higher scores on objective parentification measures than their engineering cohorts. This finding concurred with Lackie's (1982) study of 1,577 social workers, one of the largest investigations of personality variables, family of origin, and career choice. Lackie found that more than two thirds of his sample of social workers had childhood histories of "care-taking" or "go-between" roles in their families (Lackie, 1982, 1983). Lackie emphasized the positive aspects of career choices that cultivate "skills" and "inclinations" developed in childhood experiences. Using object-relations language and perspective, Lackie also argues, however, that the legacy of parentified roles can interfere with the professional's effectiveness with clients, and with overall job satisfaction.

The so-called good social worker needs to undergo a manageable disillusionment in his or her power to control reality, balanced somewhere between omnipotence and helplessness. The balanced position—the good-enough social worker—lessens the potential for splitting of clients into good ones and bad ones; the ideal would be good-enough care-takers with the capacity to tolerate coexistence with good-enough clients. (Lackie, 1983, p. 321)

In a similar vein, given the tendency for parentified individuals to enter helping professions, Blumenstein (1986) advocated therapeutic work regarding one's own family of origin for clinicians. Blumenstein maintained that without such personal work, clinicians risk perpetuating overly caretaking relationships with clients, a legacy of the therapists' childhood role, which may be predicated more on the clinicians' needs to be helpful than on what clients themselves may most benefit from in therapeutic interventions. In addition, such issues also relate to therapist self-care. Based on survey data, Blumenstein found that therapists with childhood histories of parentification were more likely to prefer individual rather than family treatment modalities. Blumenstein explained this finding by claiming that childhood parentification predisposes therapists to "care too much" and, in doing so, allows them to "retain the psychic split between the adult and childish components," with child aspects being projected onto individual clients and adult aspects being expressed by the clinician through "helping." Family treatment, on the other hand, tends to preclude such caretaking posturing between individual client and therapist because family treatment requires the clinician to relate simultaneously to the multiple perspectives of all family members.

SOCIOCULTURAL AND HISTORICAL CONTRIBUTIONS

Larger societal and historical variables must also be included as still another essential context in which to examine parentification phenomena. Bronfenbrenner's ecological model, Bowen's theory of societal regression, and Boszormenyi-Nagy and Spark's analysis of the failure of larger social systems to achieve an adequate reciprocal balance between giving to and receiving from the individual are examples of efforts to place such phenomena as parentification in the broader context of society, or even, as Bowen does, within natural evolutionary systems. It is unusual, however, for the research literature on parentification to address these phenomena in terms of their broader ecological, cultural, or historical meanings. Although social and historical factors influencing children and family life are studied extensively and written about in academic and lay literature, the specific connection to parentification usually remains implicit, if considered at all.

How child and adult functioning is defined and understood varies culturally, as indicated by cross-cultural descriptions of child rearing practices and related research issues surrounding social relationships and ethnicity (Gabriel & McAnarney, 1983; Harkness & Super, 1983; Harrison, Wilson, Pine, Chan, & Buriel, 1990; see also Chapter 9 in this volume). Some have questioned the legitimacy of using the construct of parentification at all beyond the context of specified economic classes and an Anglo-European–based cultural perspective. Others maintain that the careful delineation of a continuum of healthy and unhealthy parentification allows use of the construct in varied cultural and ethnic settings while also cautioning that "social legitimacy" according to cultural traditions must be examined in the light of moral and ethical values (e.g., via human rights and feminist understandings) (Jurkovic, 1997).

Bronfenbrenner's ecological model calls for multilevel analysis of human development conceptualized through a range of individual, family, community, and societal contributions. A Bowenian perspective emphasizes that society and its problems must be perceived in terms of its embedded emotional processes and not simply in terms of a collection of "symptoms" (i.e., problems). Emotional processes operative in individuals and families also operate in larger society "as a family." These processes include "multi-generational transmission, chronic anxiety, emotional triangles, cutoffs, projection processes, and fusion/differentiation struggles" (Friedman, 1991, p. 164). Bowen's notion of societal regression as demonstration of reactive and undifferentiated emotional relations on a societal scale implies that the very issues contributing to triangulation or exploitation of children (and adults) at the individual family level operate at the societal level as well and serve to reinforce problematic functioning. Through a Bowenian lens of emotional processes, consider, for instance, the political struggle surrounding federal support of programs benefiting children's well-being, problems and controversies related to schools and education, child care, employment, and the reactive "family values" political agenda.

In recent years, there has been a proliferation of popular press literature attributing an enormous variety of adult functional ills to deficits in adequate parenting. In fact, entire companies have come into existence, and specialized divisions within traditional publishing firms have been established, with the sole purpose of publishing and marketing self-help material for overcoming childhood deficits, and thus living happier adult lives. The market popularity of such material attests the American public's ongoing fascination with the parent-child relationship, and more broadly, the relationship of childhood to adulthood.

Greenleaf (1978) argued that this fascination with childhood has been expressed in various ways and with different emphases for centuries. What seems to make the current fascination with the parent-child relationship unique, at least in the popular press, is its focus on what adults of former generations *ought* to have given their children and how, in their narcissism, they failed children and destined them to problematic adulthood. In former centuries and decades, the concerns were focused more on how adults should guide and control children, and in return, what they should expect from their offspring (Aries, 1960/1962; Greenleaf, 1978). The Victorian emphasis on shaping the "man-in-the-child" in one's children has been replaced with the contemporary popularity of nurturing the "child-in-the-man" in one's adulthood. This shift, although at times subtle, may also reflect a present-day tendency of adults to invest in their children or guide them inadequately, while at the same time continuing to expect a great "return" in the form of cooperation, loyalty, and happiness from them.

As presented at the beginning of this chapter, interactive and intergenerational cycles of abdicating fulfillment of personal, developmentally appropriate needs in childhood (and at other life stages as well) precedes and promotes abdicating of responsibilities at later stages in other areas. Inverted cycles of giving up one's needs and giving up one's responsibilities is a hallmark of the legacy of losing one's childhood to premature adult functioning but cannot be compensated for at a later time at the expense of actual adult responsibility in appropriate care, structuring, and protection of children. Pain of not being able to give what we have not sufficiently received persists and becomes the scaffolding for a range of exploitive and insensitive adult-child interactions. Abdication of responsibility manifests in many guises. Overinvolvement or underinvolvement with one's children is, nevertheless, a distortion and forfeiting of balanced and appropriate parental nurturance.

From the perspective of Boszormenyi-Nagy's concept of reciprocity, all human relationships, including parent-child, must be balanced in what is given and received by all involved in the relationship. In general, dysfunction is defined as imbalances over time in the functioning of this reciprocity. Greenleaf (1978) and Aries (1960/1962) showed historically that acknowledgment of childhood as a status distinct from adulthood did not occur until the late 18th and early 19th centuries. Prior to that time, children were perceived as simply miniature adults and were quickly integrated into daily activities with adults. In this light, a concept similar to "parental child" was actually a historical norm, not simply a function of recent social and economic conditions. Blending child and adult worlds had its advantages and disadvantages. Failure to recognize childhood and youth as distinct developmental stages provided the context for varieties of child labor, abandonment, and physical abuses (Zigler & Hall, 1989). On the other hand, based on trends to segregate children from adults since the early 1800s, Greenleaf argues that children in the United States are now prevented from contributing to their families' or communities' financial and social well-being. With the rationale of "romancing" childhood as a period of carefree happiness, and thereby protecting children from adult-like burdens, American society has rendered its children worthless to a functioning human community. Economic disadvantage excludes huge numbers of children and adolescents from such a romantic disengagement, yet their expendability is exhibited in high rates of accidental injury and death, violence, substance abuse, and gang involvement. Having children in the second half of the 20th century, for the first time in human history, is a liability and not an advantage economically, at least in America and other highly industrialized countries.

One can speculate that if children are not given the social means to be helpful by performing useful tasks that they are capable of developmentally and recognized for doing, then several consequences are possible:

1. Children are consigned to a separate sphere of operation apart from the adult world.

2. In this segregated and less-functional status, children become burdens to their parents/society, and are perceived as depleting their parents/society directly or indirectly of emotional, physical, and financial resources.

3. Because of this depletion, parents/society will have less to give to their children.

4. In their depletion, parents/society may look covertly to their children to fulfill needs for them that children are unable to fulfill, or parents may spend an inordinate amount of energy looking for other adults to meet these needs, with little consideration given their children. Children, in this scenario, are asked to sacrifice.

Studying parentification in a context of social and cultural issues requires embracing ideas about growth and maturation that are perceived frequently as paradoxical, and, more negatively, as mutually exclusive. Addressing problems of parentified children requires a psychological focus on individuation/self-differentiation *and* a cultural perspective emphasizing collectivism and inter-dependence, with both perspectives merging to ensure promotion of healthy human attachment and functioning.

Boszormenyi-Nagy and his colleagues saw the breakdown of communities of support as contributing to parentification of children. Little supportive involvement with extended family, friends, and organizations results in "overloading the life of the nuclear families with expectations for excessive commitments and satisfaction" (Boszormenyi-Nagy & Spark, p. 162). Other writers, such as Schneider (1995), Edelman (1987), Pipher (1994, 1997), and Elkind (1982), have not mentioned parentification directly but nevertheless have expressed serious concerns about conditions such as poverty, one-parent families, teenage pregnancy, violence, and substance abuse as factors that, in Bronfenbrenner's (1970) words, "make it increasingly difficult for parents to behave as parents" (p. 78). The consensus in the literature on the history and current conditions of families in society is that if parents are not supported adequately in the process of raising their children, and if children themselves are not involved in the functioning of family and community life, then strains will be placed on the parent-child relationship that make its participants vulnerable to microlevel and macrolevel exploitation.

RECOMMENDATIONS FOR FURTHER RESEARCH

The construct of parentification has been reviewed in this chapter as it appears in three literature areas: individual and family dynamics theory, empirical research studies, and sociohistorical perspectives. The two greatest gaps in understanding parentification are failure to place such individual and family level phenomena in the context of larger cultural and historical forces, and failure to identify and address parentification in its various manifestations among both child and adult clients in clinical settings.

Empirical studies, basing their investigations on data collected through self-report instruments as well as projective measures, have produced varying results in their attempts to test hypotheses about the long-term effects of pathological parentification. Knowledge gleaned from these investigations has been fruitful, but not sufficient in understanding covert and complex phenomena associated with parentification. Furthermore, efforts to develop and validate sensitive assessment instruments have also been a factor in most empirical work on parentification (Burt, 1992; Fullinwider-Bush & Jacobvitz, 1993; Goglia, 1982; Mika, Bergner, & Baum, 1987; Sessions & Jurkovic, 1986). Just as observations have been made that studies of clinical and nonclinical adult children of alcoholics are limited by design and methodological problems, the empirical research on parentification needs to be reviewed more carefully for similar limitations (Claydon, 1987; El-Guebaly & Offord, 1977; West & Prinz, 1987).

Qualitative investigations of parentification, on the other hand, may actually offer more insight than quantitative measures, but to date have not often been undertaken. Although many case study descriptions of parentification have been published by clinicians with recommendations for treatment, only two formal and extensive qualitative analyses of naturalistic data have been undertaken (Henry, 1965; Karpel, 1977).

Finally, investigations of parentification usually approach the topic from the perspective of its pathology rather than its normal or healthy dimensions, even though studies and theories readily admit to the natural and "ubiquitous" aspect of parentification. What would be gained by examining the advantages and strengths of such phenomena? The closest efforts at this are probably cross-cultural and historical studies of child-rearing practices that emphasize the use and importance of children as active participants in the functioning of families and communities (Edelman, 1987; Greenleaf, 1978, Whiting & Whiting, 1975). These studies point to the paradox inherent in parentification that baffles clinicians, scholars, and policymakers: How is it that children can be underused and undervalued in society while at the same time being exploited and over-focused upon in their families? This question implies a necessary understanding of distinctions between instrumental and expressive parentification, and it suggests again the importance of establishing the "right" balance between demands and supports between parents and children, and between societies and families.

Current debates in our society about welfare policy, affirmative action, civil rights for gay and lesbian persons, health reform, and insurance coverage for persons with addictions and mental illnesses all have revealed dominant cultural ambivalences about various marginalized populations. Children and adolescents, too, are a marginalized population in America's economy, courts, and perhaps even families. Consideration of pathological parentification concepts and phenomena reveal the extent to which children have been consigned culturally to a sort of "separate but equal" status predisposing them to exploitation analogous to the vulnerability of other marginalized groups. When generational boundaries in the family are too diffuse or too rigid, a polarization occurs that leads in either extreme to confusing incongruities in parent-child roles. Diffuse boundaries suggest overinvolvement, with the risk of exploitation, whereas rigid boundaries suggest adult underinvolvement, with the implication that children turn to each other for support and guidance. In contrast, healthy forms of responsible adult-child involvement may actually serve to demarginalize children's place in society and reframe their involvement in family, and broadly in the human community, in ways more congruent to chronological and developmental status. For this reason, the constructs and concepts of parentification must be better understood and are ripe for further investigation in terms of their impact on adults, children, and the functioning of community.

REFERENCES

Ackerman, N. (1966). *Treating the troubled family.* New York: Basic Books.

Ainsworth, M. D. S. (1989). Attachments beyond infancy. *American Psychologist, 4,* 709-716.

Alexander, P. C. (1992). Application of attachment theory to the study of sexual abuse. *Journal of Consulting and Clinical Psychology, 60,* 185-195.

Aries, P. (1962). *Centuries of childhood: A social history of family life* (R. Baldick, Trans.). New York: Vintage. (Original work published 1960)

Bateson, G., Jackson, D., Haley, J., & Weakland, J. (1956). Toward a theory of schizophrenia. *Behavioral Science, 1,* 251-264.

Beavers, W. R. (1985). *Successful marriage: A family systems approach to couples therapy.* New York: W. W. Norton.

Bekir, P. , McLellan, T., Childress, A., & Gariti, P. (1993). Role reversals in families of substance misusers: A transgenerational phenomenon. *The International Journal of the Addictions, 28*(7), 613-630.

Benoit, D., & Parker, K. C. H. (1994). Stability and transmission of attachment across three generations. *Child Development, 65,* 1444-1454.

Berman, W. H., & Sperling, M. B. (1991). Parental attachment and emotional distress in the transition to college. *Journal of Youth and Adolescence, 20,* 427-440.

Betchen, S. J. (1996). Parentified pursuers and childlike distancers in marital therapy. *The Family Journal: Counseling and Therapy for Couples and Families, 4*(2), 100-108.

Black, C. (1979). Children of alcoholics. *Alcohol, Health and Research World, 4*(1), 23-27.

Black, C. (1981). *It will never happen to me.* Denver: Medical Administration Corporation.

Blumenstein, H. (1986). Maintaining a family focus: Underlying issues and challenges. *Clinical Social Work Journal, 14*(3), 238-249.

Boszormenyi-Nagy, I., & Krasner, B. R. (1986). *Between give and take: A clinical guide to contextual therapy.* New York: Brunner/Mazel.

Boszormenyi-Nagy, I., & Spark, G. (1973). *Invisible loyalties: Reciprocity in intergenerational family therapy.* New York: Harper & Row.

Bowen, M. (1960). Family concept of schizophrenia. In D. Jackson (Ed.), *The etiology of schizophrenia* (pp. 346-372). New York: Basic Books.

Bowen, M. (1974). Alcoholism as viewed through family systems theory and psychotherapy. *Annals of the New York Academy of Science, 233,* 115-118.

Bowen, M. (1978). *Family therapy in clinical practice.* New York: Jason Aronson.

Bowlby, J. (1973). *Attachment and loss: Separation.* New York: Basic Books.

Bowlby, J. (1979). *The making and breaking of affectional bonds.* London: Tavistock.

Bowlby, J. (1980). *Attachment and loss: Vol. 3. Loss, sadness, and depression.* New York: Basic Books.

Brody, E., & Spark, G. (1966). Institutionalization of the aged: A family crisis. *Family Process, 5,* 76-90.

Bronfenbrenner, U. (1970). *Two worlds of childhood: U.S. and U.S.S.R.* New York: Basic Books.

Bronfenbrenner, U. (1977). Toward an experimental ecology of human development. *American Psychologist, 32,* 513-531.

Burkett, L. P. (1991). Parenting behaviors of women who were sexually abused as children in their families of origin. *Family Process, 30,* 421-434.

Burt, A. (1986). *Generational boundaries in the families of alcoholics.* Unpublished master's thesis, Georgia State University, Atlanta, GA.

Burt, A. (1992). *Generation boundary distortion: Implications for object relations development.* Doctoral dissertation, Georgia State University, Atlanta, GA.

Campbell, E., Adams, G. R., & Dobson, W. R. (1984). Familial correlates of identity formation in late adolescence: A study of the predictive utility of connectedness and individuality in family relations. *Journal of Youth and Adolescence, 13,* 509-525.

Cermak, T. L. (1986). *Diagnosing and treating co-dependence.* Minneapolis: Johnson Institute Books.

Chase, N. D., Deming, M. P., & Wells, M. C. (1998). Parentification, parental alcoholism, and academic status among young adults. *The American Journal of Family Therapy, 26*(2), 105-114.

Claydon, P. (1987). Self-reported alcohol, drug and eating disorder problems among male and female collegiate children of alcoholics. *Journal of American College Health, 36,* 111-116.

Cole, P., & Woolger, C. (1989). Incest survivors: The relation of their perceptions of their parents and their own parenting attitudes. *Child Abuse and Neglect, 13,* 409-416.

Copans, S. (1989). The invisible family member: Children in families with alcohol abuse. In L. Combrinck-Graham (Ed.), *Children in family contexts: Perspectives on treatment* (pp. 277-298). New York: Guilford.

Cotroneo, M. (1987). Women and abuse in the context of the family. *Journal of Psychotherapy and the Family, 3,* 81-96.

Dawson, F. (1980). *The parental child in single and dual parent families.* Unpublished master's thesis, Georgia State University, Atlanta, GA.

Downey, G., & Coyne, J. C. (1990). Children of depressed parents: An integrative review. *Psychological Bulletin, 108,* 50-76.

Dulfano, C. (1981). Recovery: Rebuilding the family. *Alcoholism, 1*, 33-39.

Edelman, M. W. (1987). *Families in peril: An agenda for social change.* Cambridge, MA: Harvard University Press.

El-Guebaly, N., & Offord, D. R. (1977). The offspring of alcoholics: A critical review. *The American Journal of Psychiatry, 134*, 357-365.

Elkind, D. (1982). *The hurried child: Growing up too fast, too soon.* Reading, MA: Addison-Wesley.

Erikson, E. H. (1959). *Identity and the life cycle.* New York: International Universities Press.

Erikson, E. H. (1963). *Childhood and society* (2nd ed.). New York: Norton.

Erikson, E. H. (1968). *Identity: Youth and crisis.* New York: W. W. Norton.

Evans, A. L. (1979). An Eriksonian measure of personality development in child-abusing mothers. *Psychological Reports, 44*, 963-966.

Fish, M., Belsky, J., & Youngblade, L. (1991). Developmental antecedents and measurement of intergenerational boundary violation in a nonclinic sample. *Journal of Family Psychology, 43*, 278-297.

Frances, V., & Frances, A. (1976). The incest taboo and family structure. *Family Process, 15*, 235-244.

Freud, A. (1965). *Normality and pathology in childhood.* New York: International Universities Press.

Friedman, A. S. (1964). The "well" sibling in the sick family: A contradiction. *International Journal of Social Psychiatry, 2*(Special edition), 47-53.

Friedman, E. H. (1991). Bowen theory and therapy. In A. S. Gurman & D. P. Kniskern (Eds.), *Handbook of family therapy* (Vol. 2, pp. 134-170). New York: Brunner/Mazel.

Fullinwider-Bush, N., & Jacobvitz, D. B. (1993). The transition to young adulthood: Generational boundary dissolution and female identity development. *Family Process, 32*(1), 87-103.

Gabriel, A., & McAnarney, E. R. (1983). Parenthood in two subcultures: White, middle-class couples and black, low income adolescents in Rochester, New York. *Adolescence, 8*(71), 595-608.

Garbarino, J. (1981). An ecological approach to child maltreatment. In L. H. Pelton (Ed.), *The social context of child abuse and neglect* (pp. 228-267). New York: Human Sciences Press.

Gilbert, R., Christensen, A., & Margolin, G. (1984). Patterns of alliances in nondistressed and multiproblem families. *Family Process, 23*, 75-87.

Goglia, L. R. (1982). *An exploration of the long-term effects of parentification.* Unpublished master's thesis, Georgia State University, Atlanta, GA.

Goglia, L. R. (1985). Personal characteristics of adult children of alcoholics (Doctoral dissertation, Georgia State University). *Dissertations Abstracts International, 47*, 1774B.

Goglia, L. R., Jurkovic, G., Burt, A., & Burge-Callaway, K. (1992). Generational boundary distortions by adult children of alcoholics: Child-as-parent and child-as-mate. *The American Journal of Family Therapy, 20*(4), 291-299.

Greenleaf, B. K. (1978). *Children through the ages: A history of childhood.* New York: McGraw-Hill.

Haley, J. (1967). Toward a theory of pathological systems. In G. Zuk & I. Boszormenyi-Nagy (Eds.), *Family therapy and disturbed families* (pp. 11-27). Palo Alto, CA: Science and Behavior Books.

Haley, J. (1976). *Problem-solving therapy.* San Francisco: Jossey-Bass.

Harkness, S., & Super, C. M. (1983). The cultural construction of childhood: A framework for the socialization of affect. *Ethos, 11*, 221-231.

Harrison, A. O., Wilson, M. N., Pine, C. J., Chan, S. Q., & Buriel, R. (1990). Family ecologies of ethnic minority children. *Child Development, 61*, 347-362.

Held, B., & Bellows, D. (1983). A family systems approach to crisis reactions in college students. *Journal of Marital and Family Therapy, 9*, 363-373.

Henry, J. (1965). *Pathways to madness.* New York: Random House.

Jacobvitz, D. B., & Bush, N. (1996). Reconstruction of family relationships: Parent-child alliances, personal distress, and self-esteem. *Developmental Psychology, 32*, 732-743.

Jacobvitz, D. B., Morgan, E., Kretchmar, M., & Morgan, Y. (1991). The transmission of mother-child boundary disturbances across three generations. *Development and Psychopathology, 3*, 513-527.

Jacobvitz, D. B., & Sroufe, L. A. (1987). The early caregiver-child relationship and attention-deficit disorder with hyperactivity in kindergarten: A prospective study. *Child Development, 58*, 1496-1504.

Johnston, J. R. (1990). Role diffusion and role reversal: Structural variations in divorced families and children's functioning. *Family Relations, 39*, 405-413.

Jones, R., & Wells, M. C. (1996). An empirical study of parentification and personality. *The American Journal of Family Therapy, 24*, 145-152.

Jurkovic, G. J. (1997). *Lost childhoods: The plight of the parentified child.* New York: Brunner/Mazel.

Jurkovic, G. J., Jessee, E. H., & Goglia, L. R. (1991). Treatment of parental children and their families: Conceptual and technical issues. *American Journal of Family Therapy, 19*, 302-314.

Kalucy, R. S., Crisp, A. H., & Harding, B. (1977). A study of 56 families with anorexia nervosa. *British Journal of Medical Psychology, 50*, 381-395.

Karpel, M. A. (1977). Intrapsychic and interpersonal processes in the parentification of children (Doctoral dissertation, University of Massachusetts). *Dissertation Abstracts International, 38*, 365 (University Microfilms No. 77-15090)

Keele, R. L. (1984). Executive families: From pitfalls to payoffs. In N. M. Hoopes, F. L. Fisher, & S. H. Barlow (Eds.), *Structured family facilitation programs: Enrichment, education, and treatment* (pp. 209-229). Rockville, MD: Aspen System Corporation.

Kerfoot, M. (1972). Parent-child role reversal and adolescent suicidal behavior. *Journal of Adolescence, 2*, 337-343.

Kohut, H. (1971). *Analysis of the self.* New York: International Universities Press.

Kohut, H. (1977). *The restoration of the self.* New York: International Universities Press.

Kohut, H., & Wolf, E. S. (1978). The disorders of the self and their treatment: An outline. *International Journal of Psychoanalysis, 59*, 413-421.

Lackie, B. (1982). *Family correlates of career achievement in social work.* Unpublished doctoral dissertation, Rutgers University. (University Microfilm No. 8221687)

Lackie, B. (1983). The families of origin of social workers. *Clinical Social Work Journal, 11*(4), 309-322.

Latham, M. (1988). *Relationship patterns of female offspring of alcoholics: An examination of intimacy and individuation in marriage.* Unpublished doctoral dissertation, Georgia State University, Atlanta. (University Microfilm No. 8825091)

Levang, C. A. (1989). Interactional communication patterns in father/daughter incest families. *Journal of Psychology and Human Sexuality, 1*, 53-68.

Lowen, A. (1985). *Narcissism: Denial of the true self.* New York: Macmillan.

Madanes, C. (1981). *Strategic family therapy.* San Francisco: Jossey-Bass.

Mahler, M. (1968). *On human symbiosis and the vicissitudes of individuation.* New York: International Universities Press.

Mahler, M., Pine, F., & Bergman, A. (1975). *The psychological birth of the human infant.* New York: Basic Books.

Mahler, M. S., & Rabinovitch, R. (1956). The effects of marital conflict on child development. In V. E. Eisenstein (Ed.), *Neurotic interaction in marriage.* New York: Basic Books.

Main, M., & Goldwyn, R. (1984). Predicting rejecting of her infant from mother's representation of her own experience: Implications for the abused-abusing intergeneration cycle. *Child Abuse and Neglect, 8*, 203-217.

Main, M., & Hesse, E. (1990). Parents' unresolved traumatic experiences are related to infant disorganized attachment status: Is frightened and/or frightening parental behavior the linking mechanism? In M. Greenberg, D. Cicchetti, & M. Cummings (Eds.), *Attachment in the preschool years* (pp. 161-182). Chicago: University of Chicago Press.

Masterson, J. R., & Costello, J. L. (1980). *From borderline adolescent to functioning adult: The test of time.* New York: Brunner/Mazel.

Mika, P., Bergner, R. M., & Baum, M. C. (1987). The development of a scale for the assessment of parentification. *Family Therapy, 14*, 229-235.

Miller, A. (1981). *Prisoners of childhood: The drama of the gifted child and the search for the true self.* New York: Basic Books.

Minuchin, S. (1974). *Families and family therapy.* Cambridge, MA: Harvard University Press.

Minuchin, S., Montalvo, B., Guerney, B. G., Rosman, B., & Schumer, F. (1967). *Families of the slums: An exploration of their structure and treatment.* New York: Basic Books.

Minuchin, S., Rosman, B., & Baker, L. (1978). *Psychosomatic families: Anorexia nervosa in context.* Cambridge, MA: Harvard University Press.

Mitchell, G., & Cronson, H. (1987). The celebrity family: A clinical perspective. *The American Journal of Family Therapy, 15*(3), 235-241.

Morris, M. G., & Gould, R. W. (1963). Role reversal: A necessary concept in dealing with the battered child syndrome. *American Journal of Orthopsychiatry, 33*, 298-299.

Olson, M., & Gariti, P. (1993). Symbolic loss in horizontal relating: Defining the role of parentification in addictive/destructive relationships. *Contemporary Family Therapy, 15*(3), 197-208.

Parsons, T. (1954). The incest taboo in relation to social structure and the socialization of the child. *British Journal of Sociology, 5*, 101-117.

Parsons, T., & Bales, R. F. (1955). *Family, socialization and interaction process.* Glencoe, IL: Free Press.

Pipher, M. (1994). *Reviving Ophelia.* New York: Ballantine.

Pipher, M. (1997). *The shelter of each other: Rebuilding our families.* New York: Ballantine.

Robinson, B. E., & Post, P. (1995). Work addiction as a function of family of origin and its influence on current family function. *Family Journal, 3*, 200-206.

Rosenbaum, M. (1963). Psychological effects on the child raised by an older sibling. *American Journal of Orthopsychiatry, 33*, 515-520.

Rutter, M. (1987). Psychosocial resilience and protective mechanisms. *American Journal of Orthopsychiatry, 57*(3), 316-331.

Schmideberg, M. (1948). Parents as children. *Psychiatric Quarterly Supplement, 22*, 207-218.

Schneider, D. (1995). *American childhood: Risks and realities*. New Brunswick, NJ: Rutgers University Press.

Searles, H. F. (1973). Concerning therapeutic symbiosis. *The Annual of Psychoanalysis: A Publication of the Chicago Institute for Psychoanalysis, 1*, 247-262.

Searles, H. F. (1975). The patient as therapist to his analyst. In P. Giovacchini (Ed.), *Tactics and techniques in psychoanalytic therapy: Vol. 2. Countertransference* (pp. 95-151). New York: Jason Aronson.

Sessions, M. W. (1986). Influence of parentification on professional role choice and interpersonal style (Doctoral dissertation, Georgia State University). *Dissertation Abstracts International, 47*, 5066. (University Microfilms No. 87-06815)

Sessions, M. W., & Jurkovic, G. J. (1986). *The parentification questionnaire*. (Available from Gregory J. Jurkovic, Department of Psychology, Georgia State University, 1 University Plaza, Atlanta, GA 30303)

Slipp, S. (1973). The symbiotic survival pattern: A relational theory of schizophrenia. *Family Process, 12*, 377-398.

Sroufe, L. A., & Fleeson, J. (1986). Attachment and the construction of relationships. In W. Hartup & Z. Rubin (Eds.), *Relationships and development* (pp. 51-72). Hillsdale, NJ: Erlbaum.

Sroufe, L. A., Jacobvitz, D., Mangelsdorf, S., DeAngelo, E., & Ward, M. J. (1985). Generational boundary dissolution between mothers and their preschool children: A relationship systems approach. *Child Development, 56*, 317-332.

Sroufe, L. A., & Ward, J. J. (1980). Seductive behaviors of mothers of toddlers: Occurrence, correlates and family origin. *Child Development, 51*, 1222-1229.

Stierlin, H. (1974). *Separating parents and adolescents: A perspective on running away, schizophrenia and waywardness*. New York: Quadrangle, The New York Times Book Company.

Tharp, R. G. (1965). Marriage roles, child development and family treatment. *American Journal of Orthopsychiatry, 35*, 351-358.

Walsh, F. W. (1979). Breaching of family generation boundaries by schizophrenics, disturbed, and normals. *International Journal of Family Therapy, 1*(3), 254-275.

Wegscheider, S. (1981). *Another chance: Health and hope for the alcoholic family*. Palo Alto, CA: Science and Behavior Books.

Wegscheider, S. (1983). Chemical dependency—A system illness. *Focus on Alcohol and Drug Issues, 6*, 2-5.

Weiss, R. S. (1979). Growing up a little faster: The experience of growing up in a single parent household. *Journal of Social Issues, 35*, 97-111.

West, M. L., & Keller, A. E. R. (1991). Parentification of the child: A case study of Bowlby's compulsive care-giving attachment pattern. *American Journal of Psychotherapy, 45*(3), 425-431.

West, M. O., & Prinz, R. J. (1987). Parental alcoholism and childhood psychopathology. *Psychological Bulletin, 102*, 204-218.

Whiting, B., & Whiting, J. (1975). *Children of six cultures.* Cambridge, MA: Harvard University Press.

Winnicott, D. W. (1958). *Through pediatrics to psychoanalysis.* London: Hogarth.

Winnicott, D. W. (1965). *The family and individual development.* New York: Basic Books.

Winnicott, D. W. (1971). *Playing and reality.* New York: Basic Books.

Wolkin, J. (1984). Childhood parentification: An exploration of long-term effects (Doctoral dissertation, Georgia State University). *Dissertation Abstracts International, 45*, 2707-B.

Womack, M. (1991). *Issues of parental identification among adult children of alcoholics.* Unpublished doctoral dissertation, Georgia State University. (University Microfilm No. 912254)

Wood, B. L. (1987). *Children of alcoholism: The struggle for self and intimacy in adult life.* New York: New York University Press.

Zeanah, C. H., & Klitze, M. (1991). Role-reversal and the self-effacing solution: Observations from infant-parent psychotherapy. *Psychiatry, 54*, 346-357.

Zigler, E., & Hall, N. W. (1989). Physical child abuse in America: Past, present, and future. In D. Cicchetti & V. Carlson (Eds.), *Child maltreatment: Theory and research on the causes and consequences of child abuse and neglect* (pp. 38-75). New York: Cambridge University Press.

Zuk, G. H., & Rubenstein, D. (1965). A review of concepts in the study and treatment of families of schizophrenics. In I. Boszormenyi-Nagy & J. L. Frame (Eds.), *Intensive family therapy: Theoretical and practical aspects* (pp. 1-31). New York: Harper & Row.

CHAPTER 2

Cross-Sex and Same-Sex Family Alliances

Immediate and Long-Term Effects on Sons and Daughters

Deborah Jacobvitz
Shelley Riggs
Elizabeth Johnson

Family theorists describe healthy family patterns as hierarchically organized, whereby parents guide and nurture their children's development, and children, in turn, seek comfort and advice from their parents. When this hierarchy breaks down, children may assume a parental role in response to a mother or father who turns to them for support instead of to a partner or other adult. Clinicians and researchers have noted the negative effects on children when the generational boundary between parent and child breaks down. For example, 42-month-old sons who were observed to fulfill their mothers' needs for intimacy at the expense of receiving needed guidance and emotional support for themselves were more impulsive, inattentive, and overly active in kindergarten, first grade, and second grade, according to teacher reports (Carlson, Jacobvitz, & Sroufe, 1995; Jacobvitz & Sroufe, 1987). Similarly, females who remembered meeting their fathers' needs for intimacy and support without receiving appropriate parental nurturance in return had more difficulty achieving a stable sense of identity (Fullinwider-Bush & Jacobvitz, 1993) and reported more symptoms of depression, anxiety, and lowered self-esteem (Jacobvitz & Bush, 1996). This chapter will elaborate how boundaries between parent and child become blurred and the differential effects on males and females of parent-child role reversal, whereby the child assumes emotional and instrumental responsibility for the parent. It will then explore the effects of role reversal on children within the context of other family relationships. Finally, it will discuss the clinical implications of these family dynamics.

MAINTENANCE AND BREAKDOWN
OF PARENT-CHILD BOUNDARIES

The concept of "boundaries" represents the usually implicit emotional and psychological limits or rules that define various family relationships. For example, boundaries define who participates in family interaction and discourse, as well as the role each member plays (Minuchin, 1974). Perhaps the most important differentiation of roles is the generational hierarchy that places the parents in control of their children. Family theorists generally have assumed that the maintenance of cross-generational boundaries is essential to the overall health of the family system and its individual members (Boszormenyi-Nagy & Spark, 1973; Bowen, 1978; Jurkovic, 1997, in press; Minuchin, 1974). Clear, but flexible, parent-child boundaries in which parents respond to the child's needs for both dependence and independence are particularly important for optimal development during childhood. A central developmental task for children during toddlerhood and adolescence is both to stay connected to their parents and to develop an independent sense of self. Parents who provide their children with nurturance and, at the same time, encourage autonomy foster their toddlers' developing capacity to regulate impulses and emotions and the adolescents' ability to achieve an independent sense of identity.

The maintenance and breakdown of generational boundaries exist on a continuum. Some degree of role reversal may be a normal, and probably inevitable, developmental experience between parent and child (Boszormenyi-Nagy & Spark, 1973; Minuchin & Montalvo, 1967). A child may learn to identify with responsible roles and to internalize the image of self as a potentially nurturant parent (Boszormenyi-Nagy & Spark, 1973). An important question, then, is when are these cross-generational alliances pathogenic? Changes in the composition of the family unit—for example, an increasing number of single parents, unmarried couples with children, and gay and lesbian couples—require an adjustment in clinical and theoretical biases about the optimal organization of a healthy family system. In determining the point at which generational boundary dissolution becomes pathological, it is important to consider at least three factors: (a) the dynamic significance of the relationship within the family, (b) the timing and persistence of family patterns over time, and (c) the extent to which the parent relinquishes the protective function of caregiving.

With respect to the first factor, the dynamic significance of the relationship within the family, it is important to consider the extent to which one relationship in the family affects other relationships within the same family. More specifically, an overly involved relationship between one parent and child may compromise the child's relationship with the other parent or a sibling, creating emotional distance or even animosity. The child may then have to cope not only with an intrusive, controlling parent but also with the difficulties that ensue with other family members.

The timing (in relation to the family life cycle) and relative permanence of the family patterns must be considered to assess the appropriateness of role reversal (Wood & Talmon, 1983). For example, in families in transition after parental death or divorce, one family member is likely to assume those roles previously held by the absent parent, and perhaps those held by a distressed and inadequately functioning custodial parent as well. In these stressful circumstances, changes in the distribution of roles that affect the hierarchical structure of the family may be crucial to the process of successful family adaptation. According to Wood and Talmon (1983), as long as the reversal of roles between parent and child is temporary and adaptive, such patterns are not pathological. The more rigid this role assignment proves to be, however, the more damaging it is to the individual family members.

Finally, one of the primary goals of caregiving is to protect the child from harm. Bowlby (1973) proposes that infants are pre-adapted to turn to the caregiver for comfort and safety when alarmed. Infants who have caregivers who are perceptive and respond quickly and appropriately to their signals of distress are likely to form a secure attachment to them (Ainsworth, Blehar, Waters, & Wall, 1978). On the other hand, those whose caregivers are either emotionally unavailable, unpredictable and interfering, or even frightening when calm reassurance is needed are likely to form an anxious or insecure attachment relationship. Longitudinal studies following children over 10 years have shown that infants classified as insecure at 12 and 18 months (vs. those classified as secure) had more difficulty exploring the environment at 24 months (Matas, Arend, & Sroufe, 1978), persisting on challenging tasks at 42 months (Sroufe, 1983), and making friends in middle childhood (Sroufe & Jacobvitz, 1989).

Other longitudinal studies have shown that infants who did not have a strategy for gaining comfort from their caregiver when distressed were classified at age 6 as "controlling" with their mothers, in either a punitive or a caregiving way (Main & Cassidy, 1988; Wartner, Grossman, Fremmer-Bombik, & Suess, 1994). Main and Cassidy (1988) explain that these children seemed "to actively attempt to control or direct the parent's attention and behavior and assume a role which is usually considered more appropriate for a parent with reference to a child" (p. 418).

In semistructured interviews with mothers about their relationships with their 6-year-olds, George and Solomon (1996) found that mothers of "controlling" children more often took a helpless stance than did the other mothers. In some cases, the mothers' helplessness involved failing to provide reassurance and protection to their children, while in other cases, the helpless stance included fear either of their children or of their own loss of control. Other mothers described feeling that their children were in control of the relationship, either because of their child's precocious positive capabilities or because of their child's unmanageability. Controlling children, in turn, were more likely than other children to depict themselves as helpless and their caregiver as frightening (Solomon, George, & de Jong, 1995). Solomon and colleagues (1995) asked 6-year-olds to respond to a set of doll-play stories, including one about a child separated from a caregiver and another about a child with a hurt knee. They found that the responses of "controlling" children was characterized by themes of catastrophe and helplessness, including nightmares and violent fantasies, or by a complete inhibition of play. Thus, parent-child boundaries can be considered disturbed when children are expected to care for the parent, or control the parent by other means, at the expense of receiving the comfort and protection they need.

Parent-Child Boundary Disturbances

At the clinical extreme, boundary disturbances generally can be characterized as a parent's failure to respect or encourage a child's autonomy, becoming overly involved, controlling, or intrusive, and even expecting the child to care for the parent. During toddlerhood, caregivers may interfere with the child's ongoing interests, moods, and activities even though parental guidance is unnecessary. Impressive longitudinal studies have demonstrated that children whose caregivers interfered during the first year of life were often classified as insecure (vs. secure) compared with children whose mothers were perceptive of their infants' signals and responded with sensitivity. Children whose mothers were intrusive when they were 6 months, compared to those who experienced maternal sensitivity, were less persistent and became frustrated more easily on challenging tasks when they were $3\frac{1}{2}$ years old. Rather than try to solve a problem independently, they immediately sought help (Egeland, Pianta, & O'Brien, 1993).

Parents with an interfering caregiving style may, in turn, expect the child to satisfy the parent's psychological needs by providing the parent with guidance, nurturance, and companionship or by taking on household responsibilities that are beyond the child's developmental competencies (e.g., managing household finances, caring for siblings). Conversely, the parent takes on a complementary child-like or spousal role in relation to the child. For example, Main and Goldwyn (1998) describe parents who may seem bewildered or incompetent in the parental role. According to Bowlby (1980), the parent may disguise the role-reversed pattern with overprotectiveness or oversolicitousness, but the parent expects the child to act in a particular way to meet the parent's needs at some cost to the child development. These children do not receive adequate physical and emotional nurturance and protection from the parent, and the child's parental role is not explicitly recognized or supported, and may even be punished. The costs to the child, as will be described in more detail, is an inability to develop separately from the parent (i.e., differentiate or individuate) and develop an autonomous sense of self (Boszormenyi-Nagy & Spark, 1973; Jacobvitz, Morgan, Kretchmar, & Morgan, 1991; Mika, Bergner, & Baum, 1987; Minuchin, 1974; West & Keller, 1991).

Intergenerational Origins of Boundary Disturbances

A growing body of theory and research has focused on the intergenerational origins of boundary disturbances. Boszormenyi-Nagy and Spark (1973) coined the term "parentification" to describe a boundary distortion that they propose develops over multiple generations. Parentification involves a distortion of roles such that the adult believes that the spouse is a parent, seeking the guidance and support that he or she did not receive during childhood at the expense of developing a more mutual, give-and-take, relationship. Adults who turn to their spouse for such parenting will almost inevitably become disappointed with their partner, and either marital conflict or emotional distance is likely to ensue. The adult then turns to the child to fulfill the parental role. Adults experience their unmet need for nurturance and guidance during childhood as "accounts due" or "debits" and look to their spouse and child for parenting as a way of balancing the ledger. Parentified children are likely to grow up and repeat these boundaries disturbances with their spouse and child.

Sroufe and Fleeson (1986) explain how the sense of self supports continuity and reenactment of role-reversed relationship patterns. Based on early relationship experiences with significant others, children develop expectations of others, relationships, and the self that they carry forward to future relationships. These expectations influence the way the child will later approach others, as well as his or her feelings, thoughts, and behaviors with respect to important relationships.

Empirical support for the transmission of mother-daughter role reversal and entanglement across multiple generations derives from a study of 55 family triads consisting of mothers, adult daughters, and 6-month-old infants. Mothers who recalled that their own mothers (i.e., the great-grandmothers of the infants) were overly protective and failed to encourage their autonomy during childhood had adult daughters who also recalled that the mothers were overly protective of them, stifling their independence and prohibiting exploration (Jacobvitz & Kretchmar, 1996). Also, in a 30-minute series of problem-solving tasks, observations of mother-daughter role reversal and entanglement were recorded. The authors anticipated that daughters who recalled that their mothers were overly protective during childhood would have difficulty asserting their needs and would reenact childhood patterns. Instead, however, diffusion of boundaries between mothers and their adult daughter took three forms, including the mother's continuing intrusiveness and interference, a reversal of mother-daughter roles whereby the daughters were intrusive and controlling, and a peer-like mother-daughter relationship.

As predicted, one group of mothers continued to be interfering and intrusive with their adult daughters. For example, one mother spent most of the time telling her daughter that she needed to go to church more often, that she had become a sinner, and that the Lord should be her guide. In another dyad, the daughter tried to tell her mother politely that she did not like her coming to her home and taking over the household chores without the daughter's permission. The mother responded by telling the daughter how she should arrange her daily schedule. Other daughters in the study (in fact, the majority that were rated high on boundary distortions), however, were intrusive with their mothers; they lectured and scolded them, instructing them on how they should have behaved when the daughter was young and what they now expected of their mothers, and some discussed the mother's intimate relationships even when their mother tried to move away from the topic. For example, in one mother-daughter pair, the daughter was observed shaking her finger at her mother and scolding her, saying "I told you we were just fine, the two of us, when I was young. Why did you have to go and marry him? He was never any good for you!" The mother physically inched away from the daughter on the couch, shrugged her shoulders, hung her head low, and responded in a high-pitched, weak voice, "Oh, I know. I know. You are right. I know." Coders noted that the mothers seemed uncomfortable and that these interactions were painful to watch. Such a dynamic is consistent with the idea that relationships are wholes and that each person in a relationship learns both roles. For example, Troy and Sroufe (1987) found that children who were victimized by their parents carry forward to their peers both the victim and the victimizer role. The adult daughters in the study conducted by Jacobvitz and Kretchmar (1996) have learned both roles, the controlling and intrusive mother and the unassertive, withdrawn child.

Other mother-daughter dyads talked openly and freely, more like friends than like parent and child. In fact, it often was difficult to determine who was the mother and who was the daughter. When asked to discuss what they enjoy most about each other, some pairs responded "We wear the same clothes" or "We go to parties together." In some cases, they finished each other's sentences, said the same phrase simultaneously, and/or spoke for the other.

This last group of mother-daughter dyads illustrates the subtlety of some cases of boundary diffusion that involve shifting roles such that the parental function is not entirely abdicated by the parent. Family members may insist that no problem exists and that, in fact, mother and daughter are just unusually close. In fact, as women grow older, they may be likely to develop balanced friendships with their mothers. Yet, Jacobvitz and Kretchmar (1996) propose that until the mother's health or emotional or mental state declines, there still remains some hierarchical generational boundary whereby the mother is expected to provide the daughter with nurturance and guidance. The mothers in the study conducted by Jacobvitz and Kretchmar (1996) ranged in age from 40 to 57 years; they were not elderly.

One way to determine whether qualities of the mother-daughter relationship do in fact constitute boundary distortions is to examine the effects of such experiences on the daughter. Jacobvitz and colleagues (1991) anticipated that adult daughters who showed boundary disturbances in their relationships with their mothers would have difficulty encouraging autonomy in their children. Adult daughters were videotaped playing with and feeding their infants for about 30 minutes when their infants were 6 and 9 months old. Those adult daughters who recalled that their mothers were overly protective and stifled their autonomy during childhood and/or had role-reversed or peer-like relationships with their mothers during adulthood were observed to be more intrusive and interfering with their infants than the other adult daughters. Moreover, these women (the adult daughters) tended to view the world as unsafe, reported having difficulty trusting others, and became so distressed when their infants cried that they could not comfort them (Jacobvitz et al., 1991). In sum, although boundary distortions in the relationships across the three generations manifested differently—parental intrusiveness, parental overprotection, and parent-child role reversal—they all involved mothers continuing entanglement with their children at the expense of fostering their children's autonomy and individuation.

Other studies have found similar results. Based on 1-hour interviews about the quality of care they received during childhood (i.e., "the Adult Attachment Interview"; George, Kaplan, & Main, 1996), mothers were identified who appeared still angrily preoccupied or entangled with their relationship with their parents during childhood. These mothers were observed to be intrusive and unpredictable with their infants who were subsequently classified as insecurely attached. Daughters parentified during childhood appear to continue to worry about their mothers during adulthood, become intrusive and interfering with their infants, and have children who develop an insecure attachment (Benoit & Parker, 1994; Fonagy, Steele, & Steele, 1991; Jacobvitz & Kretchmar, 1996).

In sum, present research finds that mothers may be controlling, intrusive, or overprotective with their children, discouraging their children from exploring and developing an independent sense of self. In so doing, the mother keeps her child nearby to gratify her needs and bear the emotional responsibility for the relationship. When the child grows older, he or she may attempt to depend on others, either a spouse or child, to satisfy unmet needs and thereby reenact early relationship experiences.

Less is known about the breakdown of generational boundaries between fathers and sons. Some researchers speculate that because cultural expectations for females, more than males, involve taking care of others, girls are more likely than boys to become enmeshed and entangled with their mothers (Brody, 1996). It may be possible, however, that fathers parentify their sons but do so differently from mothers and daughters. Perhaps fathers expect sons to take on major household responsibilities, such as holding a job at a younger age, attempt to live vicariously through their sons' athletic and academic achievements, and even encourage their sons to engage in sexual experiences at an early age. Further research is needed to identify whether fathers and sons engage in reversals of roles and, if so, both the form these reversals take and the consequences of such a dynamic on boys.

Boundary Distortions:
From Dyadic to Triadic Interactions

Parent-child boundary disturbances often take place in the context of other relationships within the same family, such as the marriage. Dozens of studies attest the negative effects of marital discord on children (Belsky, Rovine, & Fish, 1989; Cox, Owen, Lewis, & Henderson, 1989; Howes & Markman, 1989; Jouriles, Murphy, & O'Leary, 1989) or the differential effects of caregiving qualities on children (Maccoby, 1992). Surprisingly few researchers, however, have systematically studied relations among relationships within the same family (e.g., links between the marriage and parent-child relationship). Jacobvitz, Fullinwider, and Loera (1989) have shown that examining the marital and parent-child relationships in combination better predicted children's development than looking at the parent-child relationship alone.

Family theory has long stated that dyadic relationships can be understood only by looking at the family system of relationships, and that each dyadic relationship necessarily is linked to every other relationship within the family. Little is known, however, about the process by which family relationships are interconnected. We propose that parentification often occurs as part of a number of family patterns characterized by either distance or conflictual marital interactions, or even the physical or psychological absence of one or both parents. In such cases, the child may form an alliance with a sibling to cope with parental absence. Alternatively, a cross-generational alliance between one parent and a child may occur combined with distance between the other parent and the child. The experience and outcomes of parentification vary depending both on the sex of the parentified child and on whether the cross-generational alliance is same-sex or cross-sex. In the latter case, role reversal often takes the form of spousification, in which the child is expected to take on spousal functions of intimacy, emotional support, and, in the extreme, sexual gratification.

In addition to interconnected relationships within the nuclear family, parentification can result from an attempt to balance "accounts due" arising from parents' experiences in their family of origin (Boszormenyi-Nagy & Spark, 1973). Because participants in a close relationship learn both roles of a relationship pattern, a dialectic dynamic results in which one can play either role of a dyadic pattern. This switching between one of two complementary roles can occur over time within one relationship or between generations. A woman who was parentified as a child may, with her own child, take on the role of needy adult and thereby replicate the relationship that she experienced as a child, this time assuming her mother's role.

These dialectic dynamics can occur on the level of individuals, nuclear families, and extended family networks (Boszormenyi-Nagy & Spark, 1973). Within individuals, close relationships always evoke some degree of contradictory feelings, or ambivalence. Some people have difficulty managing their ambivalent feelings and use a strategy of "splitting" to resolve the tension (Juni, 1995). In this process, the individual splits his or her ambivalent feelings between two relationships, keeping one positive and close, and projecting negative feelings to the second relationship. Juni (1995) suggests that this process of splitting and projecting ambivalent feelings underlies family triangles. In Juni's conceptualization, the inability to manage ambivalence lies within one individual, and that individual manipulates a network of relationships to create a triangle. One could also conceive of this process as occurring on a family level, with family members, including both parents and siblings, co-constructing black and white family roles when feelings of ambivalence within the family are intense.

Examples of this splitting on a family level can be drawn from retrospective accounts by women who experienced spousification through incestuous and seductive relationships with their fathers. Reporting results of comparisons of 40 women who experienced incest with their fathers and 20 women whose fathers had been seductive but not overtly sexual, Herman and Hirschman (1981) observed that in both groups the women often viewed their mothers, and indeed most women, with contempt, and idealized the power and charm of their fathers. One woman whose father had been seductive commented that "My mother's a bitch and a nag. I don't know why Daddy stays with her; she makes his life miserable. Daddy and I really understand each other. If my mother doesn't like it, too bad" (Herman and Hirschman, 1981, p. 114).

The next sections describe some of our work examining relations among relationships within a family. This work is based on the rich descriptions provided by family systems theorists and clinicians of how the marital and parent-child relationships influence each other and the effects of triadic relationships on family members.

Parent-Child Alliances

In our research, we have delineated two kinds of family alliances, same-sex and cross-sex intergenerational alliances, that occur and develop their meaning within the context of the family system, and as such are affected by and have implications for other relationships within the family. In particular, the marital relationship has been shown to be intimately involved in the development of parent-child alliances. Minuchin (1974) proposed that these rigid family structures may provide short-term relief from the stress associated with a troubled marriage. Parent-child alliances also interfere, however, with the ability of spousal partners to resolve conflicts and, by inappropriately placing the child in the middle of the marital subsystem, may jeopardize the child's psychological growth. Interactions between couples in troubled marriages vary. Some couples display heightened conflict and negativity, while others become emotionally distant and withdrawn. These two marital interaction patterns appear to affect the parent-child relationship in different ways depending on the gender of the child. For example, high levels of marital conflict have been associated with parent-child alliances that form along gender lines. In a sample of 522 adolescents, Buchanan, Maccoby, and Dornbusch (1991) found that daughters, more often than sons, reported feeling caught between battling parents and tended to establish coalitions with their mothers against the more aggressive fathers. Moreover, the more caught adolescents felt, the more depressed and anxious they were, and the more they engaged in deviant behavior (e.g., took drugs, cheated on a class test, carried weapons to school, got in trouble with the police). Similarly, Kerig, Cowan, and Cowan (1993) found that in families characterized by high marital conflict, mothers were observed to respond more positively toward their daughters (e.g., expressing pleasure, giving praise, and providing acknowledgment) than toward their sons. In another study, Jacobvitz and Bush (1996) found that young adult women's memories of marital conflict during elementary school covaried with their accounts of overly involved and entangled relationships with their mothers and emotionally distant relationships with their fathers.

A similar pattern has been found for males. When marital discord exists, sons are more likely than daughters to model their father's aggressive conflict resolution affect (Camara & Resnick, 1988) and fathers to respond with more negativity to their daughters (e.g., complaining, ignoring or rejecting them) than to sons (Kerig et al., 1993). Thus, when parents fight, children appear to identify with same-sex parents and experience tension or emotionally distant relationships with cross-sex parents.

Cross-Sex Parent-Child Alliances

An emotionally distant marital relationship in which the spouses do not rely on each other for support or express affection is a critical feature of cross-sex alliances. Unable to obtain emotional sustenance from the partner, one parent may withdraw from the family and turn to the opposite-sex child for intimacy and closeness. At the same time, these parents do not provide their children with the needed parental guidance and support. Spousification can be thought of as a form of parentification whereby the parent seeks companionship from the child. The central feature of the spousification pattern, however—seeking intimacy and, perhaps, even sexual gratification—distinguishes spousification from parent-child role reversal. Although this type of family pattern may temporarily relieve the stress generated by marital tension, it also may limit the ability of parents to overcome differences and may interfere with the child's psychological development. The negative effects of such family dynamics on children have been documented.

Most of the research on the effects of cross-gender alliances on children comes from studies of incest victims, cases in which fathers turn to their daughters, instead of their wives, to gratify their need for companionship, affirmation, sex, and nurturing. Females who have experienced intrafamilial sexual abuse during childhood more often report symptoms of depression and anxiety (Finkelhor & Hotaling, 1985) and are more likely to engage in boundary disturbances with their children (Burkett, 1991). Similarly, in a study of young adult women, Jacobvitz and Bush (1996) found that those who reported emotional distance in their parent's marriage coupled with intimate and caretaking exchanges with their fathers during elementary school more often showed symptoms of depression and anxiety, and experienced lower self-esteem, compared with women who did not recall these family dynamics.

Moreover, Fullinwider-Bush and Jacobvitz (1993) found that boundary violations, characterized by role reversal, enmeshment, and overinvolvement, with either parent compromised identity development in young adult women. Women who were excessively attuned to meeting the needs of their parents were unable to explore their own needs freely, particularly in intimate relationships. Interestingly, weak boundaries with each parent predicted distinct styles of identity exploration and commitment. Women who participated in cross-sex alliances with their fathers were more likely to report feeling indifferent and apathetic toward establishing, or even seeking to establish, a stable sense of identity. Women who participated in same-sex alliances, on the other hand, were more likely to prematurely commit to parental values without ever exploring personal alternatives. Thus, overinvolved and intrusive relationships appear to have detrimental effects on females' ability to master the critical developmental task of adolescence, identity exploration and commitment.

Women's reports of having experienced an alliance with their fathers during childhood also showed a significant association with observational ratings of their capacity to express feelings, reveal vulnerabilities, and stay emotionally attuned to their boyfriends. Interestingly, women's reports of a current alliance with their father were not related to the nature of their relationship with their boyfriends, and memories of an alliance with their father at any time in their lives, childhood or adulthood, were not related to the quality of women's interactions with their closest female friend. Furthermore, females' reconstructions of the entire network of family relationships during childhood, including connections between each parent-child relationship and the marital relationship, were related more strongly to their ability to form intimate and trusting relationships with men and women during adulthood than were their memories of their relationship with either mother or father alone (Jacobvitz et al, 1991).

Regarding relationships between mothers and sons, longitudinal research shows that women exploited by their fathers during childhood tend either to engage in a reversal of parent-child roles or to spousify their sons, touching them inappropriately, whispering secrets, and giggling together (Sroufe, Jacobvitz, Mangelsdorf, DeAngelo, & Ward, 1985). The negative effects of such treatment with sons on their emotional and behavioral development have been documented. Sons who had a history of parentification or spousification with their mothers at 24 and 42 months of age were more likely to show inattentive, impulsive, and hyperactive behavior problems in kindergarten (Jacobvitz & Sroufe, 1987) and in 2nd and 6th grade (Carlson et al., 1995). In addition, sons with a history of mother-son role reversal and spousification were less popular with peers during preadolescence and more often violated gender boundaries on the playground.

SIBLINGS

When cross-generational relationships are stronger than within-generational relationships, the "collapsed" or "reversed" generational hierarchy affects the entire family, extending beyond the marital and parent-child dyads to profoundly influence the character of the sibling subsystem. In a family system where one child is recruited as a member of the parental or spousal subsystem, that child is elevated to a higher status in the family hierarchy and is, in effect, removed from his or her rightful position in the sibling subsystem. This situation affects not only the parentified/spousified child but also other siblings, who compete for parental attention and alliance when a strong marital bond is not present (Bank & Kahn, 1976).

When indifferent or unavailable parents show insufficient attention or understanding, siblings may turn to each other for support (Bryant & Crockenberg, 1980; Irish, 1964). In the absence of parents, siblings may provide the only opportunity for an abiding family relationship that can serve as a protective factor under stress. For instance, Jenkins (1992) found that children with a close sibling relationship in disharmonious homes demonstrated a low level of behavioral disturbance, similar to children in harmonious homes, whereas children with no close sibling relationship in disharmonious homes exhibited a very high level of symptoms. Maternal distance, helplessness, and inattention may be a cue to older children to become more resourceful and nurturing toward younger children (Bryant, 1982). Because of parental ineffectualness or unavailability, the most competent child, often the oldest, shoulders the primary role of caretaker to younger siblings. "Sibling caretaking involves roles, responsibilities, and presumably, developmental outcomes for both the children offering and receiving the sibling caretaking" (Bryant, 1982, p. 106). In this type of situation, the sibling relationship is burdened with tasks and issues that normally belong to the dynamics of the parent-child relationship.

Although adult responsibilities can be a creative force for growth, enhancing interpersonal skills, and providing an arena in which the child can practice leadership and self-sufficiency, parentified children may lose the opportunity to experience the egalitarian exchange characteristic of reciprocal sibling relationships (Bank & Kahn, 1982). Not only do these children gratify parental and sibling needs while sacrificing their own, but they also forgo the chance to develop within-generational alliances and mutual loyalty in the sibling sub-system. They also may miss the opportunity to practice the capacity for empathy offered in the sibling relationship (Provence & Solnit, 1983). These missed opportunities extend to peer relationships as well, which often reflect the development of reciprocal interaction in the sibling relationship. Instead, par-entified children are locked into a rigid role as their "brother's keeper," "res-cuer," or family mediator, experiencing a type of one-way loyalty in which they give without receiving. In turn, because there are a limited number of roles available to siblings, the nonparentified children are left with a restricted range of roles in which they are likely to be the underdog. Nevertheless, the cared-for sibling may benefit from the comfort, protection, and support provided by a parental child when parents are absent or unavailable (Bryant & Crockenberg, 1980), whereas caretaker siblings lack the protective nurturance of parental care and may feel deprived and bitter that they are not taken care of similarly. As a consequence, parentified children may develop a distrust of close relationships characterized by an extreme ambivalence regarding dependency needs and a determination to remain self-sufficient.

Research consistently indicates that family factors such as the emotional climate and differential parental treatment of children are powerful predictors of the quality of sibling relationships (Brody & Stoneman, 1987; Bryant & Crockenberg, 1980; Hetherington, 1988). For example, Stocker, Dunn, and Plomin (1989) found that maternal differential responsiveness was positively correlated with competition and control factors in the sibling dyad. Social comparison theory suggests that siblings use each other as relevant standards for comparison. Pfouts (1976) found that when children differ in some highly valued characteristic, the one who is regarded as "less" may become hostile and/or ambivalent toward their siblings. By extension, preferential treatment by parents would be regarded as highly desirable by children and thus could cause conflict between siblings.

Because most mothers direct more affection, attention, control, and respon-siveness to younger siblings (Brody, Stoneman, & Burke, 1987; Bryant & Crockenberg, 1980), older parentified children may come to resent their favored younger siblings. Consequently, many parentified children may become vindic-tive and domineering, gaining compliance from their siblings through coercion (Bank & Kahn, 1982). Faced with the resistance of younger siblings, parentified children may have neither the maturity nor the psychological integrity to provide adequate discipline without resorting to high power persuasive tech-niques. The "helping" of an older sibling often contains a strong element of control that may, in the end, have a negative effect on cared-for siblings because the parentified child lacks the skills, though not necessarily the intent, to perform the job adequately (Bryant, 1982).

On the other hand, younger children may resent the authority given to the parentified child and react with hostility and a lack of cooperation. The non-triangulated sibling may feel excluded from what appears to be a more intimate and loving connection between parent and parentified/spousified child. Given research showing that siblings rated their brothers and sisters as more active in the use of physical punishment than parents (Bryant, 1982), it appears particularly likely that the parentified child will resort to physical coercion with the uncooperative sibling. Although it is possible that the sibling relationship provides an important, enduring context in which siblings have the opportunity to develop control of aggression (Bryant, 1982), research findings suggest that experiencing aggression and conflict with an older sibling shapes the development of aggressive behavior and can lead to problematic relationships with peers (Patterson, 1984). Alternatively, the cared-for sibling may learn a subservient role, becoming passive, dependent, and incompetent in the mutual exchange of social interaction (Bank & Kahn, 1982).

GENDER AND SIBLINGS

Because of a certain coherence in the parental relationships across siblings, the family experiences of both parentified/spousified and nontriangulated siblings may be influenced by gender. For instance, Sroufe and colleagues (1985) found that mothers who were seductive with sons (spousification) were significantly less intimate and more hostile and derisive toward their older daughters than were control mothers. Furthermore, Bryant (1982) found that mothers and fathers respond differentially to a child who has an older brother than to one who has an older sister. Another study reported that mothers gave more feedback and explanation to children with older brothers and that fathers with older daughters were viewed as less controlling (Cicirelli, 1976). The latter findings imply that mothers and fathers relinquish some of their caregiving functions to an older sister that they do not to an older brother.

Not surprisingly, clinical observations and empirical data confirm that girls are more likely to take on parental roles (Goglia, Jurkovic, Burt, & Burge-Callaway, 1992; Mirkin, Raskin, & Antognini, 1984), and to see themselves as caretakers (Bossard & Boll, 1960). Similarly, research findings suggest that females tend to be more nurturant and positive with their younger siblings than older brothers (Abramovitch, Corter, & Lando, 1979), and are more likely to teach and praise their siblings, whereas males are more likely to work and play with their siblings (Minnet, Vandell, & Snatrock, 1983). Consistent with these findings, other evidence indicates that siblings generally are more willing to accept an older sister in the role of teacher and caretaker (Cicirelli, 1974) and to prefer older sisters as confidantes (Furman & Buhrmester, 1992). In turn, females generally report more affection, reliable alliances, intimacy, nurturance, and satisfaction with siblings than do males (Clark-Lempers, Lempers, & Ho, 1991). The impact of societal sex roles on these findings appears clear: Girls are socialized to identify with the relationally oriented roles of nurturer and teacher, whereas boys are socialized to bring more competitive attitudes into sibling interaction (Cicirelli, 1972).

Societal sex roles also provide a type of role structure that appears to prescribe norms for same-sex and mixed-sex sibling interactions (Maccoby, 1990). Thus, it is probable that the gender composition of sibling dyads influences the type of sibling interaction experienced by parentified children and their siblings. It has been argued that same-sex siblings will exhibit greater sibling rivalry than opposite-sex siblings (Schacter, Gilutz, Shore, & Adler, 1978). For example, Minnet, Vandell, and Snatrock (1983) found that more aggression occurred in 7- to 8-year-old boys with brothers than in 7- to 8-year-old boys with sisters, and that more negative behavior and cheating occurred in 7- to 8-year-old girls with sisters than in 7- to 8-year-old girls with brothers. More recent findings, however, challenge these reports, indicating that same-sex siblings report greater companionship, intimacy, and affection than opposite-sex siblings (Buhrmester, 1992). Stocker, Dunn, and Plomin (1989) reported that same-sex dyads (consisting of 3- to 6-year-old younger sibs and 5- to 10-year-old older sibs) were less controlling and competitive and were described by their mothers as having a more positive relationship than mixed-sex dyads. The contradictory results of these studies suggest the possibility that many same-sex sibling dyads experience an intense, ambivalent relationship characterized by a remarkable mixture of closeness, rivalry, and conflict. The addition of a parenting role to the same-sex sibling dyad would likely heighten any or all of these characteristics that uniquely describe any one sibling pair.

In terms of mixed-sex pairs, although some research suggests that agonistic encounters are more common in mixed-sex dyads (Dunn & Kendrick, 1981), Cicirelli (1976) reported that older siblings were more helpful and gave more feedback to an opposite-sex younger sibling than to a same-sex sibling. Interestingly, in the same study, opposite-sex younger siblings demonstrated more independent behaviors toward older siblings than did children with older same-sex siblings. In regard to a sibling dyad in which one child is parentified, it would appear that a cared-for sibling is better off with an opposite-sex sibling taking on a parental role. Not only would the cared-for sibling receive needed help and guidance, but he or she also would function independently apart from the sibling relationship.

Taken as a whole, the findings regarding gender and parentification suggest that parentified girls and their younger siblings may be at less risk for negative outcomes than parentified boys and their siblings. Not only are girls more willing to take on parental roles, but they also are perceived as being more effective teachers and caretakers by other siblings (Cicirelli, 1973). Similarly, regardless of sex, siblings are more likely to accept sisters as caretakers and confidantes. Because the caretaker role does not conflict with the expected gender roles of society, females appear more likely to benefit from the sibling relationship in such a situation. In particular, Cicirelli's findings regarding differential helping behavior and autonomy in mixed-sex sibling dyads suggest that boys with a parentified older sister may gain the most from their sibling relationship because they would receive more help from their sister, while maintaining individual autonomy.

CONCLUSIONS

Clinicians and researchers alike have noted the negative effects on children when the generational boundary between parent and child breaks down. Among the many conditions associated with a history of parent-child role reversal and parentification are impulsivity, hyperactivity, anxiety, guilt, depressive symptoms, impaired individuation, low self-esteem, overfunctioning, distrust of relationships, and ambivalence regarding dependency needs. Parentification is likely to negatively affect the child's individuation and separation from the involved parent, particularly during toddlerhood and adolescence. In some families, problems may not surface until the child leaves home for the first time and experiences difficulty adjusting to an independent lifestyle in which the primary role of parental child is no longer an organizing force.

Young adult females' experiences of parentification during childhood also appears to influence the quality of care they provide their children. We propose that adults are likely to reenact the family alliances experienced during childhood with their own partner and spouse. Although virtually no empirical studies exist on this topic, we can draw on attachment and family theorists to understand the intergenerational transmission of family alliances. A child is likely to fulfill the parent's expectations of him or her as a way of gaining closeness. Although the act of caring for the parent may provide a sense of security to the child, in the process of meeting the parent's needs and having his or her own needs ignored, the child may come to feel unworthy of love, and his or her self-worth can suffer. Subsequent disruption of the process of identity formation may lead these children to develop an overfunctioning (Bowen, 1978) or compulsive caregiving personality (Bowlby, 1977) in which the child continuously provides for others' needs, while sacrificing his or her own. Empirical findings by Valleau, Bergner, and Horton (1995) support the link between childhood parentification and the adult caregiving style of relating to others.

Not all children who participate in family alliances, however, develop emotional or behavioral problems or show difficulties separating and individuating from their parents. Parent-child alliances appear to be a risk factor increasing the likelihood of later emotional or behavioral difficulties, with other factors either elevating the risk or buffering the effects of such early caregiving experiences on the child. The task for further research is to identify other experiences that need to be considered to better predict the effects of family alliances on children.

In determining an intervention strategy, structural family therapy (Minuchin, 1974) recommends preserving and strengthening the generational hierarchy.

This goal is accomplished by removing the parentified child from the parental/marital subsystem and returning the child to his or her rightful position in the sibling subsystem, moving him or her toward greater involvement with more egalitarian relationships with siblings and friends (Minuchin, 1974; Minuchin & Fishman, 1981).

In addition, the concept of boundaries can help family therapists attend to parent-child role reversal in the family system of emotion regulation, whereby children are expected to meet their parents' needs for emotional support and intimacy. To break this pattern, parents may need to make changes in their current relationship with their own parents in order to balance emotional debts carried forward from childhood (Boszormenyi-Nagy & Spark, 1973).

Parentification of a child generally implies the presence of marital dysfunction (Minuchin, 1974), in which case marital therapy is essential to address the problems that have led to the displacement of parental and spousal roles onto children, particularly when spousification has led to incest (Taylor, 1984). In the case of a single-parent family, it might be helpful to work individually with the custodial parent, specifically in the areas of appropriate parent-child relations and the fair distribution of family chores and responsibilities among family members.

Additionally, family therapists should keep in mind that when one child has been assigned a rigid family role, it is likely that other siblings also have been assigned roles that may be deleterious to the evolving sibling relationship, as well as their ongoing individual development. Clinicians working with children in these families may benefit from actively involving siblings in the diagnosis and treatment of identified patients (Hamlin, 1983). Siblings not only have the advantage of a unique perspective on family interaction patterns, but also may benefit from therapeutic intervention themselves.

Finally, it is important to understand the function and meaning of family behaviors and interactions. Parentification may take different forms, including intrusiveness, controlling behavior, parent-child role reversal, and overprotection, all which function to inhibit the child's autonomy and increase the likelihood that the child will stay nearby and care for the parent. Further research is needed to understand both the ways in which parentification is manifest and the conditions that give rise to its various forms. One possibility is that parentification will manifest differently depending on the age of the child. For example, parents may be intrusive and controlling with their infants and toddlers and, as the child grows older, expect them to assume emotional responsibility for the parent. In the meantime, preventive programs can be developed that help parents and children to integrate both positive and negative feelings toward each other and to manage the anxiety associated with experiencing ambivalence. Such interventions promise to help prevent parent-child alliances from forming and thereby reduce the onset of emotional and behavior problems in family members in the current generation as well as the next.

REFERENCES

Abramovitch, R., Corter, C., & Lando, B. (1979). Sibling interaction in the home. *Child Development, 50,* 997-1003.

Ainsworth, M. D., Blehar, M. C., Waters, E., & Wall, S. (1978). *Patterns of attachment: A psychological study of the strange situation.* Hillsdale, NJ: Erlbaum.

Bank, S., & Kahn, M. D. (1976). Sisterhood-brotherhood is powerful: Sibling subsystems and family therapy. *Annual Progress in Child Psychiatry and Child Development,* 493-519.

Bank, S., & Kahn, M. D. (1982). *The sibling bond.* New York: Basic Books.

Belsky, J., Rovine, M., & Fish, M. (1989). The developing family system. In M. Gunnar (Ed.), *Minnesota Symposia of Child Psychology: Vol. 22. Systems and development* (pp. 119-166). Hillsdale, NJ: Erlbaum.

Benoit, D., & Parker, K. C. H. (1994). Stability and transmission of attachment across three generations. *Child Development, 65,* 1444-1454.

Bossard, J., & Boll, E. (1960). *The sociology of child development* (3rd ed.). New York: Harper & Row.

Boszormenyi-Nagy, I., & Spark, G. M. (1973). *Invisible loyalties: Reciprocity in intergenerational family therapy.* Hagerstown, MD: Harper & Row.

Bowen, M. (1978). *Family therapy in clinical practice.* New York: Jason Aronson.

Bowlby, J. (1973). *Attachment and loss: Vol. 1. Attachment.* New York: Basic Books.

Bowlby, J. (1977). The making and breaking of affectional bonds. *British Journal of Psychiatry, 130,* 201-210.

Bowlby, J. (1980). *Attachment and loss: Vol. 3. Loss, sadness, and depression.* New York: Basic Books.

Brody , G. H., & Stoneman, Z. (1987). Sibling conflict: Contributions of the siblings themselves, the parent-sibling relationship, and the broader family system. *Journal of Children in Contemporary Society, 19,* 39-53.

Brody, G. H., Stoneman, Z., & Burke, M. (1987). Child temperaments, maternal differential behavior, and sibling relationships. *Developmental Psychology, 23,* 354-362.

Brody, L. R. (1996). Gender, emotional expression and parent-child boundaries. In R. D. Kavanaugh, B. Zimmerberg, & S. Fein (Eds.), *Emotion: Interdisciplinary perspectives* (pp. 139-170). Hillsdale, NJ: Erlbaum.

Bryant, B. K. (1982). Sibling relationships in middle childhood. In M. E. Lamb & B. Sutton-Smith (Eds.), *Sibling relationships: Their nature and significance across the lifespan* (pp. 87-121). Hillsdale, NJ: Erlbaum.

Bryant, B., & Crockenberg, S. (1980). Correlates and dimensions of prosocial behavior: A study of female siblings with their mothers. *Child Development, 43,* 282-287.

Buchanan, C. M., Maccoby, E. E., & Dornbusch, S. M. (1991). Caught between parents: Adolescents' experience in divorced homes. *Child Development, 62,* 1008-1029.

Buhrmester, D. (1992). The developmental courses of sibling and peer relationships. In F. Boer & J. Dunn (Eds.), *Children's sibling relationships: Developmental and clinical issues* (pp. 19-39). Hillsdale, NJ: Erlbaum.

Burkett, L. P. (1991). Parenting behaviors of women who were sexually abused as children in their families of origin. *Family Process, 30,* 421-434.

Camara, K. A., & Resnick, G. (1988). Interparental conflict and cooperation: Factors moderating children's post-divorce adjustment. In E. M. Hetherington & J. D.

Arasteh (Eds.), *Impact of divorce, single parenting, and stepparenting on children* (pp. 169-195). Hillsdale, NJ: Erlbaum.

Carlson, E., Jacobvitz, D., & Sroufe, L. A. (1995). A developmental investigation of inattentiveness and hyperactivity. *Child Development, 66,* 37-54.

Cicirelli, V. G. (1972). Concept learning of young children as a function of sibling relationships to the teacher. *Child Development, 43,* 282-287.

Cicirelli, V. G. (1973). Effects of sibling structure and interaction on children's categorization style. *Developmental Psychology, 9,* 132-139.

Cicirelli, V. G. (1974). Relationship of sibling structure and interaction to younger siblings' conceptual style. *Journal of Genetic Psychology, 125,* 37-49.

Cicirelli, V. G. (1976). Mother-child and sibling-sibling interactions on a problem-solving task. *Child Development, 47,* 588-596.

Clark-Lempers, D. S., Lempers, J. D., & Ho, C. (1991). Early, middle, and late adolescents' perceptions of their relationships with significant others. *Journal of Adolescent Research, 6,* 296-315.

Cox, M. J., Owen, M. T., Lewis, J. M., & Henderson, V. K. (1989). Marriage, adult adjustment, and early parenting. *Child Development, 60,* 1015-1024.

Dunn, J., & Kendrick, C. (1981). Social behavior of young siblings in the family context: Differences between same-sex and different-sex dyads. *Child Development, 52,* 1265-1273.

Egeland, R., Pianta, B., & O'Brien, M. A. (1993). Maternal intrusiveness in infancy and child maladaptation in early school years. *Development and Psychopathology, 5,* 359-370.

Finkelhor, D., & Hotaling, G. T. (1985). Sexual abuse in the National Incidence Study of Child Abuse and Neglect: An appraisal. *Child Abuse and Neglect, 8,* 23-32.

Fonagy, P., Steele, H., & Steele, M. (1991). Maternal representations of attachment during pregnancy predict the organization of infant-mother attachment at one year of age. *Child Development, 62,* 891-905.

Fullinwider-Bush, N., & Jacobvitz, D. B. (1993) The transition to young adulthood: Generational boundary dissolution and female identity development. *Family Process, 32,* 87-103.

Furman, W., & Buhrmester, D. (1992). Age and sex differences in perceptions of networks of personal relationships. *Child Development, 63,* 103-115.

George, C., Kaplan, N., & Main, M. (1996). *Adult Attachment Interview* (3rd ed.). Unpublished manuscript, University of California, Berkeley.

George, C., & Solomon, J. (1996). Representational models of relationships: Links between caregiving and attachment. *Infant Mental Health Journal, 17,* 198-216.

Goglia, L. R., Jurkovic, G. J., Burt, A. M., & Burge-Callaway, K. G. (1992). Generational boundary distortions by adult children of alcoholics: Child-as-parent and child-as-mate. *American Journal of Family Therapy, 20,* 291-299.

Hamlin, E. R. II. (1983). A study of sibling role relationships. *Journal of Social Service Research, 6,* 95-108.

Herman, J. L., & Hirschman, L. (1981). *Father-daughter incest.* Cambridge, MA: Harvard University Press.

Hetherington, E. M. (1988). Parents, children and siblings six years after divorce. In R. A. Hinde & J. Stevenson-Hinde (Eds.), *Relations within families: Mutual influences* (pp. 311-331). New York: Oxford University Press.

Howes, P., & Markman, H. J. (1989). Marital quality and child functioning: A longitudinal investigation. *Child Development, 60,* 1044-1051.

Irish, D. P. (1964). Sibling interaction: A neglected aspect in family life research. *Social Forces, 42,* 279-288.

Jacobvitz, D. B., & Bush, N. (1996). Reconstructions of family relationships: Parent-child alliances, personal distress, and self-esteem. *Developmental Psychology, 32,* 732-743.

Jacobvitz, D., Fullinwider, N., & Loera, L. (1991, April). *Representations of childhood family patterns and intimacy in romantic relationships.* Paper presented at the biennial meeting of the Society for Research in Child Development, Seattle.

Jacobvitz, D. B., & Kretchmar, M. D. (1996, August). *Breakdown and maintenance of mother-daughter boundaries.* Paper presented at the 25th International Conference on Psychology, Montreal.

Jacobvitz, D., Morgan, E., Kretchmar, M., & Morgan, Y. (1991). The transmission of mother-child boundary disturbances across three generations. *Development and Psychopathology, 3,* 513-527.

Jacobvitz, D., & Sroufe, L. A. (1987). The early caregiver-child relationship and Attention-Deficit Disorder with Hyperactivity in kindergarten: A prospective study. *Child Development, 58,* 1488-1495.

Jenkins, J. (1992). Sibling relationships in disharmonious homes: Potential difficulties and protective effects. In F. Boer & J. Dunn (Eds.), *Children's sibling relationships: Developmental and clinical issues* (pp. 125-137). Hillsdale, NJ: Erlbaum.

Jouriles, E. N., Murphy, C. M., & O'Leary, K. D. (1989). Interspousal aggression, marital discord, and child problems. *Journal of Consulting and Clinical Psychology, 57,* 453-455.

Juni, S. (1995). Triangulation as splitting in the service of ambivalence. *Current Psychology: Research & Reviews, 14,* 91-111.

Jurkovic, G. J. (1997). *Lost childhoods: The plight of the parentified child.* New York: Brunner/Mazel.

Jurkovic, G. J. (in press). Destructive parentification in families: Causes and consequences. In L. L'Abate (Ed.), *Handbook of family psychopathology.* New York: Guilford.

Kerig, P. K., Cowan, P. A., & Cowan, C. A. (1993). Marital quality and gender differences in parent-child interaction. *Developmental Psychology, 29,* 931-939.

Maccoby, E. (1990). Gender and relationships. *American Psychologist, 45,* 513-520.

Maccoby, E. (1992). The role of parents in the socialization of children. *Developmental Psychology, 28,* 1006-1017.

Main, M., & Goldwyn, R. (1998). *Adult Attachment Classification System. Version 7.0.* Unpublished manuscript, Department of Psychology, University of California, Berkeley.

Main, M., & Cassidy, J. (1988). Categories of response to reunion with the parent at age 6: Predicted from infant attachment classifications and stable over a 1-month period. *Developmental Psychology, 24,* 415-426.

Matas, L., Arend, R. A., & Sroufe, L. A. (1978). Continuity of adaptation in the second year: The relationship between quality of attachment and later competence. *Child Development, 49,* 547-556.

Mika, P., Bergner, R. M., & Baum, M. C. (1987). The development of a scale for the assessment of parentification. *Family Therapy, 14,* 229-235.

Minnet, A. M., Vandell, S. L., & Snatrock, J. W. (1983). The effects of sibling status on sibling interaction: Influence of birth order, age spacing, sex of child, and sex of sibling. *Child Development, 54,* 1064-1072.

Minuchin, S. (1974). *Families and family therapy.* Cambridge, MA: Harvard University Press.

Minuchin, S., & Fishman, H. C. (1981). *Family therapy techniques.* Cambridge, MA: Harvard University Press.

Minuchin, S., & Montalvo, B. (1967). Techniques for working with disorganized, low socio-economic families. *American Journal of Orthopsychiatry, 37,* 800-887.

Mirkin, M., Raskin, P., & Antognini, F. (1984). Parenting, protecting, preserving: Mission of the adolescent runaway. *Family Process, 23,* 63-74.

Patterson, G. R. (1984). Siblings: Fellow travellers in coercive family processes. *Advances in the Study of Aggression, 1,* 173-214.

Pfouts, J. H. (1976). The sibling relationship: A forgotten dimension. *Social Work, 21,* 200-204.

Provence, S., & Solnit, A. J. (1983). Development-promoting aspects of the sibling experience: Vicarious mastery. *Psychoanalytic Study of the Child, 38,* 337-351.

Schacter, F., Gilutz, G., Shore, E., & Adler, M. (1978). Sibling deidentification judged by mothers: Cross-validation and developmental studies. *Child Development, 49,* 543-546.

Solomon, J., George, C., & de Jong, A. (1995). Children classified as controlling at age six: Evidence of disorganized representational strategies and aggression at home and at school. *Development and Psychopathology, 7,* 447-463.

Sroufe, L. A. (1983). Infant-caregiver attachment and patterns of adaptation and competence. In M. Perlmutter (Ed.), *Minnesota symposia in child psychology* (Vol. 16, pp. 41-81). Hillsdale, NJ: Erlbaum.

Sroufe, L. A., & Fleeson, J. (1986). Attachment and the construction of relationships. In W. Hartup & Z. Rubin (Eds.), *Relationships and development* (pp. 51-72). Hillsdale, NJ: Erlbaum.

Sroufe, L. A., & Jacobvitz, D. (1989). Diverging pathways, developmental transformations, multiple etiologies and the problem of continuity in development. *Human Development, 32,* 196-203.

Sroufe, L. A., Jacobvitz, D., Mangelsdorf, S., DeAngelo, E., & Ward, M. J. (1985). Generational boundary dissolution between mothers and their preschool children: A relationship systems approach. *Child Development, 56,* 317-332.

Stocker, C., Dunn, J., & Plomin, R. (1989). Sibling relationships: Links with child temperament, maternal behavior, and family structure. *Child Development, 66,* 715-727.

Taylor, R. L. (1984). Marital therapy in the treatment of incest. *Social Casework, 65,* 195-202.

Troy, M., & Sroufe, L. A. (1987). Victimization among preschoolers: Role of attachment relationship history. *Journal of the American Academy of Child and Adolescent Psychiatry, 26,* 166-172.

Valleau, M. P., Bergner, R. M., & Horton, C. B. (1995). Parentification and caretaker syndrome: An empirical investigation. *Family Therapy, 22,* 157-164.

Wartner, U. G., Grossman, K., Fremmer-Bombik, E., & Suess, G. (1994). Attachment patterns at age six in south Germany: Predictability from infancy and implications for preschool behavior. *Child Development, 65,* 1014-1027.

West, M. L., & Keller, A. E. R. (1991). Parentification of the child: A case study of Bowlby's compulsive care-giving attachment pattern. *American Journal of Psychotherapy, 11*, 425-431.

Wood, B., & Talmon, M. (1983). Family boundaries in transition: A search for alternatives. *Family Process, 22*, 347-357.

CHAPTER 3

Workaholic Children
One Method of Fulfilling
the Parentification Role

Bryan E. Robinson

INTRODUCTION

I asked Sandra how things went during her Thanksgiving holidays. "Not so good," she replied. "My mama and uncle yelled at me because the turkey didn't turn out right."

Asked to explain, she said, "I cooked the turkey too long and it was too dry, so they fussed at me. I just went into my room and closed the door and hit my bed and cried."

I responded, "That's a pretty big job for a 10-year-old."

Sandra looked at me as if I were half crazy. "I always cook Thanksgiving dinner, 'cause my mama's too drunk!"

Not only does Sandra cook all the meals, she also looks after her 6-year-old sister and gets her off to school each morning. She cleans the house, does the laundry, and performs any other chores that are necessary for her survival. Sandra's mother is not a working mother, she is an alcoholic mother. Sandra is not a child, she is her mother's parent.

At age nine, Zak goes overboard with schoolwork and in everything he does, judges himself harshly for the most minute flaws, has few friends, and rarely plays with other children. He goes above and beyond what the teacher assigns. An assignment of a 5-page report turns out to be 10 pages long. If his teacher asks him to make a poster, he makes three. If she wants him at school for a special event at 8:00 a.m., he's there at 7:30. If she wants him to help with the erasers, he straightens the desks, does a bulletin board, helps clean floors, and stacks books too. He is willing to stay until the teacher leaves for the day. Even if it means staying until 5:00 p.m., he doesn't mind because he's doing what is right and he's getting her approval. Zak makes sure that whatever he does is

TABLE 3.1 Overly Functioning Children

Type	Author	Field
Resilient/invulnerable children	Anthony (1978)	Psychiatry
Transcendent children	Rubin (1996)	Sociology
Hurried children	Elkind (1981)	Psychology
Family heroes	Wegscheider (1979)	Social work
Responsible children	Black (1982)	Substance abuse/treatment
Type A children	Matthews and Angulo (1980)	Health and behavioral medicine
Workaholic children	Robinson (1998)	Family therapy

over, above, and beyond the call of duty. He wants to be the best, to do the most, and to get the most recognition.

By the time they had reached school age, Sandra and Zak had already carved a path of overfunctioning that stalked them into adulthood, manifesting as workaholism and interfering with their physical and mental health and personal relationships. This chapter examines the workaholic child who grows into the work addicted adult as a result of parentification in the formative years. First, I will discuss the traits of workaholic children and how they fit into the literature on overly functioning children. Next, I will examine the origins of workaholism in childhood. The literature on Type A children also will be presented as a context for understanding workaholic children. The chapter concludes with interventions and recommendations for practitioners and social scientists.

OVERLY FUNCTIONING CHILDREN

During the 1980s, social scientists identified and began studying the phenomenon of "overly functioning children"—children who function at high levels, well beyond their chronological years. Known by many labels, these children have one pattern in common: They are catapulted into the stressful and sometimes complicated adult world to function with children's emotions (see Table 3.1).

The first type of overly functioning children is called *resilient children* or *invulnerable children*. Their most common characteristic is their stress resistance. Despite the fact that resilient children are reared in extremely traumatic and stressful surroundings, they are said to thrive in spite of their problems (Robinson & Fields, 1983). Anthony (1978) describes the differences between children who are vulnerable and who are invulnerable. To explain the effects, he compared children with three kinds of dolls—glass, plastic, and steel. Glass dolls are shattered by the stressful experiences in childhood. Plastic dolls are permanently dented, and steel dolls are invulnerable, resisting the harmful effects of their surroundings. Glass (or vulnerable) children break down completely, plastic children sustain some serious injury, and steel (invulnerable) children thrive on the trouble and turmoil in their world.

Resilient children share a number of common traits. They have good social skills. They are at ease and make others feel comfortable. They are friendly and well liked by their classmates and adults. They have positive self-regard, and they have a feeling of personal power for influencing events around them. This contrasts with the feelings of helplessness that vulnerable children have. Not only do invulnerable children feel in control, they also want to help others needier than themselves.

One of the most comprehensive studies on resilience was conducted by Werner (1986), who followed 49 offspring of alcoholic parents over 18 years. She discovered that some children developed severe psychological disorders, whereas others appeared resilient to their alcoholic upbringing. Children were judged resilient by their outward appearance through interviews and examination of records, showing good grades and no mental or behavioral problems. Resilient children did well in school, at work, and in their social lives, and they had realistic goals and expectations for the future.

Lillian Rubin (1996) describes another similar type of child as *transcendent children*, those who triumph over traumatic childhoods to become healthy adults. These children are able to transcend bad beginnings because they feel separate from their families at a very early age, they have a sense of mission in life, and they have what she calls "adoptability," a knack for attracting and benefiting from mentors and surrogate parents.

David Elkind (1981) coined the term *hurried children* to refer to youngsters forced to grow up too fast. They are pushed to take on adult responsibilities before they are developmentally ready for these burdens. They are thrust into an adult world in which they are emotionally and intellectually unprepared to cope. Not only do they acquire adult responsibilities, but they also are recipients of the stress and tension that come with the territory.

Hurried children have many of the same characteristics as another group of overly functioning children called *family heroes*, whose role is to bring order and balance to a dysfunctional household by performing well and proving to the world that everything is normal at home, despite the odds (Robinson & Rhoden, 1998; Wegscheider, 1979). Usually the oldest children, they feel responsible for the family pain and work hard to make things better. To provide the family's self-worth, they excel in academics, athletics, or both and take on adult obligations such as putting a drunk parent to bed or taking care of younger siblings. Their well-functioning facade is a cover for the family pain as well as their own feelings of hurt, sadness, and inadequacy.

Responsible children are similar to family heroes in that their role is to give harmony and stability to the household (Black, 1982). The responsible child is usually the oldest, who assumes responsibilities for him- or herself and other family members. The responsible child becomes the parent child to brothers and sisters.

The next group of overly functioning children is called *Type A children*— young, compulsive overachievers who attempt to control others; suppress fatigue; are impatient, competitive, and achievement oriented; and have a sense of urgency and perfectionism (Matthews & Angulo, 1980). Healthwise, this compulsive need to achieve in children is linked to such cardiovascular risk factors as fluctuations in blood pressure and heart rate.

Could it be that all these labels are describing the same phenomenon: *workaholic children*? Each of these labels describes children who are 10 going on 30, in boot camp for learning the basic skills of adult workaholism. Each type of overly functioning child is described as having lived in a troublesome family of origin that somehow contributes to their overfunctioning. A common pattern in the families of these children is that children are expected to take on adult responsibilities before they are psychologically prepared. They are little adults with big burdens. Their childhoods are filled with serious issues ordinarily reserved for adulthood. Because they are more adept at most things, it is only natural that they are more skilled than most children at hiding their emotional pain, which is disguised by their extraordinary coping. Their attitude is, "Yeah! I can handle anything!" They learn to sacrifice intimacy for fixing, working, or getting the job done. They become product driven and lose an appreciation for the process, the moment.

Because achievement and competition are so highly valued in our society, workaholic children go unnoticed in terms of a need for special intervention; instead, their dysfunctional behavior patterns are reinforced and enabled at the microsystem, mesosystem, exosystem, and macrosystem levels in our society (Bronfenbrenner, 1979; Robinson, 1998a). Figure 3.1 presents a profile of workaholic children who, on the surface, appear to be functioning exceptionally well (Robinson, 1998a). They may be the most attentive, dependable, smart, and popular children in school. They follow the rules, always finish their schoolwork in the allotted time, and often are leaders in school government and extracurricular activities. They make the best grades and are sticklers for getting their work in on time—sometimes even before it is due. In high school, they can be president of the student body, star quarterback, or homecoming queen. While friends play and enjoy being carefree, the lives of workaholic youngsters are filled with serious, adult issues. Outward success conceals deeper problems of inadequacy and poor self-esteem. Underneath are overly serious children who browbeat themselves into perfectionism and judge themselves unmercifully for making human mistakes. Their overfunctioning becomes their drug that provides them good feelings about themselves while simultaneously causing them to have difficulty trusting, being intimate, and relinquishing control.

- Puts more time into school work than play time

- Has few friends and prefers the company of adults to that of other children

- Shows signs of health problems related to stress such as chronic exhaustion, headaches, or stomachaches

- Takes on such adult responsibilities as keeping the household running smoothly, cooking, cleaning, or caretaking of a younger sibling

- Strives for perfection in most things he or she does

- Stays serious much of the time and carries the burden of adult worries on his or her shoulders

- Spends little time relaxing, playing, fantasizing, having fun, and enjoying the carefree world of childhood

- Has precocious leadership abilities in the classroom and on the playground

- Seeks constant social approval from adults by striving to be a "good girl" or "good boy"

- Demonstrates compulsive overachievement in church work, schoolwork, sports, or other extracurricular activities

- Gets upset or impatient easily with himself or herself for making even the smallest mistake

- Shows more interest in the final result of his or her work than in the process

- Puts himself or herself under self-imposed pressures

- Does two or three things at once

- Has trouble asking for and receiving help

Figure 3.1. Characteristics of Workaholic Children

SOURCE: Adapted from *Chained to the Desk: A Guidebook for Workaholics, Their Partners and Children, and the Clinicians Who Treat Them*, Robinson, © copyright 1998 by New York University Press.

A FAMILY SYSTEMS MODEL OF ETIOLOGY

Family systems and psychodynamic theories suggest that adult patterns of interaction have their roots in the family of origin. A large body of research has shown that a functional family of origin is related to healthy functioning in adulthood (e.g., Canfield, 1984; Fine & Hovestadt, 1984). Research also suggests that adult work addiction is a consequence of family dysfunction in childhood and that it contributes to continued family dysfunction in adulthood (Fassel, 1990; Robinson, 1998b; Robinson & Post, 1995, 1997).

I employ a family systems model of addictions to conceptualize workaholic children as a symptom of a diseased family system (Robinson, 1998a, 1998b). The principal school of thought from this perspective is that addictions are transmitted through the breakdown of the family system, rendering it dysfunctional. Addictive behaviors are intergenerational and are passed on to future generations through family dynamics, often changing from generation to generation. Thus, through the family operation—its rules, beliefs, and behavior patterns—addictive behaviors such as alcoholism, work addiction, and co-dependent relationships can become an intergenerational cycle. From this model, work addiction in children is viewed as a learned addictive response to a dysfunctional family of origin system and employs a family of origin and family systems treatment perspective (Robinson, 1996a, 1996b).

To fully understand the origins of workaholism in children, practitioners must understand the interworkings of the child's total family system. They must look at the family as a composite because each member, as part of a functioning system, is interdependent on the others. As the family works together to run smoothly, any change in one part of the family will result in changes in the other parts. A family system will always try to keep itself balanced and will organize around its problems, often causing them to continue. Dysfunctional families alter how they function to accommodate family problems, which throw the whole family off kilter and cause them to shift the way they function to keep them in stasis and to maintain a closed system.

Work addiction develops most frequently in children who get a roller coaster ride through childhood, compared to those whose bounces and jostles are buttressed by steady parental hands. Because of various family situations, they are propelled into the adult world where, although unprepared, they are expected to cope without the emotional and mental resources of an adult.

Lacking the emotional equipment to survive these expectations, they instinctively grab onto a life raft to carry them through the storm. For many, it is the security of schoolwork, housework, homework, church work, and perfectionism. Examples of family patterns that can cause kids to become hooked on work are parental separation or divorce, with children placed in the middle of a tug of war; death of a parent, shattering family unity and spirit and perhaps never talked about; devastating unemployment, creating an economic seesaw; a traumatic family move, uprooting the children; parental substance abuse, throwing the family roles and expectations off kilter; parental schizophrenia or mental illness that send conflicting Dr. Jekyll/Mr. Hyde messages to children; and emotional incest in which one parent is physically or psychologically absent and the other parent elevates one of his or her young children to emotionally replace the absent parent as confidant and partner (Robinson, 1998a; Robinson & Kelley, 1998).

When the generation lines that insulate children from the parental adult world get violated or blurred, children can become what family therapists call *parentified* (Robinson, 1998b). They become parents to their own parents and sacrifice their own needs for attention, comfort, and guidance in order to accommodate and care for the emotional needs and pursuits of parents or another family member. Workaholic children are often child caretakers of younger siblings, or of emotionally dependent, alcoholic, or mentally and physically disabled parents, requiring them to become overly responsible at a young age before they are fully emotionally constructed themselves.

Workaholics, who are parentified as kids, often pass their parentification to their own offspring, who are sometimes chosen to be emotional surrogates for the missing workaholic parent. A typical example is the child who is elevated into an adult position within the family system to accommodate a parent's emotional need for intimacy by becoming the adult of the house during the workaholic parent's physical or emotional absence. Another scenario exists when the nonworkaholic spouse is consumed in the single parent role during the workaholic's absence: Children (usually the oldest) become parentified when required to become overly responsible at a young age before they are fully emotionally constructed themselves (Robinson, 1998a, 1998b). Examples include assuming household chores or caretaking responsibilities for younger siblings to bring homeostasis to the family system. Adult family members whose own needs were not met in childhood turn to their children to get these needs satisfied. The chosen child may be made into a confidant or an emotional caretaker, or required to live out parental dreams—even if these go against the child's desires and best interests. The child, to balance out the family, is used to establish family justice by providing parents whatever they never got from their own families. Children then begin to mold their identities around fulfilling the needs of parents and other adults: "Parentified children take care of their parents in concrete, physical ways by comforting them emotionally, and also by shaping their own personalities to meet the expectations of the parents, thereby increasing the parents' self-esteem" (Jones & Wells, 1996, p. 145). The gap of having to forfeit childhood—leaving youngsters void of feelings of approval, reassurance, love, and the comfort and protection from adult pressures—shows up years later as an oft-described "empty hole inside." The hole is the loss of childhood that workaholics missed, and it is continued into adulthood through deference and subjugation of self to work or caring for others: "The structure of a person's interactions with the parent is carried forward into adulthood and serves as a template for negotiating current relationships" (West & Keller, 1991, p. 426).

RESEARCH ON TYPE A BEHAVIOR
AS IT APPLIES TO WORK ADDICTION

In contrast to the scant research on work addiction, there is a vast body of research on Type A behaviors, children of Type A parents, and Type A children (Robinson, 1997). The reason for this is that the Type A behavior pattern, like alcoholism, has demanded research attention, because it is viewed as a medical problem—a condition that has been linked to coronary-prone heart disease. The Type A pattern emphasizes such generalized behaviors as the rapid pace of living, impatience, hostility, and competitive drive, whereas work addiction refers to more specific, compulsive work habits manifested in work performance. Friedman and Rosenman (1974) describe Type A individuals as hard-driven, competitive, hostile, and hurried. They invented the term to describe a personality type that—compared with Type B behavior types who are relaxed, easygoing, and not overly ambitious—is more prone to heart disease. The Type A personality pattern and work addiction describe the same high stress level and the aftermath of physical and health problems. Both depict a hard-driving, urgent, and impatient approach to life. Despite similarities, however, all Type A personalities are not necessarily workaholics, and there are different beliefs about the origins and treatment of Type A behavior and work addiction.

Work addiction is one way that obsessive-compulsive individuals manifest their obsessional tendencies. It is possible to be Type A or obsessive compulsive and manifest those traits in other, more diverse ways. A growing number of scientists believe that the tendency for Type A behavior is biologically inherited from parents (Weidner, Sexton, Matarazzo, Pereira, & Friend, 1988), whereas work addiction is viewed as the result of childhood upbringing (Robinson & Post, 1995, 1997). Whereas Type A behavior is most commonly treated with behavioral medicine, work addiction is most often and effectively treated through a nonmedical model of treatment from a family of origin and structural family therapy systems perspective. Because Type A behaviors parallel the pace and style of the workaholic, I have drawn heavily from this field of research to help clinicians, theorists, and researchers to better understand workaholic children.

Research on the Origins of Type A Behaviors

It is generally believed that Type A workaholic personality types are passed from parents to children through either family dynamics, genetics, or both (Woodall & Matthews, 1989). Type A behaviors are often described as a continual drive to succeed, acute desire for competition, need to achieve and be recognized, continual necessity for time restrictions, the aptitude or ability to increase the rate of execution of physical and mental functions, increased mental and physical alertness, and aggressive and hostile feelings (Houston, 1988; Raikkonen & Jarvinen, 1992; Yamasaki, 1990).

According to Paul Visintainer and Karen Matthews (1987), Type A kids often suppress their fatigue and become compulsive overachievers. They try to control others, and they are impatient, competitive, and achievement oriented and have a sense of urgency and perfectionism. Whereas Type A children tend to choose the performances of others as standards against which to compete, Type B children (those kids with an absence of Type A behaviors) tend to choose their own previous performance as a standard (Lopes & Best, 1987). Visintainer and Matthews traced the origins of Type A behavior and its association with coronary artery and heart disease to childhood. They observed Type A traits among schoolchildren as young as 5 years of age, and these traits endured over a 5-year period.

Healthwise, this compulsive need to achieve in children is linked to such cardiovascular risk factors as fluctuations in blood pressure and heart rate (Visintainer & Matthews, 1987). Type A children as young as 6 years of age have shown significantly greater cardiovascular responsivity with systolic rise than Type B children, a finding that suggests a precursor to adult cardiac disease (Brown & Tanner, 1987).

Despite their achievements, in the social domain hard-driving Type A children tend to be losers instead of winners. Studies indicate that peer relationships are negatively affected by Type A behaviors in early elementary school. Type A children, for example, have more difficulty making and keeping friends (Jose, 1986), a problem that appears to persist into adulthood. Other studies indicate that Type A behaviors in school-age children have been significantly associated with lack of social competence and social skills (Jose & Langer, 1989; Kliewer, 1991). Figure 3.2 shows the similarities between Type A children and workaholic adults.

Parallels drawn from the research between factors typical of Type A children and those of workaholic adults are strikingly similar. Hostility and anger factors are prominent in both Type A children (Matthews & Angulo, 1980) and adult workaholics (Haymon, 1993). Interpersonal and social skills are truncated in Type A children (Kliewer, 1991) and in workaholic adults (Robinson & Post, 1995), and both populations have difficulty establishing and maintaining relationships (Robinson, 1998a).

Health risks are high among Type A children (Visintainer & Matthews, 1987) and among workaholic adults (Spence & Robbins, 1992). There is a tendency among both Type A children (Leiken, Firestone, & McGrath, 1988) and workaholic adults (Matthews, Siegel, Kuller, Thompson, & Varat, 1983) to ignore and underreport warning signs of physical symptoms. Hyperactivity and overdoing are present among Type A children (Rickard & Woods-de-Rael, 1987) and among workaholics (Robinson & Post, 1994). Type A children, furthermore, have shorter reaction times than Type B children (Corrigan & Moskowitz, 1983). Impatience-aggression has been observed among Type A children (Vega-Lahr & Field, 1986) and workaholic adults (Haymon, 1993; Robinson, 1989). Type A children exhibit stronger efforts to excel (Matthews & Volkin, 1981) and tend to be more competitive (Eagleston et al., 1986) and hard driving (Yamasaki, 1994), whereas adult workaholics tend to be more driven than nonworkaholics (Spence & Robbins, 1992). Type A children have more of a sense of urgency and perfectionism than Type B children (Visintainer & Matthews, 1987), as do adult workaholics when compared to nonworkaholics (Robinson

---

- Hostility and anger are present in both Type A children and adult workaholics

- Interpersonal and social skills are truncated in Type A children and in workaholic adults, and both groups have difficulty establishing and maintaining relationships

- Health risks are high among Type A children and among workaholic adults

- There is a tendency among both Type A children and workaholic adults to ignore and underreport warning signs of physical symptoms

- Hyperactivity and overdoing are present among Type A children and among workaholics; Type A children also have shorter reaction times than Type B children

- Impatience and aggression have been observed among Type A children and workaholic adults

- Type A kids make stronger efforts to excel and tend to be more competitive and hard driving, whereas adult workaholics tend to be more driven than nonworkaholics

- Type A children are more anxious and stressed than non–Type A children, as are workaholic adults compared to non–workaholic adults

- Type A children have more of a sense of urgency and perfectionism than Type B children, as do adult workaholics in comparison to nonworkaholics

---

Figure 3.2. Portrait of the Similarities Between Type A Kids and Workaholic Adults

& Post, 1994; Spence & Robbins, 1992). This profile of Type A children and adult workaholics suggests that work addiction has its roots in one's family of origin, and Type A behaviors in childhood may be temperamental antecedents to adult Type A behavior and work addiction (Steinberg, 1985).

Research on Children of Type A Parents

Children with Type A behaviors tend to come from authoritarian families void of positive interpersonal climates, emotional support, and involvement. Lack of parental emotional warmth and involvement are antecedents to childhood anger, hostility, and greater cardiovascular responses to stress in boys that place them at risk for cardiovascular disease in adulthood. Type A behaviors are more prevalent among boys and adult men than girls and adult females, although both genders are at risk in Type A families (Haynes, Levine, Scotch, Feinleib, & Kannel, 1978; Matthews & Avis, 1983).

Type A behaviors have been traced as far back as the preschool years (Vega-Lahr & Field, 1986) and even to birth. One study reported that Type A behavior mothers tended to have Type A babies, whereas Type B mothers tended to have Type B babies (Fackelmann, 1992). Correlations of Type A behaviors between parent-child pairs are especially notable in father-son relationships, where paternal aspirations strongly influence Type A behavior in boys (Kliewer & Weidner, 1987; Weidner et al., 1988; Yamasaki, 1994). In general, these studies show that fathers of Type A sons were more competitive and set higher goals for their boys than fathers of Type B sons and that these goals are out of reach and unattained by the children (Blaney, Blaney, & Diamond, 1989; Weidner et al., 1988). Overall, Type A parents expect higher performance of and more independent behaviors from their children (Raikkonen, 1993; Thoresen & Pattillo, 1988). When sons of Type A parents were unable to achieve the goals, fathers used punitive actions and critical statements, and sons felt that paternal acceptance was contingent on their performance.

Family environments in which parents have big achievement expectations or evaluate their children's performance compared to others are believed to promote the development of such Type A behaviors as competitiveness, aggressiveness, and hostility, as well as losses in self-esteem and perceived control in some children (Harralson & Lawler, 1992; Price, 1982). Type A parents tend to be more controlling and dominating and to give specific directions and criticisms to their children, who turn out to be more competitive, angry, and stressed out than offspring whose parents do not pressure them to succeed (Thoresen & Pattillo, 1988). Although Type A children struggle and work harder, they do not accomplish any more than the children who approach tasks with a calm and more relaxed style. Other studies support the idea that cardiac prone behavior can be identified early in life and is related to socialization practices (Cassel, 1985; Kilbey & Davis, 1983; Visintainer & Matthews, 1987).

Hostile child-rearing practices among Type A parents who ignore children, are punitive and irritable, perceive the child as a burden, and are verbally hostile predispose children to Type A behaviors (Raikkonen & Jarvinen, 1992; Treiber et al., 1990). Other studies indicate that the children's perception of rejection and lack of emotional warmth from their Type A parents may be a developmental antecedent to youngsters' competitiveness, achievement striving, and time urgency (Emmelkamp & Karsdorp, 1987). Yamasaki (1990) found that fathers and mothers of Type A boys showed less concern for their children than parents whose boys were classified as Type B. Because Type A parents are self-absorbed in their own lives and show less interest in family members, their Type A children appear to be striving to prove themselves to get more attention and expression of concern and affection from their parents in order to gain self-confidence (Price, 1982; Yamasaki, 1990). Other studies support the relationship between Type A parents and lower self-esteem in their offspring, compared

---

- Parental rejection and lack of emotional warmth[2]

- Lack of parental attention and concern for children[8, 12, 13]

- High expectations and pressures for achievement and performance that are perceived by children as impossible to attain[1, 3, 5, 7, 9]

- Parental authoritarianism combined with unsupportive family climate and lack of positive family affiliation[4, 11]

- Parental control, domination, and criticism[9]

- Punitive, hostile, and irritable child-rearing practices by Type A mothers who perceive their children as burdens[8, 10]

- Hypertension and risk for cardiovascular disease[6]

Figure 3.3. Traits of Type A Parents That Serve as Antecedents to Type A Behaviors in Children

SOURCE: 1 = Blaney, Blaney, and Diamond (1989); 2 = Emmelkamp and Kaisdorp (1987); 3 = Harralson and Lawler (1992); 4 = Houston (1988); 5 = Kliewer and Weidner (1987); 6 = Lawler and Allen (1981); 7 = Raikkonen (1993); 8 = Raikkonen and Jarvinen (1992); 9 = Thoresen and Pattilo (1988); 10 = Treiber et al. (1990); 11 = Woodall and Matthews (1989); 12 = Yamasaki (1990); 13 = Yamasaki (1994).

to children of non-Type A parents (Houston, 1988; Raikkonen, Jarvinen, & Pietikainen, 1991).

RESEARCH ON WORK ADDICTION AND THE FAMILY SYSTEM

Only two studies have been conducted on work addiction and the family system. The first study ever conducted on workaholism in the family developed from a desire to know if there was a relationship between work addiction and family of origin or current family functioning (Robinson & Post, 1995, 1997). My colleagues and I administered a battery of tests to 107 participants from Workaholics Anonymous representing five regions of the United States and Canada. The average age of participants was 44 years, and 65% were women.

Findings indicated that workaholics who had sought counseling for their condition, compared to those who had not, were more likely to rate their families of origin as dysfunctional and lower in intimacy. Maintaining social and intimate relationships was a problem for workaholics in the overall sample because of work interference, with the social relationships of men more affected than the social relationships of women. Moreover, work addiction was positively linked to current family functioning in workaholic-headed families. The work addiction wreaked havoc on the family functioning such that the more serious the work addiction, the worse the family was at communicating, solving problems, expressing feelings, valuing others' concerns, and functioning as a unit.

Based on scores from the Work Addiction Risk Test (Robinson, 1998a), three groups were established from the sample: low, medium, and high risk for work addiction. Individuals in the high risk group were more likely to rate their families as having problems in communication or in the exchange of information among family members than those in the low or medium risk categories. They were more likely to rate their families as having unclearly defined family roles and believed their families were less likely to have established behavior patterns for handling repetitive family functions than those in the other groups. They also said their families were less likely to appropriately express feelings in response to various events that occurred in the family. High risk adults said their families were less likely to be interested in and value each other's activities and concerns. High risk individuals also were perceived to be more likely to have problems in the general functioning and overall health and pathology of their families than individuals at low or medium risk for work addiction. The study's strongest confirmation appeared to be in supporting clinical observations that work addiction is associated with ineffective communication, which can lead to brittle family relationships, contribute to marital conflict, and create dysfunction within the family system.

The second study on children of workaholics indicated that the family of origin dysfunction may get passed on to offspring. My colleagues and I asked 211 young adults to rate their parents on the Work Addiction Risk Test. Based on their ratings, parents were grouped as either workaholic (scores of one standard deviation above the mean) or nonworkaholic. We then tested the young adults (average age 24) on depression, anxiety, self-concept, and locus of control. Results showed that adult children of workaholic fathers suffered greater depression, anxiety, and external locus of control than the comparison group of children of nonworkaholic fathers. These findings corroborate similar findings among children of alcoholic populations, compared to adult children of nonalcoholics (Robinson & Rhoden, 1998). There were no differences on self-concept, and children of workaholic mothers scored no differently from children of nonworkaholic mothers. These findings match those from the Type A research, which suggests that fathers are more prominent in passing on to their children Type A behaviors (Weidner et al., 1988; Yamasaki, 1994).

Although research in this area is still embryonic, results of this study suggest that children are affected by parental work addiction in negative ways that are mentally unhealthy and can leave scars well into young adulthood. Other clinical accounts also suggest that children of workaholics often become workaholics themselves—using performance as a measure of their self-worth

(Robinson, 1998a). They are described as self-critical, perfectionistic, overly self-demanding, and chameleons in adult relationships—eager to forfeit the self for the approval of others.

SUGGESTIONS FOR PRACTITIONERS

Children have a basic need for psychological insulation during their vulnerable childhood years, to be provided by their caregivers, whose job it is to keep them safe and separate in their carefree worlds against intrusions of the adult world. When this security is breached, children learn that they cannot depend on adults to give them the insulation they need and that their absolute control over people and situations are essential for their psychological and physical survival. Constant disruptions require children to take charge of a life that feels like it is crumbling around them. Workaholic children learn to take control of everything around them to keep their worlds from coming unglued. They overcompensate for the confusion, become overconciliatory, and ultimately transfer these qualities into their jobs. They grow into adults who believe that they cannot count on anyone else and that their very emotional, financial, and physical survival requires them to do everything themselves. These traits serve workaholics by providing them the psychological insulation of certainty and security that they manufactured to survive childhood (Robinson, 1998a).

Workaholic children and adults are damaged by these traits because their refusal to ask for help and inability to delegate puts them at risk for burnout. Paradoxically, the insulation of parentified children becomes their isolation because, as adults, it is difficult for them to become fully involved in intimate relationships. They tend to be suspicious and unforgiving of people who procrastinate or who fail to follow through on commitments. Having renounced their own childhood need for care to attend to a designated family member, they pay a price in adulthood, where they carry forward a pattern of subjugation of self by attending to their work. As practitioners recognize the problem, children can receive the attention they need, and the dysfunctional behavior patterns can be circumvented before they become entrenched.

Several approaches can be taken to help workaholic children who are overfunctioning, driving themselves for approval. Outwardly, they appear immune from the effects of their hard-driving, competitive approach. Anxiety, depression, or the feeling that the control of their lives is outside themselves may be masked by resiliency, perfectionism, overresponsibility, or self-reliance to the point of having difficulty asking for help.

Positive school and social experiences could be mitigating factors that contribute to children overcoming their legacy. Practitioners often fail to assist compliant and accomplished children and may even reward them for their super-achievements, turning their attentions instead to children who have more obvious behavior problems (Robinson & Rhoden, 1998). School counselors and teachers, for example, can be on the lookout for "overly competent" children who appear to be functioning at their maximum.

It is important to point out that not all successful or competent children are suffering inside. Practitioners need to scrutinize for an *overdeveloped* sense of accomplishment, responsibility, and perfectionism and make sure these children get as much attention as other children who may have an easier time of showing their needs or asking for help. Workaholic children need challenges that match their developmental abilities but help in not taking on more than they can handle. Supportive adults who refrain from unreasonably high expectations and from saddling children with adult responsibilities, even when they are eager to accept them, can help to mitigate parental control and pressures to achieve. Providing unconditional regard for children—not just measuring their worth by what they produce or achieve—can be a major step forward for youngsters who have spent their lives measuring their value by the standards and approval of others.

Children can be provided with opportunities for noncompetitive games so that they can enjoy the sheer fun of play and learn to relax and enjoy their childhood with other youngsters rather than spending it with grownups in adult activities. Some children need to learn to play and enjoy the carefree world of childhood. Practitioners can encourage parents and teachers to welcome laughter and fun by structuring creative and process-oriented activities (such as story-telling, music, art, and sports) that teach children the value of the present moment as a balance to activities that are future-oriented and driven by the end product.

Workaholic children often grow into adults who are envied by everyone: responsible, achievement oriented, able to take charge of any situation success-fully. At least that is how they might appear to the outside world. Inside, they often feel like little children who never do anything right, while holding themselves up to standards of perfection without mercy, judging themselves harshly for the most minor flaws.

It has been said that "Work addiction is the pretty addiction. Not only does it look good on adults, but it is becoming on children as well" (Robinson, 1998a). Practitioners need to apprise themselves of the hidden dangers of childhood workaholism (see, for example, Robinson, 1996a, 1996b). It is important to screen for potential anxiety and depression among children and to look beyond the surface to the devastation of this "pretty addiction." Clinicians can help clients lower perfectionistic standards to more reachable goals and to delegate tasks in the office or at home. Helping workaholic children to be less self-critical and to strengthen their inner nurturing voice, and teaching them to affirm them-selves for "who they are" and not just for "what they do," are also important.

Practitioners can screen for stress and burnout and, where appropriate, teach stress-relief exercises or other relaxation techniques to help them live more in the moment. Developing flexibility and the ability to allow for spontaneous, spur-of-the-moment activities are worthy goals.

Family of origin work is essential for understanding the legacy of childhood workaholism. Practitioners can use a family systems approach to help workaholic children and adult workaholics examine more deeply the family-of-origin wounds that continue to drive them. It is important, for example, to examine the origins of their inadequacies, depressions, or anxieties.

More empirical research is needed on the psychological problems and adjustment of workaholic children. Although we have a body of research on Type A children, few studies exist on workaholic children. Future studies need to address the entire family system, including spouses and younger children of workaholics, in order to draw more conclusive results.

One reason the research is so woefully incomplete is that "workaholism" has not been accepted into the official psychiatric and psychological nomenclature (Pietropinto, 1986). During the 1970s, the term "workaholism" was coined by Wayne Oates (1971) as an analogy to alcoholism because the two addictions were believed to be similar in etiology and symptomatology. Despite this analogy, the connotation of the term has in many ways minimized the disorder and perpetuated society's denial. During the late 1980s and early 1990s, a perceptual shift occurred in which the terms *work addiction* and *work addict* were used to describe the seriousness of the disorder, and it was seen as a legitimate type of compulsive disorder that was related to family dysfunction (Pietropinto, 1986; Robinson, 1989; Spruell, 1987). Still, in research and clinical practice, no consensus exists on the meaning of work addiction, its definition, or how it is measured. Because "work addict" and "workaholic," and "workaholism" and "work addiction" are used interchangeably in the literature, more standardization of these terms is needed in social science research and clinical practice.

REFERENCES

Anthony, E. J. (1978). A new scientific region to explore. In E. J. Anthony, C. Koupernik, & C. Chiland (Eds.), *The child and his family: Vol. 4. Vulnerable children*. New York: Wiley.

Black, C. (1982). *It will never happen to me*. Denver: M.A.C. Publications.

Blaney, N. T., Blaney, P. H., & Diamond, E. (1989). Intrafamilial patterns reported by young Type A versus Type B males and their parents. *Behavioral Medicine, 10*, 161-166.

Bronfenbrenner, U. (1979). *The ecology of human development*. Cambridge, MA: Harvard University Press.

Brown, M. S., & Tanner, C. (1987). *Type A behavior and cardiovascular responsivity in preschoolers.*. Washington, DC: Biomedical Research Service.

Canfield, B. S. (1984). Family-of-origin experiences and selected demographic factors as predictors of current family functioning (Doctoral dissertation, East Texas State University). *Dissertation Abstracts International, 44*, 3281-A.

Cassel, R. N. (1985). Changing the Type A prone person to a Type C coping one using the Type-A proneness assessment program. *College Student Journal, 19*, 330-334.

Corrigan, S. A., & Moskowitz, D. S. (1983). Type A behavior in preschool children: Construct validation evidence for the MYTH. *Child Development, 54*, 1513-1521.

Eagleston, J., Kirmil-Gray, K., Thoresen, C., Wiedenfeld, S., Bracke, P., Heft, L., & Arnow, B. (1986). Physical health correlates of Type A behavior in children and adolescents. *Journal of Behavioral Medicine, 9*, 341-362.

Elkind, D. (1981). *The hurried child.* Reading, MA: Addison-Wesley.

Emmelkamp, P. M. G., & Karsdorp, E. P. (1987). The effects of perceived parental rearing style on the development of Type A pattern. *European Journal of Personality, 1*, 223-230.

Fackelmann, K. A. (1992). Type A: From the nursery to the boardroom. *Science News, 141*, 183.

Fassel, D. (1990). *Working ourselves to death.* Center City, MO: Hazelden.

Fine, M., & Hovestadt, A. J. (1984). Perceptions of marriage and rationality by levels of perceived health in the family of origin. *Journal of Marital and Family Therapy, 10*, 193-195.

Friedman, M., & Rosenman, R. (1974). *Type A behavior and your heart.* New York: Knopf.

Harralson, T. L., & Lawler, K. A. (1992). The relationship of parenting styles and social competency to Type A behavior in children. *Journal of Psychosomatic Research, 36*, 625-634.

Haymon, S. (1993). The relationship of work addiction and depression, anxiety, and anger in college males (Doctoral dissertation, Florida State University). *Dissertation Abstracts International, 53*, 5401-B.

Haynes, S. G., Levine, S., Scotch, N., Feinleib, M., & Kannel, W. B. (1978). The relationship of psychosocial factors to coronary heart disease in the Framingham study: 1. Methods and risk factors. *American Journal of Epidemiology, 107*, 362-383.

Houston, B. K. (1988, March). *Hostility, insecurity, stress and health.* Paper presented at the meeting of the Society of Behavioral Medicine, Boston, MA.

Jones, R. A., & Wells, M. (1996). An empirical study of parentification and personality. *The American Journal of Family Therapy, 24*, 145-152.

Jose, P. E. (1986, August). *Effects of sex-roles and Type A behavior on children's friendships choices.* Paper presented at the Annual Conference of the American Psychological Association, Washington, DC.

Jose, P. E. (1991, April). *Family correlates of children's Type A behavior.* Paper presented at the Biennial Meeting of the Society for Research in Child Development, Seattle, WA.

Jose, P. E., & Langer, B. A. (1989, April). *Type A behavior and teacher ratings of social skills.* Paper presented at the Biennial Meeting of the Society for Research in Child Development, Kansas City, MO.

Kilbey, M., & Davis, J. (1983, March). *Sex-role identification and parental rearing practices: Determinants of Type A behavior in college age women and men.* Paper presented at the Annual Meeting of the Southeastern Psychological Association, Atlanta, GA.

Kliewer, W. (1991). Coping in middle adulthood: Relations to competence, Type A behavior, monitoring, blunting, and locus of control. *Developmental Psychology, 27*, 689-697.

Kliewer, W., & Weidner, G. (1987). Type A behavior and aspirations: A study of parents' and children's goal setting. *Developmental Psychology, 23*, 204-209.

Lawler, K. A., & Allen, M. T. (1981). Risk factors for hypertension in children: Their relationship to psychophysiological responses. *Journal of Psychosomatic Research, 23*, 199-204.

Leiken, L., Firestone, P., & McGrath, P. (1988). Physical symptom reporting in Type A and B children. *Journal of Consulting and Clinical Psychology, 56,* 721-726.

Lopes, A. K., & Best, D. L. (1987, April). *Physiological reactivity and comparison behavior in Type A children.* Paper presented at the Biennial Meeting of the Society for Research in Child Development, Baltimore, MD.

Matthews, B., & Halbrook, M. (1990). Adult children of alcoholics: Implications for career development. *Journal of Career Development, 16,* 261-268.

Matthews, K. A., & Angulo, J. (1980). Measurement of the Type A behavior pattern in children: Assessment of children's competitiveness, impatience-anger, and aggression. *Child Development, 51,* 466-475.

Matthews, K. A., & Avis, N. E. (1983). Stability of overt Type A behaviors in children: Results from a one-year longitudinal study. *Child Development, 54,* 1507-1512.

Matthews, K. A., Siegel, J., Kuller, L., Thompson, M., & Varat, M. (1987). Determinants of decisions to seek medical treatment by patients with acute myocardial infarction symptoms. *Journal of Personality and Social Psychology, 6,* 1144-1156.

Matthews, K. A., & Volkin, J. I. (1981). Efforts to excel and the Type A behavior pattern in children. *Child Development, 52,* 1283-1289.

Oates, W. (1971). *Confessions of a workaholic.* New York: World Publishing Company.

Pietropinto, A. (1986). The workaholic spouse. *Medical Aspects of Human Sexuality, 20,* 89-96.

Price, V. A. (1982). *Type A behavior pattern: A mode for research and practice.* New York: Academic Press.

Raikkonen, K. (1993). Predictive associations between Type A behavior of parents and their children: A 6-year follow-up. *Journal of Genetic Psychology, 154,* 315-328.

Raikkonen, K., & Jarvinen, L. K. (1992). Mothers with hostile, Type A predisposing child-rearing practices. *Journal of Genetic Psychology, 153,* 343-354.

Raikkonen, K., Jarvinen, L. K., & Pietikainen, M. (1991). Type A behavior and its determinants in children, adolescents and young adults with and without parental coronary heart disease: A case-control study. *Journal of Psychosomatic Research, 35,* 273-280.

Rickard, K. M., & Woods-de-Rael, C. (1987). The relationship between Type A behavior and hyperactivity in children as measured by the Conner's hyperactivity and MYTH-O scales. *Journal of Social Behavior and Personality, 15,* 207-214.

Robinson, B. E. (1989). *Work addiction.* Deerfield Beach, FL: Health Communications.

Robinson, B. E. (1996a). The psychosocial and familial dimensions of work addiction: Preliminary perspectives and hypotheses. *Journal of Counseling and Development, 74,* 447-452.

Robinson, B. E. (1996b). Relationship between work addiction and family functioning: Clinical implications for marriage and family therapists. *Journal of Family Psychotherapy, 7,* 13-29.

Robinson, B. E. (1997). Work addiction: Implications for EAP counseling and research. *Employee Assistance Quarterly, 12,* 1-13.

Robinson, B. E. (1998a). *Chained to the desk: A guidebook for workaholics, their partners and children, and the clinicians who treat them.* New York: New York University Press.

Robinson, B. E. (1998b). The workaholic family: A clinical perspective. *American Journal of Family Therapy, 26,* 63-73.

Robinson, B. E., & Fields, N. H. (1983). Casework with invulnerable children. *Social Work, 28*, 63-65.

Robinson, B. E., & Kelley, L. (1998). Adult children of workaholics: Self-concept, anxiety, depression, and locus of control. *American Journal of Family Therapy, 26*, 35-50.

Robinson, B. E., & Post, P. (1994). Validity of the Work Addiction Risk Test. *Perceptual and Motor Skills, 78*, 337-338.

Robinson, B. E., & Post, P. (1995). Work addiction as a function of family of origin and its influence on current family functioning. *The Family Journal, 3*, 200-206.

Robinson, B. E., & Post, P. (1997). Risk of work addiction to family functioning. *Psychological Reports, 81*, 91-95.

Robinson, B. E., & Rhoden, L. (1998). *Working with children of alcoholics: The practitioner's handbook* (2nd ed.). Thousand Oaks, CA: Sage.

Rubin, L. (1996). *The transcendent child: Tales of triumph over the past.* New York: Basic Books.

Spence, J. T., & Robbins, A. S. (1992). Workaholics: Definition, measurement, and preliminary results. *Journal of Personality Assessment, 58*, 160-178.

Spruell, G. (1987). Work fever. *Training and Development Journal, 2*, 47.

Steinberg, L. (1985). Early temperamental antecedents of adult Type A behaviors. *Developmental Psychology, 21*, 1171-1180.

Thoresen, C. E., & Pattillo, J. R. (1988). Exploring the Type A behavior pattern in children and adolescents. In B. K. Houston & C. R. Snyder (Eds.), *Type A behavior: Research, theory & intervention* (pp. 98-145). New York: Wiley.

Treiber, F. A., Mabe, A., Riley, W. T., McDuffie, M., Strong, W. B., & Levy, M. (1990). Children's Type A behavior: The role of parental hostility and family history of cardiovascular disease. *Journal of Social Behavior and Personality, 5*, 183-199.

Vega-Lahr, N., & Field, T. (1986). Type A behavior in preschool children. *Child Development, 57*, 1333-1348.

Visintainer, P., & Matthews, K. A. (1987). Stability of overt Type A children: Results from a two- and five-year longitudinal study. *Child Development, 58*, 1586-1591.

Wegscheider, S. (1979). *The family trap.* Palo Alto, CA: Science and Behavior Books.

Weidner, G., Sexton, G., Matarazzo, J., Pereira, C., & Friend, R. (1988). Type A behavior in children, adolescents and their parents. *Developmental Psychology, 24*, 118-121.

Werner, E. E. (1986). Resilient offspring of alcoholics: A longitudinal study from birth to age eighteen. *Journal of Studies on Alcohol, 47*, 34-40.

West, M. L., & Keller, A. (1991). Parentification of the child: A case study of Bowlby's compulsive care-giving attachment pattern. *American Journal of Psychotherapy, 155*, 425-431.

Woodall, K. L., & Matthews, K. A. (1989). Familial environment associated with Type A behaviors and psychophysiological responses to stress in children. *Health Psychology, 8*, 403-426.

Yamasaki, K. (1990). Parental child-rearing attitudes associated with Type A behaviors in children. *Psychological Reports, 67*, 235-239.

Yamasaki, K. (1994). Similarities in Type A behavior between young children and their parents in Japan. *Psychological Reports, 74*, 347.

CHAPTER 4

Parentification of Siblings of Children With Disability or Chronic Disease

Suzanne Lamorey

Approximately four million American children have developmental disabilities such as mental retardation, behavior disorders, autism, physical impairments, cerebral palsy, sensory impairments, and learning disabilities (Meyen, 1995). Another 10 million children in the United States suffer from some form of chronic illness, with almost one million of these chronically ill children needing significant medical support (Andrews & Nielson, 1988; Sirvis & Caldwell, 1995). The majority of the children affected with these diseases and disabilities are living at home with their families. In supporting the various medical, educational, and psychosocial needs of these children, family members may find it necessary to renegotiate traditional roles and responsibilities of brother, sister, parent, and spouse.

Much has been written about parent response to a child with disability or disease in terms of effects such as stress, depression, social isolation, marital dissatisfaction, and the parent's grieving process (Beckman, 1983; Dyson, 1991; Innocenti, Huh, & Boyce, 1992; Mahoney, O'Sullivan, & Robinson, 1992). Much still needs to be learned about the experiences of the siblings of children with disabilities or chronic disease in terms of these siblings' attempts to accommodate to "differentness" (often a very drastic "differentness") and in terms of their search for support of their own psychosocial needs within the context of their families.

As medical crises wax and wane, as diagnosis of disability or disease creates recurring waves of grief and acceptance, family members gather what resources they possess and reallocate those resources in terms of time, money, energy, and expectations. Perhaps the affected child's medical needs necessitate family involvement in extensive treatments and therapies, diet regimens, doctor and clinic visits, lengthy hospitalizations, trips to the emergency room, home monitoring devices, accommodations for equipment such as wheelchairs and lifts, extensive tutoring, and behavior management techniques—all in addition to the usual family functions. It is rare that these families have access to home-based assistive services for more than a few hours each week, so that addressing a child's special needs often results in exceptional demands on mothers, fathers, siblings, and extended family members.

This chapter reviews the research literature on disability and disease relevant to siblings in a search for understanding the dynamics of family accommodation to the demands of "differentness." Sibling accommodation in meeting the family needs created by the impact of disability and disease is the specific focus of this examination. The family system model (Turnbull, Summers, & Brotherson, 1984), ecological model (Bronfenbrenner, 1979), and transactional model (Sameroff & Chandler, 1975) all suggest that as one family member is affected by disability or disease, so must each family member individually adjust to the impact of disability or disease. In this light, family dynamics may recreate instrumental roles as well as expressive roles for siblings of children with special needs.

During periods of stress and crisis in families, parent-child roles as well as sibling roles undergo adaptive redefinition. Siblings of young children with disabilities or diseases may have positive opportunities to handle added responsibility, develop greater nurturing skills, and experience healthy identity formation with a heightened sense of self-esteem. If, however, the family dynamics chronically demand adult-like caregiving services and behaviors from siblings of young children with disability or disease, these demands may compromise siblings' development in terms of parentifying the roles as well as the identity of siblings. The extreme helpfulness, hyper-responsibility, and pseudo-maturity exhibited by some siblings may be accompanied by a flip-side clinical picture of depression, shame, excessive guilt, unrelenting worry, social isolation, psychosomatic problems, and conduct disturbances that characterize the parentified child.

In terms of discussing parentified siblings, it does a huge disservice to families of children with disability or disease to burden them with yet another sense of "differentness" or assault them with a label that smacks of deficit or dysfunction. As in any time of family crisis or stress—whether it be the birth of an infant with a significant disability, the diagnosis of parent or child illness, divorce, unemployment, financial hardship, or a death in the family—all family members attempt to accommodate and adapt to circumstances. Regarding the impact of family crises on siblings and their roles in the family, there is a continuum of adaptations that range from developmentally appropriate and healthy in one region of the caregiving continuum to compromised and even crippling adaptations at the other end of that continuum. In the light of the need to respect and support family members' responses to the birth or diagnosis of a child with disability or disease, this chapter consists of a review of the research literature regarding the impact of disability or disease on young siblings and a discussion of these studies with a focus on prevention of the harmful effects of parentification. The goal of this chapter is to strengthen family systems by asking how parents, teachers, and other helping professionals can be more aware of, and provide support to, siblings of children with disability or disease in meeting their own individual developmental needs in the context and climate of special family needs.

REVIEW OF STUDIES

Table 4.1 provides an overview of selected studies that have focused on the psychosocial status of siblings of children with disabilities or disease. These studies were selected primarily on the basis of methodology in terms of the researchers' inclusion of a control group of siblings of healthy children. A computer-based search of the literature using Psych Lit and ERIC yielded a total of 33 studies focused on siblings of children with disability or disease which used control groups. Twenty-one of these controlled studies investigated siblings of children with developmental disabilities. Three examined a mix of siblings of chronically ill children and children with developmental delays. Nine studies examined siblings of children with chronic illness.

Of the 33 studies, 12 focused on sibling self-concept, and only three of these found decrements in the self-concept of siblings of children with disability or disease. Ten studies measured internalizing symptoms of siblings, and six of these found increased sibling risk levels in the areas of depression, social isolation, anxiety, and insecurity. Ten studies measured externalizing symptoms of siblings, and seven of these found increased risk in terms of aggression, oppositional behavior, delinquency, and peer difficulties. Sixteen studies investigated general levels of sibling symptoms, with eight finding increased symptoms for children of siblings with disability or disease, and two finding enhanced outcomes for siblings. A total of 14 studies also examined topics such as sibling duties, responsibilities, and roles. Ten of these studies found asymmetry among sibling relationships, increased child care responsibilities carried out by siblings, increased household tasks assigned to siblings, or decreased leisure time. The overall results of these studies, as well as a summary of landmark early research, are discussed in the following sections. For a more detailed discussion of many of these studies, the reader is advised to consult Howe (1993) and Gallo and Knafl (1993).

REVIEW OF EARLY STUDIES OF SIBLINGS OF
CHILDREN WITH DISABILITY

The majority of the early studies investigating the effects of a child with disability on siblings indicated a high level of psychosocial risk for negative sibling outcomes. These studies varied in terms of methods and measures used,

TABLE 4.1 Studies on the Psychosocial Status of Siblings of Children With Disabilities or Disease

	Child Type[a]	Self-Concept	Internalizing Symptoms	Externalizing Symptoms	General Adjustment	Roles and Duties
Bagenholm and Gillberg (1991)	DD		At risk		At risk	
Bishchoff and Tingstrom (1991)	DD	No effect			No effect	Hierarchical status and power
Boyce, Barnett, and Miller (1991)	DD					Increased duties
Breslau (1982)	DD and CI				Younger male siblings at risk	
Breslau and Prabucki (1987)	DD and CI		At risk	At risk	At risk	
Breslau, Weitzman, and Messenger (1981)	DD and CI			At risk	Younger males and older females at risk	
Brody, Stoneman, Davis, and Crapps (1991)	DD					Role asymmetry; increased duties
Burton and Parks (1994)	DD				Enhanced	
Cadman, Boyle, and Offord (1988)	CI	No effect	At risk		At risk	No effect
Carr (1988)	DD				Enhanced	
Coleby (1995)	DD		Younger siblings at risk	Older siblings at risk		

Study						
Cuskelly and Gunn (1993)	DD			Sisters at risk		No effect on duties
Dallas, Stevenson, and McGurk (1995)	DD					Hierarchical relationships
Daniels, Miller, Billings, and Moos (1986)	CI	No effect			At risk	
Drotar, Doershuk, Stern, Boat, Boyer, and Matthews (1981)	CI			No effect		
Dyson, Edgar, and Crnic (1989)	DD	No effect				
Dyson and Fewell (1989)	DD	Enhanced				
Ferrari (1984)	CI	No effect			No effect	
Gath and Gumley (1987)	DD	At risk			No effect	No effect
Harvey and Greenway (1984)	DD	At risk				
Hoare (1984)	CI	No effect			At risk	
Kazak and Clark (1986)	DD	No effect				
Lavigne and Ryan (1979)	CI			At risk	No effect	
Lavigne, Traisman, Marr, and Chasnoff (1982)	CI			No effect	No effect	
Lobato, Barbour, Hall, and Miller (1987)	DD	No effect		At risk	At risk	Sisters had more duties
McHale and Gamble (1989)	DD	Sisters at highest risk	Sisters at highest risk			More duties for sisters

(continued)

TABLE 4.1 Continued

	Child Type[a]	Self-Concept	Internalizing Symptoms	Externalizing Symptoms	General Adjustment	Roles and Duties
McHale, Sloan, and Simeonsson (1986)	DD					Highly variable
Stoneman, Brody, Davis, and Crapps (1987)	DD					Sisters had more teaching and managing roles
Stoneman, Brody, Davis, and Crapps (1988)	DD					More duties associated with more conflict
Stoneman, Brody, Davis, Crapps, and Malone (1991)	DD					Asymmetric relationships
Summers, Summers, Ascione, and Braeger (1989)	DD					Asymmetric relationships
Tritt and Esses (1988)	CI	No effect		At risk		
Vance, Fazan, Satterwhite, and Pless (1980)	CI	At risk		Enhanced	No effect	

a CI = chronically ill; DD = developmentally delayed

variables studied, and the ages of siblings targeted in the research samples. Results of work by Farber (1959, 1960), Farber and Jenne (1963), Gath (1973, 1974), and Grossman (1972) indicated that siblings generally reported negative effects of their roles as caregivers. For example, Farber's work examined the role tension experienced by siblings who assumed responsibilities of caregiving. Role tension was described as a feeling of frustration, tension, or anxiety based on maternal report of sibling personality traits. Farber reported that siblings of children with disabilities experienced higher role-tension scores, with sisters experiencing higher role tension than brothers, particularly when the child with disabilities was more dependent. The results of Farber's work also suggested that sisters assumed a great many adult responsibilities in terms of sharing the burden of care with the mother. Similarly, in some of Gath's early work (1973, 1974), older sisters in large families appeared to bear the brunt of the caregiving burden and were determined to be at greatest risk for psychiatric disorder (in particular, neurotic and antisocial behaviors on the Rutter Behavioral Scale). Grossman (1972) reported that sisters of children with mental retardation had higher levels of anxiety than comparison groups, particularly when the child with disabilities needed greater care and assistance.

These early results strongly suggested a relationship between negative outcomes for some siblings and a family role characterized by increased responsibility of caring for a disabled sibling. This review of early studies is included to provide a sense of historical perspective, as these studies were conducted prior to the legislation that created special education services. The educational, political, and medical context of disability in the 1960s and 1970s incorporated little of the advocacy, intervention and habilitation efforts, normalization, and inclusion that characterize more current views of disability. When disability was viewed as a condition to be hidden and devalued, research about its impact on family members yielded more unequivocally negative results. As indicated in the following current review of controlled studies, when individuals with disabilities moved into the mainstream of society, research findings regarding the impact of disability began to be characterized by more diverse results.

Many of the controlled studies in Table 4.1 investigated general levels of sibling psychosocial symptoms and these studies yielded examples of mixed results. The majority of the studies reported adjustment difficulties, yet these results indicated only mild effects. When differences were reported, trends seem to indicate that younger males and older females had poorer adjustment scores than control groups of siblings (Breslau, 1982; Breslau, Weitzman, & Messenger, 1981), that peer relationships were affected (Bagenholm & Gillberg, 1991; Cadman, Boyle & Offord, 1988), that more impairment was noted when siblings with disabilities were more dysfunctional (Daniels, Miller, Billings, & Moos, 1986), and that some siblings found psychological strength in the context of disability (Burton & Parks, 1994; Carr, 1988).

CURRENT STUDIES OF SIBLINGS OF
CHILDREN WITH DISABILITIES

In terms of internalizing and externalizing symptoms of siblings of children with disability, 60% to 70% of the controlled studies that were reviewed indicated some level of increased risk. Increased levels of anxiety and depression were identified, as well as increased aggression, delinquency, withdrawal, and irritability. Sisters were more often affected (Cuskelly & Gunn, 1993; McHale & Gamble, 1989), and in one study the younger siblings were more often affected (Coleby, 1995). In terms of self-concept, only about one fourth of the studies indicated decrements, with the study by McHale and Gamble (1989) reporting that sisters experienced the lowest self-esteem scores.

Interestingly, Gath's later work (Gath & Gumley, 1987) revealed no differences in adjustment scores of siblings of children with and without disability, and in contrast to earlier work, there was no evidence of increased responsibility of older sisters. Gath and Gumley (1987) attempted to explain the earlier finding as possibly due to lower socioeconomic status of families involved in the 1970s studies and larger family size. In another light, Dyson and Fewell (1989) reported quite different results. In their sibling groups, measures of self-concept were higher for siblings of children, with disabilities with sisters scoring higher than brothers.

SIBLINGS OF CHILDREN WITH
CHRONIC DISEASE

In terms of self-concept, only one study of siblings of children with chronic disease reported significant decrements. Vance, Fazan, Satterwhite, and Pless (1980) found that siblings of children with nephrotic syndrome showed significantly lower scores in self-concept as a group, yet none of these children scored lower than one standard deviation below the mean, indicating a mild effect. As indicated in Table 4.1, four additional studies focused on self-concept of siblings of children with chronic disease, but none found significant group differences.

Several studies that focused on internalizing symptoms of siblings of children with chronic disease found significantly increased risk levels in the areas of depression, social isolation, and parent report of anxiety. Breslau and Prabucki (1987) reported increased levels of social isolation and depression symptoms for siblings of children with congenital disabilities and chronic illness. Parents of these siblings also reported increased levels of child anxiety. The siblings in this study were followed for 5 years; over this time, they were reported to experience increased symptoms. Tritt and Esses (1988) also found increased levels of social withdrawal and personality problem scores for siblings of children with chronic disease. An impressive study was reported by Cadman, Boyle, and Offord (1988), who conducted a general population survey of more than 3,000 children in Ontario. These researchers found that siblings of children with chronic illness had a twofold risk of anxiety, depression, and obsessive-compulsive disorder and a significant increase in poor peer relationships compared with siblings of well children.

In terms of externalizing symptoms, a small group of researchers found increased risk for siblings of children with chronic disease in terms of aggression, oppositional behavior, and peer difficulties. Breslau, Weitzman, and Messenger (1981) found higher scores in fighting and delinquency for this group of siblings. Breslau and Prabucki (1987) found a slight increase in aggression and oppositional behavior in their sibling group. Vance, Fazan, Satterwhite, and Pless (1980), however, reported less conflict for siblings of children with chronic disease.

Finally, a number of studies focused on general levels of symptoms, with six studies indicating increased symptoms for siblings of children with chronic illness. In an early study conducted by Breslau (1982), two subgroups of siblings of children with chronic disease were found to be at increased risk for aggressive behavior and symptoms of depression. These high risk groups included male siblings younger than the child with a disease and female siblings older than the child with a disease. Breslau suggested that the older siblings may be pressed into early service, with the increased burden becoming overwhelming and distressful. In another vein, the younger siblings may be subject to a lack of parental attention, yielding increased aggression. Breslau and Prabucki (1987), Hoare (1984), and Cadman, Boyle, and Offord (1988) found slight increases in general adjustment difficulties for siblings of children with chronic disease. Daniels and colleagues (1986) reported a trend of more physical problems and more psychological problems noted for siblings of children with chronic diseases when the children with illness were more dysfunctional.

SIBLINGS AS CAREGIVERS

Studies have also examined the roles of siblings as caregivers in terms of the amount of time spent performing household tasks and time spent caring for siblings with disabilities. Using frequency rating scales and comparison groups of siblings of children without disabilities, researchers have reported interesting results. Lobato, Barbour, Hall, and Miller (1987) investigated preschool siblings and found that sisters had the greatest responsibility for caregiving, yet the result was not statistically significant. Stoneman, Brody, Davis, and Crapps (1987, 1988, 1989), Stoneman, Brody, Davis, Crapps, and Malone (1991), and Brody, Stoneman, Davis, and Crapps (1991) documented naturalistic information about the daily life in families with children who had disabilities. These researchers found that older sisters of children with disabilities had significantly more responsibility in tasks such as personal assistance, adaptive tasks, meal preparation, and baby-sitting. Greater levels of caregiving on the part of sisters was correlated with more sibling conflict and fewer positive

sibling interactions, while more involvement in household chores was correlated with less sibling conflict. Observations of interactions between sibling
dyads (a typical child and a sibling with a disability) reflected much role
asymmetry and indicated that the typical sibling assumed more caregiving roles
such as teaching, managing, and dominating when a sibling had a disability.
Documenting a reversal of traditional roles, these studies indicated that the
younger siblings were found to assume baby-sitting responsibilities for the
older children with disabilities. When baby-sitting their older siblings, these
younger children performed the helper role more frequently and the playmate
role less often, contributing further to a sense of role reversal. In addition, more
demands for family responsibilities were directly related to decreased time for
being with friends and participating in out-of-home activities. Similarly, Farber
and Jenne (1963) found that the activities of sisters were also limited because
of their household/caregiving responsibilities.

McHale and Gamble (1989) found that siblings of children with disabilities,
and in particular sisters, did more caregiving and household tasks, with caregiving being correlated to greater sibling anxiety. Boyce, Barnett, and Miller
(1991) used a matched case method to focus on time use of siblings of children
with and without disabilities and found that siblings of children with mental
retardation performed more child care than matched siblings, particularly
sisters who were older than the child with mental retardation. Boyce and
colleagues (1991) also reported that siblings of children with disabilities spent
significantly less time in school.

FINDINGS REGARDING MEDIATING VARIABLES

Generally, there are mixed results reported for mediating variables such as child
gender, family socioeconomic status, child birth order, and level of sibling
disability. In terms of gender, sisters generally have more domestic and caregiving responsibility than brothers, with sisters managing and directing younger
siblings more than brothers (Stoneman et al., 1987, 1988, 1989), and with
sisters reporting more negative interactions with mothers and with siblings,
including teasing and hitting (Gamble & McHale, 1989). In reviews of mediating variables, lower socioeconomic status has been correlated with less positive
outcomes in terms of straining family financial resources and family coping
abilities (Gallagher & Powell, 1989).

The category of family social process variables also yielded interesting
findings. Sibling concerns about the future, sibling concerns about parental
favoritism, and parental attitudes such as maternal negativity accounted for
significant variance in sibling depression and anxiety above variables such as
sibling caregiving and household chores (McHale & Gamble, 1989). In a similar
vein, Dyson, Edgar, and Crnic (1989) found that parental stress significantly
predicted adjustment of siblings of children with disabilities. Other related
variables including problems in the functioning of the ill child, increased

maternal depression, and increased maternal anxiety have been reported to correlate with more sibling problems in terms of higher distress levels (Treiber, Mabe, & Wilson, 1987). Some data indicate that in poorer families, disability was associated with economic losses resulting from treatment demands, with losses in family cohesion, and with increased maternal depression. Increased depression in parents, particularly mothers, has been associated with increased risk of maladjustment in children. Some data indicate that fathers of children with severe disabilities assume less caregiving responsibilities for the child with disabilities, with a suggestion that the mother's caregiving load doubles, again opening the door to parentification of the sibling because some fathers' loads may be redistributed to siblings (Bristol, Gallagher, & Schopler, 1988).

SUMMARY

In general, there is evidence of increased psychosocial risk for some siblings of children with chronic illness or disability in the following six areas.

1. Increased risk of internalizing symptoms was found in about half of the studies.
2. Increased risk of externalizing symptoms was found slightly more often.
3. General symptom levels also show increased risk for sibling psychosocial difficulties in about 50% of the studies.
4. We see a trend of role expansion for some siblings in terms of the caregiving responsibilities.
5. We also see a trend toward role reversals for some siblings in terms of younger siblings caring for the needs of older children with developmental delays.
6. Sibling difficulties in terms of self-concept were not often identified, and when these problems were found, they tended to be mild.

It is important to note that large individual differences were reported across these studies, and these differences can be interpreted to reflect a continuum of sibling outcomes ranging from an acclimated child who is supported and recognized in his or her family role to an overburdened child who is struggling with significantly inappropriate roles and responsibilities. In some cases, it seems that the overt burden of care extends disproportionately to one sibling, often an older sister, who may subsequently forgo opportunities to interact with peers and forgo opportunities to participate in age appropriate activities that would support and enhance her healthy psychosocial development. In other cases, it would seem that the burden of care may have extended to the degree that siblings not only are overburdened in terms of their roles and responsibilities in an instrumental sense, but also have internalized an expressive sense of their identity and self-worth as "little parents." The subgroup of these "little parents" have roles, responsibilities, and identities that extend beyond the healthy helper and may represent a pervasive, age inappropriate, isolating, unilateral, unacknowledged, and dysfunctional parentification process as described by Jurkovic (1997).

In the light of the mix of research findings, no single pathway or set of risk factors can be identified as contributing to parentification. Increased risk is typically mild and probably varies with the condition of the child in terms of etiology, course, and prognosis of the condition (Howe, 1993). In addition, family constellation variables such as age of the siblings, gender of siblings, birth order, and characteristics of the disability or illness have yielded mixed results in terms of predicting sibling psychological functioning. Expanding our understanding of the factors that contribute to sibling risk of parentification is obviously a high priority in terms of promoting prevention and intervention strategies. To effectively counsel families, it is essential to more completely understand the family dynamics involved in the development of the parentified sibling of children with disability or disease.

The purpose of this chapter is to investigate the parentification of siblings of children with a disability or chronic illness as family members define their needs, boundaries, roles, and responsibilities in the context of the family system. This chapter acknowledges and respects the resiliency of families as they negotiate the changing needs of members. With the current special education focus on the need to support the family, it is important to explore the needs of siblings as they strive to define and differentiate their relationships and identities within the family system. There is no need to return to the pathology-focused models of the past when examining the strengths and needs of families of children with disabilities. It is important, however, to acknowledge that there are family members who are overwhelmed, overstressed, and in need of support. One group of family members that is a focus of concern are the siblings of children with disability or disease. When parents of children with disability or disease are overwhelmed by their parenting roles and when siblings' roles and identities subsequently begin to expand beyond the healthy boundaries of the sibling subsystem, the risk of dysfunctional parentification of siblings is present. Well-designed group research results indicate the presence of some very stressed siblings, and the framework of parentification with its emerging therapy model may offer a way to understand and support these siblings.

The risk of parentification may reflect the interaction of a variety of factors that result, for some siblings in some families, in a "lost childhood," as Jurkovic (1997) describes the experience of the parentified child. This notion of a lost childhood may describe the experience of some siblings when the typical developmental experiences of childhood are sacrificed as the child assumes the role of a parent either in caring for the sibling with a disability or disease or in assuming the parent's role in carrying out other family responsibilities so that the parent can meet the needs of the child with disabilities or disease. This parentification of the sibling may have its roots in the disproportionate amount of parental attention focused on the child with a disability or chronic disease or in the expectations of increased involvement of the sibling with caregiving, teaching, training, and treatment activities focused on the more dependent child with the disability or disease. Under these circumstances, some siblings may learn to give up their needs to be parented by their mothers and fathers, and instead learn to assume the role of the "little helper" or the "little parent." Whatever the contributing variables, the driving mechanisms of sibling parentification include role confusion, guilt, anger, anxiety, frustration, and conflict experienced as a result of siblings becoming enmeshed in chronic, captivating, unilateral, and pervasive behavioral patterns that overtly reflect overresponsibility and caretaking (Jurkovic, 1997).

This parentified sibling role occurs when children become parents to their siblings at the expense of their own developmental needs. Some adults who have siblings with disabilities report the positive experiences that they have had in caring for their siblings in terms of heightened sensitivity, sharing, altruism, and compassion (Grossman, 1972). Some adults who have siblings with disability or disease, however, report that their needs came last in the family, and often their needs for time, for play, for childhood activities, and for support were not met because of the persistent needs of the sibling with disability or disease. These adults of siblings with disability or disease experienced a childhood characterized by family dynamics that were emotionally depleting and confusing for all involved, particularly when the family did not have adequate social support or financial resources, or was reeling from repeated cycles of hospitalizations, diagnostic pronouncements, or other medical emergencies incurred by the child with the disability or disease.

Parents report that they can become vastly overwhelmed by the needs of a child with a significant disability or life-threatening disease, and it is not unlikely that siblings would also experience a sense of being similarly overwhelmed, particularly when the siblings have so few tools with which to understand the nature of meanings of disability and disease. Siblings often blame themselves for these outcomes, and they take on the roles of overachiever or hero to compensate for the limitations of the disabled sibling. Super-siblings step in to take over household duties such as cooking, cleaning, and child care. Often, they may feel the need to excel academically to compensate for the shortcomings of the developmentally delayed sibling or excel in sports to compensate for the shortcomings of the sibling with limitations resulting from disease.

Protective factors have been identified that can support siblings and their families, and perhaps defuse the dysfunctional aspects of parentification. According to Jurkovic (1997), healthy family boundaries include roles and responsibilities for siblings characterized by developmental appropriateness, clear definitions, and supervision of assigned tasks. In addition, the distribution of responsibilities throughout the family including the siblings can be an important balancing factor (Minuchin, 1974). When siblings are expected to perform expanded duties in the home, the experience is more positive when siblings perceive that their jobs are necessary and are shared with parents (Goodnow, 1988). Communication between home and school can contribute positively to the sibling's healthy development, particularly in terms of social development and academic background. Often, siblings whose identities and interpersonal relationships have centered on their role as the family's caretaker need to have the support of teachers and other professionals in developing healthy peer relationships, in discovering their own personal needs and interests, and in balancing academic accomplishment with personal and social development.

We must be cautious in terms of labeling the sibling relationship as "morbid" when some of the feelings of responsibility and efforts in helping out are beneficial to the child's developing sense of belonging and contributing. When do problems occur? What factors seem to contribute to poorer outcomes for some siblings? When is this experience non-nurturing? When are the expectations above and beyond the child's abilities? When are the extra responsibilities a diversion of the child's time and energy away from developmentally appropriate activities and a threat to the child's current and future well-being? Furthermore, how can professionals respond to the needs of siblings of children with disabilities or disease in order to minimize the possibilities of parentification processes? The answers to these questions depend on the needs of individual siblings and their families, and can be addressed only when families and professionals work together to define, describe, and defuse the parentification process.

REFERENCES

Andrews, M. A., & Nielson, D. W. (1988). Technology dependent children in the home. *Pediatric Nursing, 14*(2), 111-151.

Bagenholm, A., & Gillberg, C. (1991). Psychosocial effects on siblings of children with autism and mental retardation: A population based study. *Journal of Mental Deficiency Research, 35*, 291-307.

Beckman, P. (1983). Influence of selected child characteristics on stress in families of handicapped infants. *American Journal of Mental Deficiency, 88*, 150-156.

Bischoff, L., & Tingstrom, D. (1991). Siblings of children with disabilities: Psychological and behavioral characteristics. *Counselling Psychology Quarterly, 4*(4), 311-321.

Boyce, G. C., Barnett, S., & Miller, B. C. (1991, April). *Time use and attitudes among siblings: A comparison in families of children with and without Down syndrome.* Poster presented at the Biennial Meeting of the Society for Research in Child Development, Seattle, WA.

Breslau, N. (1982). Siblings of disabled children: Birth order and age-spacing effects. *Journal of Abnormal Child Psychology, 10*, 85-96.

Breslau, N., & Prabucki, K. (1987). Siblings of disabled children: Effects of chronic stress in the family. *Archives of General Psychiatry, 44*, 1040-1046.

Breslau, N., Weitzman, M., & Messenger, K. (1981). Psychologic functioning of siblings of disabled children. *Pediatrics, 67*, 344-353.

Bristol, M. M., Gallagher, J. J., & Schopler, E. (1988). Mothers and fathers of young developmentally disabled and nondisabled boys: Adaptation and spousal support. *Developmental Psychology, 24*, 441-451.

Brody, G. H., Stoneman, Z., Davis, C. H., & Crapps, J. M. (1991). Observations of the role relations and behavior between older children with mental retardation and their younger siblings. *American Journal on Mental Retardation, 95*, 527-536.

Bronfenbrenner, U. (1979). Toward an experimental ecology of human development. *American Psychologist, 32*, 513-531.

Burton, S., & Parks, A. L. (1994). Self-esteem, locus of control, and career aspiration of college-age siblings of individuals with disabilities. *Social Work Research, 18*(3), 178-185.

Cadman, D., Boyle, M., & Offord, D. R. (1988). The Ontario Child Health Study: Social adjustment and mental health of siblings of children with chronic health problems. *Journal of Development and Behavioral Pediatrics, 9*, 117-121.

Carr, J. (1988). Six weeks to twenty-one years old: A longitudinal study of children with Down's syndrome and their families. *Journal of Child Psychology and Psychiatry, 29*(4), 407-431.

Colcby, M. (1995). The school-aged siblings of children with disabilities. *Developmental Medicine and Child Neurology, 37*, 415-426.

Cuskelly, M., & Gunn, P. (1993). Maternal reports of behavior of siblings of children with Down syndrome. *American Journal of Mental Retardation, 97*, 521-529.

Dallas, E., Stevenson, J., & McGurk, H. (1995). Cerebral-palsied children's interactions with siblings-I. Influence of severity of disability, age, and birth order. *Journal of Child Psychology, 34*(5), 621-647.

Daniels, D., Miller, J. J., Billings, A. G., & Moos, R. H. (1986). Psychosocial functioning of siblings of children with rheumatic disease. *Journal of Pediatrics, 109*, 379-383.

Drotar, D., Doershuk, C. F., Stern, R. C., Boat, T. F., Boyer, W., & Matthews, L. (1981). Psychosocial functioning of children with cystic fibrosis. *Pediatrics, 67*, 338-343.

Dyson, L. (1991). Families of young children with handicaps: Parental stress and family functioning. *American Journal on Mental Retardation, 95*, 623-629.

Dyson, L., Edgar, E., & Crnic, K. (1989). Psychological predictors of adjustment of siblings of developmentally disabled children. *American Journal of Mental Retardation, 94*(3), 292-302.

Dyson, L., & Fewell, R. R. (1989). The self-concept of siblings of handicapped children: A comparison. *Journal of Early Intervention, 13*(3), 230-238.

Farber, B. (1959). Effects of a severely mentally retarded child on family integration. *Monographs of the Society for Research in Child Development, 24*(2).

Farber, B. (1960). Family organization and crises: Maintenance of integration in families with a severely retarded child. *Monographs of the Society for Research in Child Development, 25*(1).

Farber, B., & Jenne, W. C. (1963). Family organization and parent-child communication: Parents and siblings of a retarded child. *Monographs of the Society for Research in Child Development, 28*(7).

Ferrari, M. (1984). Chronic illness: Psychosocial effects of siblings and chronically ill boys. *Journal of Child Psychology and Psychiatry, 25*(3), 459-476.

Gallagher, P. A., & Powell, T. H. (1989). Brothers and sisters: Meeting special needs. *Topics in Early Childhood Special Education, 8*(4), 24-37.

Gallo, A., & Knafl, K. (1993). Siblings of children with chronic illness: A categorical and noncategorical look at selected literature. In Z. Stoneman & P. Berman (Eds.), *The effects of mental retardation, disability, and illness on sibling relationships: Research issues and challenges* (pp. 215-234). Baltimore, MD: Paul Brookes.

Gath, A. (1973). The school-age siblings of mongol children. *British Journal of Psychiatry, 123,* 161-167.

Gath, A. (1974). Sibling reactions to mental handicap: A comparison of the brothers and sisters of mongol children. *Journal of Child Psychology and Psychiatry, 15,* 187-198.

Gath, A., & Gumley, D. (1987). Retarded children and their siblings. *Journal of Child Psychology and Psychiatry, 28*(5), 715-730.

Goodnow, J. (1988). Children's household work: Its nature and function. *Psychological Bulletin, 103,* 5-26.

Grossman, F. K. (1972). *Brothers and sisters of retarded children: An exploratory study.* Syracuse, NY: Syracuse University Press.

Harvey, D., & Greenway, A. (1984). The self-concept of physically handicapped children and their non-handicapped siblings: An empirical investigation. *Journal of Child Psychology and Psychiatry, 25,* 273-284.

Hoare, P. (1984). Does illness foster dependency? A study of epileptic and diabetic children. *Developmental Medicine and Child Neurology, 26,* 20-24.

Howe, G. (1993). Siblings of children with physical disabilities and chronic illness: Studies of risk and social ecology. In Z. Stoneman & P. Berman (Eds.), *The effects of mental retardation, disability, and illness on sibling relationships: Research issues and challenges* (pp. 185-214). Baltimore, MD: Paul Brookes.

Innocenti, M., Huh, K., & Boyce, G. (1992). Families of children with disabilities: Normative data and other considerations on parenting stress. *Topics in Early Childhood Special Education, 12*(3), 403-427.

Jurkovic, G. (1997). *Lost childhoods: The plight of the parentified child.* New York: Brunner/Mazel.

Kazak, A. E., & Clark, M. W. (1986). Stress in families of children with myelomeningocele. *Developmental Medicine and Child Neurology, 28,* 220-228.

Lavigne, J. V., & Ryan, M. (1979). Psychological adjustment of siblings of children with chronic illness. *Pediatrics, 63,* 616-627.

Lavigne, J. V., Traisman, H. S., Marr, T. J., & Chasnoff, I. J. (1982). Parental perceptions of the psychological adjustment of children with diabetes and their siblings. *Diabetes Care, 5,* 420-426.

Lobato, D., Barbour, L., Hall, L. J., & Miller, C. T. (1987). Psychosocial characteristics of preschool siblings of handicapped and nonhandicapped children. *Journal of Abnormal Child Psychology, 15,* 329-338.

Mahoney, G., O'Sullivan, P., & Robinson, C. (1992). The family environments of children with disabilities: Diverse but not so different. *Topics in Early Childhood Special Education, 12*(3), 386-402.

McHale, S. M., & Gamble, W. C. (1989). Sibling relationships of children with disabled and nondisabled brothers and sisters. *Developmental Psychology, 25*(3), 421-429.

McHale, S. M., Sloan, J., & Simeonsson, R. J. (1986). Sibling relationships of children with autistic, mentally retarded, and nonhandicapped brothers and sisters. *Journal of Autism and Developmental Disorders, 16*(4), 399-413.

Meyen, E. L. (1995). Legislative and programmatic foundations of special education. In E. Meyen & T. Skrtic (Eds.), *Special education and student disability: An introduction* (4th ed., pp. 33-96). Denver: Love.

Minuchin, S. (1974). *Families and family therapy.* Cambridge, MA: Harvard University Press.

Sameroff, A., & Chandler, M. (1975). Reproductive risk and the continuum of caretaking causality. In F. Horowitz (Ed.), *Review of child development research* (Vol. 4, pp. 187-244). Chicago: University of Chicago Press.

Sirvis, B. P., & Caldwell, T. H. (1995). Physical disabilities and chronic health impairments. In E. Meyen & T. Skrtic (Eds.), *Special education and student disability: An introduction* (4th ed., pp. 533-564). Denver: Love.

Stoneman, Z., Brody, G. H., Davis, C. H., & Crapps, J. M. (1987). Mentally retarded children and their older same-sex siblings: Naturalistic in-home observations. *American Journal on Mental Retardation, 92*(3), 290-298.

Stoneman, Z., Brody, G. H., Davis, C. H., & Crapps, J. M. (1988). Child care responsibilities, peer relations, and sibling conflict: Older siblings of mentally retarded children. *American Journal on Mental Retardation, 93*(2), 174-183.

Stoneman, Z., Brody, G. H., Davis, C. H., & Crapps, J. M. (1989). Role relations between children who are mentally retarded and their older siblings: Observations in three in-home contexts. *Research in Developmental Disabilities, 10*, 61-76.

Stoneman, Z., Brody, G. H., Davis, C. H., Crapps, J. M., & Malone, D. M. (1991). Ascribed role relations between children with mental retardation and their younger siblings. *American Journal on Mental Retardation, 95*, 537-550.

Summers, M., Summers, C. R., Ascione, F., & Braeger, T. (1989, April). *Observations of sibling's social interactions: Comparing families with and without a handicapped child.* Paper presented at the Biennial Meeting of the Society for Research in Child Development, Kansas City, MO.

Treiber, F., Mabe, P. A. I., & Wilson, G. (1987). Psychosocial adjustment of sickle cell children and their siblings. *Children's Health Care, 16*, 82-88.

Tritt, S. G., & Esses, L. M. (1988). Psychosocial adaption of siblings of children with chronic medical illnesses. *American Journal of Orthopsychiatry, 58*, 211-220.

Turnbull, A. P., Summers, J. A., & Brotherson, M. J. (1984). *Working with families with disabled members: A family systems approach.* Lawrence: University of Kansas, Kansas University Affiliated Facility.

Vance, J. C., Fazan, L. E., Satterwhite, B., & Pless, I. B. (1980). Effects of nephrotic syndrome on the family: A controlled study. *Pediatrics, 65*, 948-955.

CHAPTER 5

Assessing Childhood Parentification

Guidelines for Researchers and Clinicians

Gregory J. Jurkovic
Richard Morrell
Alison Thirkield

David, an 11-year-old who lives with his mother and two younger sisters, has long been his mother's primary source of emotional support and companionship. Since his parents' divorce, he has also assumed increased responsibility for the care of his siblings and for the management of the household. Although David's role is critical and often burdensome (e.g., interfering with his ability to complete homework and to engage in extracurricular activities), his contributions and needs are rarely acknowledged by his family. Interestingly, he is showing signs of relating to peers like family members; that is, he is overly concerned about their problems and frequently takes great pains to help them.

Rosa and her family moved to the United States from Puerto Rico several years ago to join relatives who had immigrated earlier. Most of Rosa's high school friends are amazed by the extent of her domestic responsibilities (e.g., baby-sitting, cooking, shopping, caring for an elderly grandmother, translating for her mother who speaks little English). Her friends' reaction surprises her. As Rosa told one of them, "It is the way in my family to help; we all help one another. That's how it is back home [in Puerto Rico]."

Frank's parents seldom discipline him despite his marginal academic performance and behavior problems at school and home. Rather, they rescue him from the consequences of his behavior and generally expect little of him. For example, although 12 years old, Frank has no household chores. His parents also have long-standing marital conflicts, which they reportedly have difficulty addressing because of their son's misbehavior.

Although only 28 months old, Sarah seems unusually sensitive to her mother's mood. Her mother suffers from chronic depression, which frequently renders her barely functional and unable to attend to her own needs, not to mention her daughter's. At these times, Sarah attempts to comfort her, for example, stroking her hair, bringing her food, and staying by her side. According to Sarah's mother, "My daughter has always been there for me."

These cases raise a number of questions for the clinician or researcher concerned with operationalizing and assessing destructive parentification in families. Perhaps most fundamental is whether David, Rosa, Frank, or Sarah are engaging in inappropriate levels of caretaking in their families. If so, how are these levels identified? Is the definition of destructive parentification confined to the type and extent of the child's overt responsibilities? Or does it include behaviors whose caretaking intent can only be inferred? Moreover, what are the contextual features of the parentified role? Are certain caretaking activities age appropriate? Do toddlers and even infants become active participants in the parentification process? Is parentification normative in some cultural and subcultural settings? Under what conditions is the child's parentified behavior unfair regardless of social legitimacy? Finally, are there psychometrically sound instruments and approaches for measuring parentification?

The objective of this chapter is to address the foregoing queries, if only preliminarily. Now that more helping professionals and investigators are turning their attention to destructive parentification in families, the need for theoretically based and empirically sound assessment methods has grown markedly. As will be seen, however, considerable work remains to be done in this area. Accordingly, another goal of the present chapter is to illuminate the various avenues such work might take.

PARAMETERS OF PARENTIFICATION

To capture the multifaceted nature of destructive caretaking behaviors by children as discussed by Boszormenyi-Nagy (1965, 1987; Boszormenyi-Nagy & Krasner, 1986; Boszormenyi-Nagy & Spark, 1973), Minuchin (1974; Minuchin & Fishman, 1981; Minuchin, Montalvo, Guerney, Rosman, & Schumer, 1967), Bowlby (1973, 1979, 1980), and others (e.g., Karpel, 1976; Miller, 1979/1981), while at the same time delimiting the scope of the problem, it is important to distinguish the parentified role from the context in which it is embedded (Jurkovic, 1997). This distinction sheds light on many of the conceptual concerns raised earlier and provides guidelines for our review later in the chapter of various clinical and psychometric approaches to identifying and evaluating destructively parentified youngsters.

Role Properties

Degree of Overtness. A defining characteristic of the parentified role from our perspective and that of others, particularly Karpel (1976), is the overt nature of the child's helping behavior. With the exception of Frank, all the children in the scenarios presented earlier exhibited tangible evidence of beneficent behavior. By contrast, Boszormenyi-Nagy's comprehensive definition of destructive parentification, which, in part, refers to children who are unfairly conscripted by family members to meet their needs *either directly or indirectly*, might include Frank as well. Indeed, it is possible that he colluded with his parents in detouring their marital conflict via his irresponsible behavior. The degree of inference required to discern such indirect manifestations of caretaking, along with the lack of specificity involved, greatly compromises the utility and measurability of the parentification construct. Rather than consider children such as Frank as possibly parentified, Karpel suggests that they may be more appropriately referred to as "loyal objects."

Type of Role Assignment. Another useful distinction in this area involves differentiating instrumental from expressive (or emotional) parentified role functions (Jurkovic, 1997; Jurkovic, Jessee, & Goglia, 1991). The former refer to physical maintenance and sustenance of the family (e.g., child care, grocery shopping, cooking), whereas the latter involve ministering to the socio-emotional needs of family members and the family as a whole (e.g., serving as a confidant, companion, or mate-like figure; mediating family conflict; providing nurturance and support). Minuchin's description of the "parental child" revolves largely around instrumental functioning of the kind referred to in the case of Rosa, although it is likely that many of the parental children observed by Minuchin and his colleagues engaged in expressive caretaking as well. Indeed, children such as David often perform both instrumental and expressive tasks.

Extent of Responsibility. In describing the parentified role in families, we also place importance on the degree and the duration of the parentified member's instrumental and/or expressive responsibilities. Has the role extended beyond a situational adaptation to become a chronic process? Of course, the consequences of the latter are potentially more serious. For example, without intervention, it is likely that Sarah's parentification will continue unabated, thus significantly disrupting her development.

Object of Concern. Who is the primary object of the parentified member's caretaking efforts: mother, father, siblings, other family members, spousal subsystem, or family as a whole? The beneficiaries are often multiple, as in the cases of David and Rosa. If parental figures are the focus of concern, then sex of the parent may interact with that of the child in determining the effects of the parentification process.[1]

Contextual Properties

Age Appropriateness. At what developmental stage was the youngster first parentified? The earlier the parentification, the greater the chances that children's resources are overextended and that their ability to negotiate future developmental tasks (e.g., exploration of the environment, self-differentiation) is affected. Clinical observation and empirical investigation suggest that very young children, such as Sarah, can be drawn into a destructive parentification process and that by 1 or 2 years of age may actually begin to attempt to help needy family members at the expense of their own development (see Jurkovic, 1997, for a review of relevant studies). On the other hand, assignment of instrumental and expressive responsibilities to children that are neither excessive nor developmentally inappropriate is healthy. Failure to assign age-appropriate tasks may be part of an overprotective and infantilizing parent-child dynamic. (Recall, for example, the dynamics in Frank's family.)

Internalization. Another important component of the psychological context of parentification is the extent to which the parentified individual has internalized his or her role. Has it become an enduring, self-defining characteristic or a time-limited adaptation enacted for functional or pragmatic reasons? As noted in David's case, it appears that his parentified role is becoming an integral part of his relational style and personality.

Boundaries. At a transactional level in the family of a parentified individual, it is critical to examine whether there are functional self-other and subsystem boundaries. An example of such boundaries is when children's caretaking responsibilities are supervised by parents and perhaps shared with others in the family, thus reducing their potentially deleterious effects.

Social Legitimacy. Is the parentification process a normative aspect of the family's sociocultural background? This was the case for Rosa. Although an important contextual property that may moderate the impact of the parentification of a family member, social legitimacy of this role pattern is not isomorphic with its ethical legitimacy.

Ethicality. The larger ethical context of the parentification process qualifies the other properties. Are responsibilities in the family distributed in such a way that supports relational fairness and trust in the light of members' capabilities, resources, burdens, and obligations (Boszormenyi-Nagy & Krasner, 1986)?

Excepting Rosa, none of the children described at the outset of this chapter lived in families characterized by fair and trusting relationships.

In Boszormenyi-Nagy's intergenerational view, the balancing of give and take in family relationships extends beyond one's current family to include previous and future generations. For example, parents who experienced unfair treatment during their childhood are at risk of extracting compensation, perhaps in the form of inappropriate caretaking, from their children, thus perpetuating the intergenerational cycle of injustice and distrust. From an ecological perspective, the ethicality of extrafamilial dynamics (e.g., gender socialization, social policies, racism) should also be factored into an accounting of the family ledger (Jurkovic, 1997). Destructive parentification typically is part of an interconnected system of ethically imbalanced familial and sociocultural exchanges.

COMMON PROFILES

Children's responsibilities in their families can be profiled according to the different parameters described above. Four profiles are common: destructive parentification, adaptive parentification, nonparentification, and infantilization (Jurkovic, 1997). In the worst case scenario, the caretaking behavior of *destructively parentified* children is overtly instrumental and/or expressive, extensive in terms of degree and/or duration, developmentally inappropriate, internalized, unsupervised, socially illegitimate, and unfair. If the parentified child's role is culturally prescribed, it is not destructive unless problems along the other dimensions are evident. For example, parents may exploit culturally based practices in the excessive parentification of one of their children. Or, in the case of immigrant families, socioeconomic and acculturative stressors may thrust the children into a parental role to a degree that neither the family nor other members of their culture find acceptable.

Children who are *adaptively parentified* typically discharge caretaking responsibilities, which may be considerable, during a time-limited crisis in the family. If their duties require long-term service, they do not internalize the parentified role. These youngsters, moreover, are supported as well as duly acknowledged and compensated for their caretaking activities by their families and often the larger sociocultural community.

Nonparentified children are expected to engage in culturally appropriate levels of overtly instrumental and expressive caretaking behaviors for which they are recognized. As responsible members of their families, they learn the value of fair give and take in relationships.

Infantilized children are developmentally underchallenged by parental figures, who expect them to engage in little, if any, overt caretaking behavior. They are at risk of internalizing an underfunctioning position in relationships rather than an overfunctioning one like their destructively parentified counterparts.

Unhealthy boundaries, injustice, and distrust also characterize the dynamics in their family.

ASSESSMENT METHODS

Clinicians and researchers have relied on a number of different interview, self-report, projective, and observational methods to operationalize and evaluate destructive parentification and kindred processes (e.g., parental conceptions, relational ethics, boundary dissolution). Because evaluation of the latter contributes significantly to an understanding of the complex of socioemotional, cognitive, behavioral, and ethical dimensions of parentification in children, related assessment tools also will be discussed in this section.

Interview

Adaptation of Child-Rearing Practices Scales. Burkett (1991) adapted Sears, Maccoby, and Levin's (1957) semi-structured parenting interview (Child-Rearing Practices Scales) to assess parentification. Specifically, she coded information from the entire interview to determine the degree to which mothers relied on their children for (a) companionship or (b) emotional caretaking.

In addition to establishing acceptable interrater reliability for the coding system, Burkett (1991) reported findings supporting its validity. In comparison to mothers without a history of sexual abuse, mothers with such a history reported using their children to a greater extent as companions and emotional caretakers. For example, one of the abused mothers described her relationship with her 9-year-old girl as follows:

> It's her and I, and sometimes I get support from her, and I'm not sure if she's old enough to give it. I forget that she's a child, especially when I'm confiding in her, I'm talking to her at an adult level, and I forget that she's not an adult. I've decided I can't confide in her like she's another adult because she just can't keep it to herself. (p. 429)

Parental Awareness Interview. Composed of semistructured questions and hypothetical parent-child dilemmas, the Parental Awareness Interview was developed by Newberger (1977, 1980) in the light of structural developmental considerations (Kohlberg, 1969; Selman, 1980). The interview evaluates socio-cognitive processes mediating various parenting behaviors, including abusive ones. It focuses on the deep logical structure of parents' conceptualization of children as people, the parent-child relationship, and the parental role rather than on surface attitudes and beliefs.

Newberger and her colleagues have demonstrated that the responses of parents can be classified reliably into one or more hierarchically organized levels: (a) egoistic, (b) conventional, (c) subjective-individualistic, and (d) systems.

These levels reflect progress from an exclusive orientation to self to an increasingly complex, process-oriented, and ethical understanding of children and parenting issues. Exemplifying the former is the response of one of Newberger's (1977) interviewees to a question about goals for her child: "I think to grow up into the image of what you wanted to be, or what you wanted them to be, what you wanted to be yourself" (p. 225).

Abusive parents scored lower on the Parental Awareness Interview than non-abusive parents in studies by Newberger (1977) and her colleagues (Newberger & Cook, 1983). The relation of destructively parentifying tendencies on the part of parents to scores on the Parental Awareness Interview has yet to be examined. It is probable that parents whose understanding of children and the parental role is largely egoistic in nature are at risk of parentifying their offspring.

Adult Attachment Interview. Although the use of attachment measures may not at first glance appear applicable to studying and understanding parentification, attachment theory (Bowlby, 1973, 1979) provides an illuminating perspective for viewing this phenomenon. According to Bowlby, the attachment process is one of the most crucial tasks of infancy and early childhood, centrally contributing to one's "internal working model" of relationships. In the absence of a secure relational base, young children are at risk of developing an insecure attachment. This type of attachment can assume different forms. Ainsworth, Blehar, Waters, and Wall (1978) found that in addition to a secure attachment, 12-month-olds exhibited—in a laboratory situation (discussed later)—avoidant and anxious/ambivalent patterns of attachment behavior. Subsequently, Main and Solomon (1986, 1990) identified another insecure pattern referred to as disorganized/disoriented.

Both the anxious/ambivalent and the disorganized/disoriented types may be associated with parentification or what Bowlby (1979) labels "compulsive care-giving" (Main & Cassidy, 1988; Main & Hesse, 1990; Zeanah & Klitzke, 1991). Rather than continue to seek a caring response to their attachment signals, children with such attachment behaviors may care for their parent, thereby securing for themselves relational proximity that otherwise would not be available (Bowlby, 1979). Their working model of relationships, however, is likely to include suppressing their own needs and giving of unrequited and compulsive care to others.

Main and her colleagues (Main & Kaplan, 1985) developed the Adult Attachment Interview to measure attachment processes in adults. The semistructured interview focuses on the early attachment experiences of interviewees to produce a description of their current style of attachment. The interview is coded along two dimensions (content of statements about early attachment, including events, feelings, and current interpretations, and linguistic style) to determine the interviewee's current internal working model of relationships: secure, dismissing of attachment, or preoccupied with attachment. These different working models parallel Ainsworth and colleagues' classification scheme of attachment in young children. Although the interview and coding process are time-consuming, data from a number of studies support the reliability and validity of this assessment device (e.g., Bakermans-Kranenburg & Van Ijzendoorn, 1993; Benoit & Parker, 1994). Self-report measures of adult attachment are reviewed below.

Self-Report

Parentification Questionnaire—Adult and Youth. One of the first self-report measures in this area, Parentification Questionnaire-Adult (PQ-A), was developed by Sessions and Jurkovic (1986) in a college-student population to evaluate (retrospectively) parentification during childhood and adolescence. Scale construction was influenced by theory, particularly Boszormenyi-Nagy's (Boszormenyi-Nagy & Krasner, 1986), and clinical experience with parentified children and adults. The questionnaire yields an overall parentification score based on the respondent's answers to questions about instrumental and expressive parentified role behaviors (e.g., "I often felt like a referee in my family.") and relational ethics (e.g., "In my family I often felt called upon to do more than my share."). An adaptation of this measure (Parentification Questionnaire—Youth, PQ—Y), assessing current parentification, also has been developed for preadolescents and adolescents (Godsall & Jurkovic, 1995).

Both the PQ-A and the PQ-Y have satisfactory psychometric properties. The PQ-A has been shown to discriminate college students who grew up in alcoholic homes from those who did not (Chase, Deming, & Wells, 1998; Goglia, Jurkovic, Burt, & Burge-Callaway, 1992). Godsall, Emshoff, Jurkovic, Anderson, and Stanwyck (in press) recently discovered that the PQ—Y accounted for more variance in self-esteem in adolescents than several other variables, including parental substance abuse.

Parentification Scale. This measure also originated in a college student population (Mika, Bergner, & Baum, 1987). Although the Parentification Scale does not include items of an ethical nature and includes only a few pertaining to expressive caretaking, it assesses respondents' retrospective reports of different types of parentified role actions (spousal role, parental role vis-à-vis parents, parental role vis-à-vis siblings, nonspecific adult role-taking) across two age periods (before age 14, between ages 14 and 16). Evidence for the scale's reliability and validity has been presented by Mika and colleagues (1987). More recently, Valleau, Bergner, and Horton (1995) discovered that college students scoring high in parentification—as measured by the Parentification Scale—reported excessive caretaking in their current interpersonal relationships.

Family and Parents' Relationship Questionnaires. These innovative measures (Fullinwider-Bush & Jacobvitz, 1993; Jacobvitz & Bush, 1996) were developed with college students to study the relation of women's reconstructions of family relationships during childhood and adulthood to identity development, self-esteem, and personal distress. The scales of the Family Relationship Questionnaire (Father-Daughter Enmeshment, Mother-Daughter Enmeshment, and Conflict Mediation during childhood and adulthood), along with those of the Parents' Relationship Questionnaire (Marital Conflict and Marital Support during childhood and adulthood) index dynamics implicated in the parentification process. For example, four of the six Conflict Mediation items (rated on a 7-point scale) are

> Children can try to prevent or diminish their parents' fights in a number of ways: (1) Trying to stop it by taking charge and talking to them; (2) Distracting them with unrelated topics; (3) Joking or clowning around; and (4) Misbehaving or acting up. (Jacobvitz & Bush, 1996, p. 734)

Although Jacobvitz and Bush (1996) reported that the internal and test-retest reliabilities for many of the scales are only in the .5s and .6s, they are adequate for research purposes. By combining scale scores, different structural family patterns are derivable, for example, early Father-Daughter Alliance (Father-Daughter Enmeshment score during childhood + Marital Support score during childhood) and early Mother-Daughter Triangulation (Conflict Mediation score during childhood + Mother-Daughter Enmeshment score during childhood + Marital Conflict score during childhood). Jacobvitz and Bush found, in part, that after controlling for physical abuse as a child and for current Father-Daughter Alliance, early Father-Daughter Alliance related to depression, anxiety, and low self-esteem in college women.

Adult-Adolescent Parenting Inventory. Bavolek (1984) constructed this 32-item measure to detect attitudes associated with parental abuse and neglect. Normative data are available for adolescents and adults as a function of race, gender, and abuse history. A psychometrically sound instrument, the Adult-Adolescent Parenting Inventory includes a Corporal Punishment scale and three others that are directly relevant to the parentification construct: Developmental Expectations, Empathy, and Role Reversal. Pregnant adolescents, who are at risk of parentifying their child, were found by Hanson (1990) to endorse parentifying attitudes on the Role Reversal scale.

Pictorial Assessment Inventory. Developed by Fosson and Lask (1988) for use with children, adults, and families, this assessment tool has a unique format. Drawings of different family patterns, including parent-child role reversal, are presented. Family members—either alone or conjointly—select depictions that characterize their own family systems. In contrast to the other scales discussed thus far, the validity of the Fosson and Lask instrument, at least as a measure of parentification, has yet to be demonstrated empirically.

Interparental Conflict Vignettes. Another unique approach, which may be useful in assessing parentification, involves evaluating children's responses to audio-or videotaped enactments of interparental conflict. For example, in one of the studies reported by Grych and Fincham (1993), the authors developed audiotapes of a man and a woman who disagreed about various issues. The arguments varied in intensity (high vs. low) and content (child-related vs. nonchild-related). Indicating how they would feel if the disagreement occurred between their own parents, children rated five emotions (sad, mad, worried, ashamed, and helpless) on bipolar scales. They also responded to items composing two cognitive scales, Escalation (e.g., "The disagreement will get worse.") and Involvement (e.g., "I would probably have to take sides."), as well as answering open-ended questions about what they would do if the argument occurred in their family. The latter were coded in one of nine categories (e.g., Intervene, Physical Withdrawal, Seek Support). Following the coping questions, the children rated two coping efficacy items: The degree to which their response would (a) help them feel better (emotion-focused coping) and (b) help the parents resolve their disagreement (problem-focused coping).

Other than for the Escalation and Involvement scales (coefficient alphas of .86 and .73, respectively), the authors provide little information about the psychometric properties of the different measurement techniques. Questions also can be asked about the external validity of such analogue measures. Grych and Fincham (1993), however, observe that analogue research is useful in theory testing and studying relations between variables that cannot be readily investigated in natural contexts. Along these lines, they found, in part, that 11- and 12-year-old children held a greater expectancy of helping their parents resolve conflict when it was child- rather than nonchild-related. It is likely that parentified children would expect to be helpful regardless of the content of the argument.

Sibling Inventory of Differential Experience. Measuring siblings' perceptions of their relative experiences within their families of origin, this reliable and valid inventory contains a scale (Differential Sibling Caretaking) that assesses a significant dimension of parentification (Daniels & Plomin, 1985). Data collected by Daniels and Plomin indicate that their inventory captures environmentally rather than genetically rooted familial experiences.

Adolescent and Adult Attachment: Self-Report Instruments. A variety of self-report measures of adolescent and adult attachment has been developed in recent years (see Armsden & Greenberg, 1987; Bartholomew & Horowitz, 1991; Bell, Billington, & Becker, 1986; Collins & Read, 1990; Feeney, Noller, & Hanrahan, 1994; Hazan & Shaver, 1987; Hindy, Schwarz, & Brodsky, 1989;

Simpson, 1990; Sperling & Berman, 1991; West & Sheldon, 1988; West, Sheldon, & Reiffer, 1987). See also a study by Sperling, Foelsch, and Grace (1996) evaluating the congruence of many of these instruments as well as Lyddon, Bradford, and Nelson's (1993) review in this area. Two of the measures that appear particularly relevant to parentification are discussed here.

Building on the work of Hazan and Shaver (1987), Bartholomew and Horowitz's (1991) instrument presents respondents with four short paragraphs describing different attachment styles: secure, dismissing, preoccupied, and fearful. The last of these is seen as a derivative of the disorganized/disoriented pattern identified by Main and Solomon (1986, 1990) in young children. Each paragraph is rated on a 7-point scale; the respondent also designates the one paragraph that is most descriptive of him or her. Bartholomew and Horowitz (1991) found that interview data and ratings by family and friends provided support for the validity of their measure. Their results also pointed to likely linkages between parentification and the preoccupied and fearful attachment styles.

West and Sheldon (1988) constructed a 40-item measure of adult attachment comprising four scales: Compulsive Care-Seeking, Compulsive Care-Giving, Compulsive Self-Reliance, and Angry Withdrawal. As Lyddon and colleagues (1993) observe, the latter two scales assess patterns that are analogous to Ainsworth's anxious/ambivalent and avoidant classifications of childhood attachment. From our perspective, the Compulsive Care-Giving and Care-Seeking scales appear to capture parentified-parentifying dynamics in adult relationships. Along these lines, because the measure focuses on reciprocal attachment, the respondents are instructed to use a special peer relationship, at least 6 months in duration and preferably romantic and sexual in nature, as their frame of reference in answering questions.

West and Sheldon report a high level of internal consistency for their measure and interscale relationships (i.e., moderate positive correlations between Compulsive Care-Seeking and Compulsive Care-Giving and between Compulsive Self-Reliance and Angry Withdrawal) that are to be expected theoretically. More research, however, validating this promising instrument is needed (Lyddon et al., 1993).

Relational Ethics Scale. Although not a measure of parentification per se, the Relational Ethics Scale (Hargrave, Jennings, & Anderson, 1991) draws from Boszormenyi-Nagy's theory (Boszormenyi-Nagy & Krasner, 1986) to assess the ethical underpinnings of adults' current relationships with others of equal status, such as friends or mates (Vertical dimension), and their past family-of-origin relationships (Horizontal dimension). Based on a component analysis, the authors derived six subscales: Trust and Justice, Loyalty, and Entitlement along the Vertical dimension, and the same three along the Horizontal dimension. More information about the construction and psychometric properties of the instrument, which are excellent, can be found in Hargrave, Jennings, and Anderson (1991) and Hargrave and Bomba (1993).

Projective

Child-as-Parent and Child-as-Mate. In her research of generational boundary problems in severely disturbed adults, Walsh (1979) developed a coding scheme for self-constructed stories about pictures taken in large part from the Thematic Apperception Test (TAT). The scheme codes for two types of themes—child-as-parent (the child character in a caretaking or sacrificial role) and child-as-mate (the child character in a perverse triangle or sexualized relationship with parental figures).

In addition to finding satisfactory interrater reliability for this measure, Goglia and colleagues (1992) discovered, as expected, more evidence for both types of themes in the stories of adult children of alcoholics than in those of the controls. A story by one of the participants in the experimental group illustrates the child-as-parent theme:

> The older woman is the mother, and the man is the son. The woman intensely looks out the window, hoping that her husband would return. The husband has been dead for several years, and the son knows and realizes that his father isn't coming back home. The son witnessed the death of his father, but he can't bring himself to convince his mother that he is dead because it will hurt her so much. (p. 297)

An advantage of this measure is that it circumvents the tendency of destructively parentified individuals to mute or distort their response to indices asking directly about parentification because of their extreme filial loyalty. Child-as-parent and child-as-mate story themes, however, may not symbolize actual parentified behavior but rather generational boundary distortions generally or loyal-object processes. Walsh herself did not interpret responses to her measure as prima facie evidence of parentification.

Pathogenesis Scale. Whereas Walsh's coding scheme possibly points to the individual's identification with a parentified role, the other projective approach in this area, the Pathogenesis Scale, focuses on the storyteller's inclination to ignore or exploit the needs of others in a dependent position, an inclination associated with a parentifying orientation. Interrater reliability and validity for this scale—which, like the Walsh scheme, uses the TAT—have been established in several studies (Meyer & Karon, 1967; Mitchell, 1968; VandenBos & Karon, 1971).

Behavioral Observation

Role of Child-in-Dispute Scale and Role Reversal Scale. Johnston, Gonzalez, and Campbell (1987) developed these 5-point clinical rating scales as part of their research on child disturbance and post-divorce conflict in an ethically diverse sample. Both scales measure aspects of parentification. The Role of Child-in-Dispute Scale assesses the degree to which parents involve their children in their marital conflicts (e.g., as a communication channel, as an active or passive weapon). The Role Reversal Scale contains such items as the child's diverting/rescuing the parent from distressing feelings, helping with chores/work more than is developmentally or culturally appropriate, and attempting to discipline parent/siblings.

Designed for use by clinicians who have had extended exposure to family members through counseling, mediation, play therapy, and structured observation, the scales are completed separately for the mother's and the father's interactions with the child. The authors found acceptable levels of interrater reliability and evidence for the scales' utility in predicting various behavior problems in children.

Inventory for Assessment of Parent-Child Interaction. This inventory was developed in Germany by Frank, Kopecky-Wenzel, and their colleagues (Frank & Kopecky-Wenzel, 1994) as part of their observational research of child maltreatment. It contains 21 unipolar 5-point scales covering various aspects of children's (e.g., happiness, anxiety) and parents' behavior (e.g., patience, anger), as well as qualities of the global interaction (e.g., bonding, role appropriateness) between the children and parents in videotaped free play situations in the families' homes. Ratings on each scale are based on both the interactive play and the parent-child decision-making process about what to play.

The scales have excellent interrater reliability (Frank & Kopecky-Wenzel, 1994; Graf, 1995). Working with Frank's research team, Graf also discovered, in part, more evidence of *rollenumkehr* (role reversal) on the role appropriateness scale in the interactions of abusive and neglectful mothers with their young children (ages 3-6) than in control mother-child pairs.

Dissolution of Generational Boundaries Scale. This measure of boundary dissolution created by Sroufe, Jacobvitz, Mangelsdorf, DeAngelo, and Ward (1985) rates parents' tendency to support their young children or to relate to them as a peer or child in interactive laboratory situations (e.g., tower building, tracing a pattern with an Etch-a-Sketch®). The 7-point scale was developed as part of a larger prospective study of an urban poor population (Egeland & Sroufe, 1981). The authors were interested, in part, in the role of maternal seductive behavior and of boundary dissolution more generally in mothers' attempts to meet their own emotional needs through their youngsters. Complementing Sroufe and colleagues' Nonresponsive Intimacy Scale, which measures the frequency, duration, intensity, and quality of unwarranted provocative physical contact of the mother toward the child, the Dissolution of Generational Boundaries Scale rates boundary violations that manifest in other than strictly physical terms. Despite the nonspecific nature of the scoring criteria, Sroufe and colleagues found ample agreement ($r = .87$) between independent raters. Interestingly, at follow-up testing, the combined scores on the Nonresponsive Intimacy and Dissolution of Generational Boundaries Scales (Overstimulating Care) when the children were 42 months of age predicted those who were later rated as hyperactive by their kindergarten teachers (Jacobvitz & Sroufe, 1987).

Maternal Observation of Prosocial Behavior. Zahn-Waxler and her colleagues developed a coding scheme to measure instances of prosocial and reparative behaviors on the part of 1- and 2-year-olds in the observational records of the children's mothers (Zahn-Waxler & Radke-Yarrow, 1982; Zahn-Waxler, Radke-Yarrow, Wagner, & Chapman, 1992). In the 1992 study, 30 mothers were trained to observe and report emotional events both caused and witnessed by their children throughout their second year of life. Mothers also simulated emotions and recorded their responses to these emotions at certain points during the observation period. Simulated situations were videotaped at three points to assess coder reliability. To provide another reliability check, on one occasion a home visitor simulated pain, and both the mother and the home visitor recorded the child's response. Simulated and naturally occurring distress incidents included arguments, conflicts, injuries, psychological distress, and illness, among others.

Coders listened to audiotapes or worked from typed transcripts of the mothers' reports to categorize the children's reactions to caused or witnessed distress. The reactions were categorized along seven dimensions: prosocial behavior, empathic concern, hypothesis testing, self-referential behaviors, self-distress, aggressive behavior, and positive affect. Various estimates of interrater reliability, including mother-observer reliability, were surprisingly high. Also of interest was evidence of clear signs of prosocial and reparative behavior in the responses of these young children, lending support to speculation, noted earlier, that the parentification process may begin very early in life (Jurkovic, 1997). To date, however, the innovative observational methods of Zahn-Waxler and her colleagues have not been used to study parentified children.

Structural Analysis of Social Behavior. Benjamin (1974) developed the Structural Analysis of Social Behavior (SASB) as a system for conceptualizing and evaluating interpersonal relationships and for relating these phenomena to one's self-concept. The SASB reduces the interpersonal and intrapsychic domains to three essential variables: focus, affiliation, and interdependence. Focus involves three circumplex "surfaces" involving transitive action directed from the other to the subject (Other surface), the intransitive state of the subject (Self surface), or transitive action directed at the self by the subject (Interject surface). Each surface comprises two bipolar axes, Affiliation-Disaffiliation and Independence-Interdependence. Each surface has 36 transaction codes. Benjamin has also developed eight clusters of behaviors for each of the three surfaces.

The SASB is a complex and labor-intensive assessment device. It requires preparation of a transcript of videotape including nonverbal behaviors. Coders study the videotape and mark codes on the transcript. Coders typically receive 60-80 hours of training to enable them to attend to such cues as tone of voice, posture, eye contact, and context. Coders process each message unit or thought expressed by making three decisions: Which plane, how much affiliation, and how much interdependence? The coders' results are then processed by a computer program. Cohen's weighted kappa is used to measure reliability, examining agreement between coders on an event-by-event basis.

Interested in the issue of role reversal in families with a history of sexual abuse, Burkett (1991), referred to earlier, coded family interaction tasks with the SASB. She found the SASB particularly useful because the two underlying axes of affiliation and dominance are analogous to the concepts of support and control, aspects that are central to parenting. The top plane deals with interpersonal behaviors characterized by a focus on the other person rather than on the self. Such behaviors are expected in the parental role in which one person is defined as responsible for the well-being of another. The lower plane involves self-focused interpersonal behaviors, representing behaviors considered to be reactive to another and prototypic of the role of a dependent person such as a child. Parentified children would be expected to exhibit a greater other- than self-focus, whereas the converse would be expected of their parents. Indeed, this pattern emerged in Burkett's study.

Burkett appears to be the only investigator who has used the SASB to address parentification. Although complex, it represents a promising vehicle for future research and assessment in this area. There is now a short form of the SASB, which relies on self-reports (Intrex Interpersonal Institute, 1988). This form, however, is less likely to yield the same quality of information regarding more complex parent-child interactions such as parentification.

Strange Situation. As discussed earlier, measures of adult attachment, which are relevant to the parentification process, index behavioral patterns that are commensurate with those reported by Ainsworth and colleagues. Their findings are based on observations of mother-child and child-stranger interactions before, during, and after a 20-minute separation in an unfamiliar laboratory setting. Referred to as the Strange Situation, this widely used procedure yields data that are valid and reliably capture the quality of the child's attachment (Ainsworth et al., 1978).

In the Strange Situation, securely attached children often seek physical contact with their mothers after being separated from them; at a minimum, they greet them. By contrast, avoidantly attached children ignore their mothers, exhibit little preference for them over a stranger, and behave aggressively toward them at home. The anxious/ambivalent children engage in both contact-seeking and angry behaviors upon their mothers' return. Interestingly, at the 3-month-old mark in the Ainsworth et al. (1978) study, the anxious/ambivalent group was characterized by their mothers as tending toward role reversal and inconsistent responding.

Main and her co-investigators (Main & Cassidy, 1988; Main & Hesse, 1990) also discovered that children in the disorganized/disoriented attachment category often have caretakers with a history of unresolved trauma or loss who inadvertently behave in a frightening and unpredictable fashion. These children display an incoherent strategy for coping with separation from and reunion with their mothers in the Strange Situation and, as noted earlier, also may be at risk for destructive parentification.

DISCUSSION

As is true in the early stage of any line of investigative activity, theoretical clarification of central constructs, along with the development of operational definitions, is essential. Clearly, researchers in the area of parentification are making significant progress along these lines. A more differentiated and complex conceptual definition has been proposed, encompassing both the parentified role and its context at different levels of analysis. Various procedures for operationalizing and assessing parentification also have been developed, although they have yet to encompass all the facets of this construct.

For example, none of the measures reviewed specifically differentiates instrumental and expressive dimensions of the parentified role. Even more problematic is the fact that with the exception of Johnston and colleagues' (1987) Role Reversal Scale and Bavolek's (1984) Adult-Adolescent Parenting Inventory, the current instruments evaluate parentified role behaviors independently of the sociocultural and ethical context in which they occur. In the light of this concern, we are presently revising the Parentification Questionnaire to allow isolation of not only instrumental and expressive forms of parentification but also their ethical properties. It is hoped that this revision will differentiate extensive but culturally appropriate caretaking that is duly acknowledged and supported (i.e., ethical) from extensive caretaking that is not enacted in a fair and trustworthy familial and sociocultural setting.

Further scale construction in this area should also focus on self-report measures of parentifying tendencies. Although several of the observational measures tap this aspect of the parentification process, they do not easily lend themselves to use as screening tools or in large group research. Scales on the Adult-Adolescent Parenting Inventory (Bavolek, 1984), such as Role Reversal, assess parentifying attitudes but do not ask about parentifying behaviors per se. The Compulsive Care-Seeking scale on West and Sheldon's (1988) measure evaluates this dimension in adult peer relationships but not in family of origin.

Self-report instruments for children under 11 and 12 years of age also are needed. Unfortunately, one of the measures that is available, the Pictorial Assessment Inventory (Fosson & Lask, 1988), is of questionable validity. The measure nevertheless shows promise, particularly for use with young children, because of its stimulus and response qualities, and thus warrants further development. Analogue procedures involving audio- or videotaped vignettes of marital or family stress (Grych & Fincham, 1993) may also prove useful with this age group.

It is recognized that individual self-reports about relational processes, particularly when retrospective, are suspect as measures of family process. Such information must be corroborated by evaluation of other members of the relational system. Self-report scales in this area yield, however, useful data in their own right. As discussed earlier, they may—from Bowlby's perspective—reflect the respondent's internal working model of relationships derived from family-of-origin experiences. Interestingly, Sroufe, Egeland, and Kreutzer (1990) found a 75% concordance rate between classifications of adult attachment (on Main's measure) in a group of 21-year-olds and earlier classifications of these individuals via direct observation. These data notwithstanding, it is important to remember that one's internal mapping of relationships based on early familial patterns is subject to change as a result of subsequent shifts in parent-child relating and extrafamilial experiences.

Of all the measures that address parentification, only one, the Adult-Adolescent Parenting Inventory, has been standardized for application in clinical situations. The rest were developed primarily for research purposes, although many have clinical utility. In particular, coding schemes for the different interview, observational, and projective measures reviewed provide guidelines for understanding material obtained from children and families in evaluation, mediation, and therapy sessions.

For example, a mother of an extremely parentified adolescent seen by one of us said in therapy that she tired of listening to her son's "15-year-old stuff" and expected him to continue to be her confidant because she had no one else with whom to talk. In Newberger's (1977) framework, this comment, along with others of the same genre, reflected an "egoistic" level of parental awareness. An appreciation of this mother's reasoning within the context of Newberger's developmental sequence contributed to the therapist's efforts to help her construct a more cognitively sophisticated and less parentifying perspective.

The senior author (Jurkovic, 1997) also has outlined a clinical approach (the I-D-C Model) to assessing destructive parentification, involving an adaptation of many of the evaluation methodologies discussed in this chapter. The approach entails three stages: Identify, Describe, and Contextualize. The objective of the first stage is to identify signs, symptoms, and risk factors associated with a pathological parentification process in families through the reports and ratings of teachers and others, individual and conjoint interviews with family members, and observation of family interaction. Signs and symptoms might include overcompliant behavior, pseudomaturity, chronic worrying, or excessive sibling caretaking by a child and egoistic parenting conceptions or a compulsive care-seeking pattern in parents. Examples of risk factors are large families, divorce, parental loss, substance disorder, physical or emotional disability, and abuse or neglect.

In Stage 2, the role properties of a potentially destructive form of parentification are described: overtness, type, extent, and object of concern. The goal of Stage 3 is to develop a formulation of the context of the child's parentified behaviors with an emphasis on the different dimensions discussed above (age appropriateness, internalization, family boundaries, social legitimacy, and ethicality) as well as the biopsychosocial consequences of the parentification process not only for the child but also for other family members.

In conclusion, we are just beginning to appreciate the role of parentification as a pivotal process in a variety of sociofamilial contexts. Research and clinical intervention in this area depend on our ability to detect and evaluate the parentifying-parentified dynamic at different points in the child's development. Toward this end, the continuing construction and refinement of valid and reliable measurement tools and assessment approaches, albeit tedious, are crucial.

NOTE

1. In the event of couple parentification, we also distinguish between unilateral and bilateral parentification, a distinction that Jurkovic (1997) refers to as "unilaterality of caretaking." Does one partner primarily overfunction and the other underfunction (unilateral), or does each overfunction vis-à-vis one another (bilateral)?

REFERENCES

Ainsworth, M. D. S., Blehar, M. C., Waters, E., & Wall, S. (1978). *Patterns of attachment: A psychological study of the strange situation.* Hillsdale, NJ: Erlbaum.

Armsden, G. C., & Greenberg, M. T. (1987). The inventory of parent and peer attachment: Individual differences and their relationship to psychological well-being in adolescence. *Journal of Youth and Adolescence, 16,* 427-453.

Bakermans-Kranenburg, M. J., & Van Ijzendoorn, M. H. (1993). A psychometric study of the Adult Attachment Interview: Reliability and discriminant validity. *Developmental Psychology, 29,* 870-879.

Bartholomew, K., & Horowitz, L. M. (1991). Attachment styles among young adults: A test of a four-category model. *Journal of Personality and Social Psychology, 61,* 226-244.

Bavolek, S. J. (1984). *Handbook for the adult-adolescent parenting inventory (AAPI).* Schaumburg, IL: Family Development Associates.

Bell, M., Billington, R., & Becker, B. (1986). A scale of the assessment of object relations: Reliability, validity, and factorial invariance. *Journal of Clinical Psychology, 242,* 733-741.

Benjamin, L. S. (1974). Structural analysis of social behavior. *Psychological Review*, *81*, 392-425.

Benoit, D., & Parker, K. C. H. (1994). Stability and transmission of attachment across three generations. *Child Development, 65*, 1444-1456.

Boszormenyi-Nagy, I. (1965). A theory of relationships: Experience and transaction. In I. Boszormenyi-Nagy & J. L. Framo (Eds.), *Intensive family therapy: Theoretical and practical aspects* (pp. 38-86). New York: Harper & Row.

Boszormenyi-Nagy, I. (1987). *Foundations of contextual therapy*. New York: Brunner/ Mazel.

Boszormenyi-Nagy, I., & Krasner, B. R. (1986). *Between give and take: A clinical guide to contextual therapy*. New York: Brunner/Mazel.

Boszormenyi-Nagy, I., & Spark, G. M. (1973). *Invisible loyalties: Reciprocity in intergenerational family therapy*. Hagerstown, MD: Harper & Row.

Bowlby, J. (1973). *Attachment and loss: Vol. 2. Separation*. New York: Basic Books.

Bowlby, J. (1979). *The making and breaking of affectional bonds*. London: Tavistock.

Bowlby, J. (1980). *Attachment and loss: Vol 3. Loss*. New York: Basic Books.

Burkett, L. P. (1991). Parenting behaviors of women who were sexually abused as children in their families of origin. *Family Process, 30*, 421-434.

Chase, N. D., Deming, M. P., & Wells, M. (1998). Parentification, parental alcoholism, and academic status among young adults. *American Journal of Family Therapy, 26*, 105-114.

Collins, N. L., & Read, S. J. (1990). Adult attachment, working models, and relationship quality in dating couples. *Journal of Personality and Social Psychology, 58*, 644-663.

Daniels, D., & Plomin, R. (1985). Differential experience of siblings in the same family. *Developmental Psychology, 21*, 747-760.

Egeland, B., & Sroufe, L. A. (1981). Attachment and early maltreatment. *Child Development, 52*, 44-52.

Feeney, J. A., Noller, P., & Hanrahan, M. (1994). Assessing adult attachment. In M. B. Sperling & W. H. Berman (Eds.), *Attachment in adults: Clinical and developmental perspectives* (pp. 128-152). New York: Guilford.

Fosson, A., & Lask, B. (1988). Pictorially displayed family patterns as an assessment instrument. *Journal of Family Therapy, 10*, 65-74.

Frank, R., & Kopecky-Wenzel, M. (1994). *Inventar zur beurteilung der elter-kind-interaction* [Inventory for assessment of parent-child interaction]. (Available from Reiner Frank, Institute for Child and Adolescent Psychiatry of Ludwig-Maximilians University, Lindwurmstr. 2a, 80336 Munich, Germany)

Fullinwider-Bush, N., & Jacobvitz, D. B. (1993). The transition to young adulthood: Generation boundary dissolution and female identity development. *Family Process, 32*, 87-103.

Godsall, R., Emshoff, J., Jurkovic, G. J., Anderson, L., & Stanwyck, D. (in press). Why some kids do well in bad situations: The effects of parentification and parental impairment on childhood self-esteem. *International Journal of Addictions*.

Godsall, R., & Jurkovic, G. J. (1995). *The parentification questionnaire—youth*. (Available from Gregory J. Jurkovic, Department of Psychology, Georgia State University, University Plaza, Atlanta, GA 30303)

Goglia, L. R., Jurkovic, G. J., Burt, A. M., & Burge-Callaway, K. G. (1992). Generational boundary distortions by adult children of alcoholics: Child-as-parent and child-as-mate. *American Journal of Family Therapy, 20*, 291-299.

Graf, J. (1995). *Kinder als eltern, eltern als kinder* [Children as parents, parents as children]. Unpublished master's thesis, Ludwig-Maximilians University, Munich, Germany.

Grych, J. H., & Fincham, F. D. (1993). Children's appraisals of marital conflict: Initial investigations of the cognitive-contextual framework. *Child Development, 64*, 215-230.

Hanson, R. A. (1990). Initial parenting attitudes of pregnant adolescents and a comparison with the decision about adoption. *Adolescence, 25*, 629-643.

Hargrave, T. D., & Bomba, A. K. (1993). Further validation of the Relational Ethics Scale. *Journal of Marital and Family Therapy, 19*, 292-299.

Hargrave, T. D., Jennings, G., & Anderson, W. (1991). The development of a relational ethics scale. *Journal of Marital and Family Therapy, 17*, 145-158.

Hazan, C., & Shaver, P. (1987). Romantic love conceptualized as an attachment process. *Journal of Personality and Social Psychology, 52*, 511-524.

Hindy, C. G., Schwarz, J. C., & Brodsky, A. (1989). *If this is love why do I feel so insecure.* New York: Atlantic Monthly.

Intrex Interpersonal Institute. (1988). *SASB short form user's manual* (2nd ed.). Madison, WI: Author.

Jacobvitz, D. B., & Bush, N. F. (1996). Reconstructions of family relationships: Parent-child alliances, personal distress, and self-esteem. *Developmental Psychology, 32*, 732-743.

Jacobvitz, D. B., & Sroufe, L. A. (1987). The early caregiver-child relationship and attention-deficit disorder with hyperactivity in kindergarten: A prospective study. *Child Development, 58*, 1488-1495.

Johnston, J. R., Gonzalez, R., & Campbell, L. E. G. (1987). Ongoing postdivorce conflict and child disturbance. *Journal of Abnormal Child Psychology, 15*, 493-509.

Jurkovic, G. J. (1997). *Lost childhoods: The plight of the parentified child.* New York: Brunner/Mazel.

Jurkovic, G. J., Jessee, E. H., & Goglia, L. R. (1991). Treatment of parental children and their families: Conceptual and technical issues. *American Journal of Family Therapy, 19*, 302-314.

Karpel, M. A. (1976). Intrapsychic and interpersonal processes in the parentification of children. *Dissertation Abstracts International, 38*, 365. (University Microfilms No. 77-15,090)

Kohlberg, L. (1969). Stage and sequence. In D. Goslin (Ed.), *Handbook of socialization theory and research* (pp. 347-480). New York: Holt, Rinehart & Winston.

Lyddon, W. J., Bradford, E., & Nelson, J. P. (1993). Assessing adolescent and adult attachment: A review of current self-report measures. *Journal of Counseling and Development, 71*, 390-395.

Main, M., & Cassidy, J. (1988). Categories of response to reunion with the parent at age 6: Predictable from infant attachment classifications and stable over a 1-month period. *Developmental Psychology, 24*, 415-426.

Main, M., & Hesse, E. (1990). Parents' unresolved traumatic experiences are related to infant disorganized attachment status: Is frightened and/or frightening parental behavior the linking mechanism? In M. Greenberg, D. Cicchetti, & M. Cummings (Eds.), *Attachment in the preschool years* (pp. 161-182). Chicago: University of Chicago Press.

Main, M., & Kaplan, N. (1985). Security in infancy, childhood, and adulthood: A move to the level of representation. In I. Bretherton & E. Waters (Eds.), *Monographs of the Society for Research in Child Development, 50*, 66-104.

Main, M., & Solomon, J. (1986). Discovery of an insecure-disorganized attachment pattern. In T. B. Brazelton & M. W. Yogman (Eds.), *Affective development in infancy* (pp. 95-124). Norwood, NJ: Ablex.

Main, M., & Solomon, J. (1990). Procedures for identifying infants as disorganized/disoriented during the Ainsworth strange situation. In M. Greenberg, D. Cicchetti, & M. Cummings (Eds.), *Attachment in the preschool years* (pp. 121-160). Chicago: University of Chicago Press.

Meyer, R. G., & Karon, B. P. (1967). The schizophrenigenic mother concept and the TAT. *Psychiatry, 30,* 173-179.

Mika, P., Bergner, R. M., & Baum, M. C. (1987). The development of a scale for the assessment of parentification. *Family Therapy, 14,* 229-235.

Miller, A. (1981). *The drama of the gifted child* (R. Ward, Trans.). New York: Basic Books. (Original work published 1979)

Minuchin, S. (1974). *Families and family therapy.* Cambridge, MA: Harvard University Press.

Minuchin, S., & Fishman, H. C. (1981). *Family therapy techniques.* Cambridge, MA: Harvard University Press.

Minuchin, S., Montalvo, B., Guerney, B. G., Rosman, B., & Schumer, F. (1967). *Families of the slums.* New York: Basic Books.

Mitchell, K. M. (1968). An analysis of the schizophrenigenic mother concept by means of the TAT. *Journal of Abnormal Psychology, 73,* 571-574.

Newberger, C. M. (1977). Parental conceptions of children and child-rearing: A structural-developmental analysis. *Dissertation Abstracts International, 38,* 6123. (University Microfilms No. 78-08622)

Newberger, C. M. (1980). The cognitive structure of parenthood: The development of a descriptive measure. In R. Selman & R. Yando (Eds.), *New directions in child development: Clinical developmental research* (pp. 45-67). San Francisco: Jossey-Bass.

Newberger, C. M., & Cook, S. J. (1983). Parental awareness and child abuse and neglect: A cognitive-developmental analysis of urban and rural samples. *American Journal of Orthopsychiatry, 53,* 512-524.

Sears, R. R., Maccoby, E. E., & Levin, H. (1957). *Patterns of child rearing.* New York: Row, Peterson.

Selman, R. L. (1980). *The growth of interpersonal understanding: Developmental and clinical analyses.* New York: Academic Press.

Sessions, M., & Jurkovic, G. J. (1986). *The Parentification Questionnaire.* (Available from Gregory J. Jurkovic, Department of Psychology, Georgia State University, 1 University Plaza, Atlanta, GA 30303)

Simpson, J. A. (1990). Influence of attachment styles on romantic relationships. *Journal of Personality and Social Psychology, 59,* 971-980.

Sperling, M. B., & Berman, W. H. (1991). An attachment classification of desperate love. *Journal of Personality Assessment, 56,* 971-980.

Sperling, M. B., Foelsch, P., & Grace, C. (1996). Measuring adult attachment: Are self-report instruments congruent? *Journal of Personality Assessment, 67,* 37-51.

Sroufe, L. A., Egeland, B., & Kreutzer, T. (1990). The fate of early experience following developmental change: Longitudinal approaches to individual adaptation in childhood. *Child Development, 61,* 1363-1373.

Sroufe, L. A., Jacobvitz, D., Mangelsdorf, S., DeAngelo, E., & Ward, M. J. (1985). Generational boundary dissolution between mothers and their preschool children: A relationship systems approach. *Child Development, 56,* 317-325.

Valleau, M. P., Bergner, R. M., & Horton, C. B. (1995). Parentification and caretaker syndrome: An empirical investigation. *Family Therapy, 22,* 157-164.

VandenBos, G., & Karon, B. P. (1971). Pathogenesis: A new therapist personality dimension related to therapeutic effectiveness. *Journal of Personality Assessment, 35,* 252-260.

Walsh, F. W. (1979). Breaching of family generation boundaries by schizophrenics, disturbed, and normals. *International Journal of Family Therapy, 1,* 254-275.

West, M., & Sheldon, A. (1988). Classification of pathological attachment patterns in adults. *Journal of Personality Disorders, 2,* 153-159.

West, M., Sheldon, A., & Reiffer, L. (1987). An approach to the delineation of adult attachment: Scale development and reliability. *Journal of Nervous and Mental Disease, 175,* 738-741.

Zahn-Waxler, C., & Radke-Yarrow, M. (1982). The development of altruism: Alternative research strategies. In N. Eisenberg (Ed.), *The development of prosocial behavior* (pp. 109-137). San Diego, CA: Academic Press.

Zahn-Waxler, C., Radke-Yarrow, M., Wagner, E., & Chapman, M. (1992). Development of concern for others. *Developmental Psychology, 28,* 126-136.

Zeanah, C. H., & Klitzke, M. (1991). Role reversal and the self-effacing solution: Observations from infant-parent psychotherapy. *Psychiatry, 54,* 346-357.

PART II

Clinical and
Contextual Perspectives

Object Relations Therapy for Individuals With Narcissistic and Masochistic Parentification Styles

Marolyn Wells
Rebecca Jones

Although the psychology and family therapy literatures on parentification (i.e., the rigidified reversal of parent and child roles) concur that this construct is exceedingly useful in informing clinical practice, most publications have focused on the conceptualization and treatment of parentified children. Less has been written about the effects of childhood parentification on adult personality and accompanying treatment issues. In this chapter, we hope to expand the conceptual understanding of the effects of childhood parentification on adults and offer an individualized, interactive object relations approach (Glickauf-Hughes & Wells, 1995, in press) to the treatment of two distinctive parentified personality styles (i.e., masochistic and narcissistic) previously described by Jones and Wells (1996). We focus on three core clinical issues manifested by parentified adults—shame, splitting, and projective identification.

Object relations therapy (Glickauf-Hughes & Wells, in press) is built on the premise that individual personality and psychopathology develop within the context of primary early relationships. Harmful derailments in the development of one's personality thus need to be healed within the context of a properly formed, corrective therapeutic relationship.

Following the therapeutic model proffered by Glickauf-Hughes and Wells (in press), we believe that masochistic and narcissistic forms of parentification require different therapeutic attitudes and interventions to effect a corrective healing relationship. Because each of the clinical issues (i.e., shame, splitting, projective identification) being examined can assume a distinctive form depending on whether the parentified client's presentation is more narcissistic or more masochistic, distinctions in therapeutic approach are introduced for each style.

RECENT RESEARCH ON ADULT RESPONSES
TO CHILDHOOD PARENTIFICATION

Parentification is believed to occur in response to a parent's wish to have a child gratify the parent's own unmet childhood needs. Previous research by Jones and Wells (1996) supports the hypothesis that children can be parentified either in a masochistic (self-defeating) style, by being induced to directly gratify parental needs for emotional and physical caretaking, or in a narcissistic (grandiose) style, by being induced to realize the parent's projected ego ideal.

West and Keller (1991) originally proposed that childhood parentification could result in "compulsive care giving", or masochistic personality characteristics in adulthood. According to West and Keller, children develop self-defeating, compulsive caregiving because it provides the parentified child "the best opportunity for achieving proximity to the parent" (p. 426), who may otherwise be inconsistently available, emotionally detached, or self-absorbed. This child gives up his or her rights to childhood and real self-development in order to assume the role of nurturer, mediator, organizer, protector, and general caretaker of the parent(s).

Our research also supports the existence of an alternative, narcissistic form of parentification (Jones & Wells, 1996). In narcissistic parentification, the child adapts to parental needs by internalizing a parent's projected ego-ideal (e.g., living out the parent's lifelong dream of becoming a great musician or a famous doctor or becoming the parent's own lost object of childhood). Narcissistically parentified children give up true self-actualization to become the parent's ego ideal and, thus, in fundamental ways, live out someone else's life in order to stay connected with the parent who is overwhelmed with his or her own loss or self-esteem deficiencies.

In a separate analysis, Wells and Jones (in press-b) found an empirical relationship between parentification and shame-proneness in adults. This empirical finding matches our clinical experience that parentified adult clients appear exquisitely prone to feelings of shame related to true self-expression. Shame is experienced as the absolute discrediting of one's true self by a disapproving significant other. When a child's true needs or feelings are shamed by significant others (e.g., "Don't be such a pest" or "Such an insolent girl will give me a heart attack someday"), the child learns to devote substantial psychic energy to processes and activities designed to avoid the experience of shame (and thus the experience of the true self).

In a third analysis, Wells and Jones (in press-a) found that childhood parentification is associated with defensive splitting in adults. In general, splitting is a defense mechanism that allows an individual to keep apart positive and negative feelings and images of self and other which, if mixed together, would generate intolerable anxiety. More specifically, we believe that when children are induced into a parentified role, they may split by either (a) over-idealizing the parent (even in the face of the parents' coercive and/or over-whelming demands for emotional and physical caretaking) and devaluing the self (i.e., masochistic splitting; Meyers, 1988) or by (b) creating an idealized, grandiose image of the self and devaluing others who do not provide admiration or mirroring (i.e., narcissistic splitting; Kohut 1971). The maintenance of such splitting may be encouraged by two parental attitudes: (a) parents who uncon-sciously want the child to fulfill their own needs to be aggrandized, by directly idealizing and serving them, or (b) parents who need the child to become their extension of self and live out those idealized dreams that bring the parent glory or prestige, thus enhancing the parents' experience of self.

The parentified child with masochistic tendencies, feeling pulled to take care of a parent in ways that are beyond his or her developmental capacity, learns to defend against feelings of frustration and anger toward the parent by "internal-izing the burden of badness" (Fairbairn, 1954), while maintaining an idealized view of the parent. Masochistic splitting thus results in a mental template of a "bad" self-representation with a "good" object representation. As Fairbairn noted, the child determines that it is better to feel like a sinner in a world ruled by God than an innocent in a world ruled by the devil. The masochistic child thus chooses the lessor of two evils to maintain a feeling of connectedness with the illusion of a "good parental object" that substitutes for real parents who are predominantly inconsistent, hostile, critical, or overly self-absorbed because of their own narcissistic injuries. This split fuels the masochistically parentified child's underlying feelings of shame as well as his or her motivation to earn love and approval by caretaking the parent or significant other.

In contrast, the narcissistically parentified child defends against feelings of rage and shame over the parents' lack of attunement to the child's real self by constructing a grandiose false self representation (i.e., by internalizing the parents' ego ideal) that is admired by the parent(s). Narcissistic splitting thus results in an experience of "wonderful me" (although false self–based) and devalued other. Others are generally dismissed when not providing narcissistic supplies or emotional homage for this grandiose self. This child determines that it is better to identify with an illusion of invulnerable greatness than to identify with a devalued and seemingly worthless true self experience.

Both the narcissistic and masochistic parentified styles are invoked by the child as a means to maintain relationships with needed, yet unattuned, care-givers. In each case, the child internalizes a self-other relationship model or template that demands the sacrifice of the true self for the sake of relational maintenance. In each form of parentification, shame of the real self is defended against through specialized splitting and projective identification.

We could find no empirical research findings linking parentification and projective identification. Our clinical experience, however, leads us to believe

that clients who were parentified as children will recreate the family parentification process by reenacting prototypic interactions with the therapist (projective identification). Because of our clinical experience, we include in the
following section descriptions of typical projective identification enactments
that are likely to occur with parentified clients, and a method of working
through projective identifications in individual treatment.

TREATMENT ISSUES

This section outlines treatment issues with adult clients who were parentified
as children. Specifically, emphasis is placed on the following important treatment goals: (a) establishing a working alliance, (b) resolving shame and splitting, and (c) working with prototypic projective identifications (which often
incorporate both shame and splitting mechanisms).

Establishing a Working Alliance

Because of the parentified adult client's tendencies to experience shame and
use splitting to defend against relational anxiety, one of the first therapeutic
challenges is to help these clients understand the importance of establishing an
authentic working alliance that can support the client's real self-activation.
These clients are often terrified that any real self-expression will induce either
shaming degradation or abandonment by the valued other. They need to learn
that they can directly express thoughts and feelings reflecting the real self with
a therapist who will maintain a holding environment. This is accomplished by
the therapist providing emotional and relationship safety through empathy,
appropriate limit-setting, clarification, a larger perspective, and relational expertise.

In the beginning, this process often requires these clients to gradually
acknowledge ways that they do not trust the therapist and how hard it is for them
to admit their lack of trust (e.g., they are afraid of hurting the therapist and being
abandoned, or devaluing the therapist and then having to leave). One of the most
challenging aspects of working with these clients is to establish a real working
alliance where shame and related feelings of anger, helplessness, and inferiority
can be safely acknowledged and expressed.

Narcissistically parentified clients are likely to attempt to create a narcissistic collusion rather than a reality based therapeutic alliance. For example, one
client repeatedly complimented the therapist for her "pure gold" interventions,
but never used these insights to further his own self-understanding. The therapist noted that although she appreciated the compliments, she also wondered
if, in some way, the client needed to experience her observations as "pure gold"
so that he could feel safe being vulnerable, while relying on her to be strong.
They then explored the fact that the client was unable to rely confidently on his
parents, because his father was manic-depressive and his mother, alcoholic. The

therapist normalized the client's yearning for a "strong competent parent figure." She also noted that by idealizing the therapist, he was able to avoid any anxiety about the fact that both the therapist and the client were regular people with real frailties.

The masochistic client is likely to form a false self-collusion with the therapist that is more subtle. For example, the therapist may experience a reluctance to "rock the boat" by raising controversial issues with this client. As a result, the therapist may fail to challenge the client's caretaking of the therapist. More specifically, when such a client empathically lets the therapist off the hook (e.g., by never getting angry with the therapist despite the therapist's lateness), the overstressed therapist may feel a genuine sense of gratitude. The problem is that these clients are compulsively gracious and forgiving and need the therapist's help to feel safe to express their irritation or resentment. They need to learn that they can get angry and that the therapist will not withdraw the relationship or emotionally disconnect. To this end, the therapist might note: "I both appreciate your graciousness with me and realize that if I were you I would probably feel a little irritated that I had to wait for my appointment. Would it be hard to tell me if a part of you felt annoyed with me?"

Attempts at false self collusions need to be empathically addressed as they arise in order for these clients to recognize how their adaptations to the demands in their families of origin now defeat their ability to have real self-activation, honest emotional expression, and authentic relationships with others. The rest of therapy depends on the creation of this foundation. Otherwise, the client who is in a false self collusion with the therapist has only the option of a transference cure—that is, getting better to please the therapist—which undermines true separation-individuation processes (Glickauf-Hughes & Wells, 1997).

Working Through Shame and Splitting

Wells and Jones (in press) have outlined a therapeutic approach to working with the shame-based identities of masochistically and narcissistically parentified clients. This approach first advises the therapist to be sensitive to the inarticulateness of shame-related experiences. The therapist must help the patient identify and name shame when it is experienced. Then the therapist can normalize the difficulty the client has in talking about this area of experience, resulting both from the intensity of the emotional discomfort that accompanies shame and from the lack of language or words for the experience.

Kaufman (1989) discusses the importance of creating a safe enough holding environment so that the client eventually can talk about the shame-based experiences in detail. It is in sharing the emotionally laden details with a safe, supportive, and empathic other that healing occurs. Shame induces individuals to talk about shame-related issues in a superficial, globalized, and glossed over manner that denies the depth and breadth of the experience. Therapists often need to slow these clients down, letting them know that this is material that they may need to go over many times in some detail before they have worked it through. The therapist can reassure these clients that they can work together to pace the experience so that it will not be overwhelming.

Empathy is one of the primary antidotes to shame (Jordan, 1997). Several issues are important in empathizing with shame. For example, individuals with shame-based identities (who feel shame over their real self and who believe that they are bad at their core) are likely to feel shame even about their shame. Thus, when responding to shame, timing and tact are extremely important, so that the individual does not feel shamed by the interpretation itself.

Whereas masochistically parentified individuals are more likely to be aware of shame feelings and leak code words or phrases (e.g., "I should be a better person"), narcissistically parentified clients often are unconscious of shame. They are likely to focus consciously on being perfect, rather than on feeling filled with shame. With these clients, the first step in resolving shame may be to observe and empathize with the client's sensitivity to self-esteem injury. In addition, it is important to address defensive splitting (e.g., when the client experiences the *other* as disgusting or contemptible and devalues him or her).

Although accurate empathy is important in healing shame, empathic failures, rather than being detrimental, can actually become gold mines in this treatment process, if properly worked through (Jordan, 1997). In one case, after several minor empathic failures on the therapist's part, a client responded by devaluing the therapist and telling her that no one could really understand him because he was so complex. Because this was a pattern that the therapist and client had explored previously, the therapist offered the following summary observations and interpretations:

> When you feel criticized by me either directly or by implication, you defend against feeling shame by becoming critical of me. In the past we've come to understand that you devalue me and dismiss what I'm saying because it feels rejecting. It seems like you need to reject me and make me unimportant because you are feeling subtly rejected by me—like you reject me before I can reject you.

The client nodded affirmatively and looked interested. The therapist continued:

> I think we are beginning to understand how you try to get others to see you as a great thinker, because in your family you learned that any deviation from this image brought rejection of you as a person. This made you feel ashamed of yourself, as if you were only o.k. if you were brilliant.

The client continued to nod and look sad, so the therapist continued:

> I can see why it has been important for you to fend off anything or anyone that feels at all critical, especially of your intellect, because it was so prized in your family. The problem is that when you can only be a great thinker, we miss out on many other parts of you that also have value and we need to get to know better.

You have already spent a lot of your life feeling like you had to be exceptional to be OK. Our challenge now is to help you feel more comfortable being yourself, whether that's a great thinker or just a beginner at something new.

As empathy is an antidote to shame, so is respect and mutuality. Shame is disrespectful, discrediting, and isolating, and therefore leads individuals to limited experiences of relationships. Masochistically parentified clients tend to view relationships in terms of a dominance-submission (master-slave) continuum, whereas narcissistically parentified clients tend to view relationships in terms of a superior-inferior (admired-dismissed) continuum. Helping parentified clients develop alternative relationship models based on mutuality, respect, and general equity often is useful.

These clients usually are very sensitive to the general inequities in relationships and to the obvious power differential in the therapeutic relationship in particular. For example, whereas clients are asked to expose themselves, therapists generally are cautious about self disclosure. In addition, there is a potential and often real imbalance in emotional investment, with the client having only one therapist and the therapist having many clients. Leaving the safety of the "caretaker" or the "special/grandiose" role to be truly oneself (with a mixture of "good and bad" characteristics) in order to find the parameters and pleasures of mutuality can be frightening. The built-in inequities of the therapeutic relationship can stimulate fears of unrequited love and, once again, a sense of hopelessness in ever finding mutuality. Although there may be a measure of reality in the client's complaint, the fear that is generated is the very obstacle that has prevented such clients from risking themselves in other relationships. Helping the client to build a sense of self-resiliency so that potential and real disappointments do not become devastating can help the client to tolerate the risks of pursuing genuine relationships based primarily on mutuality and respect.

For parentified clients, healing toxic, relational shame requires coming to terms with two other difficult issues. Working through these two issues can help parentified clients to understand and begin to form more mutual, respectful relationships. One has to do with how individuals feel loved, and the other has to do with how individuals make peace with the inevitable disappointments or irreconcilable differences we all must face in relationships (e.g., when two people have competing desires or needs, such as one wanting to buy a house and the other wanting to rent an apartment, one wanting to be easy-going, the other wanting control).

Learning to Feel Loved/Learning to Cope With Relationship Disappointments. When parentified clients are disappointed in their relationships, they are particularly vulnerable to experiencing shame and reactive, defensive splitting, as noted above. As clients learn to cope better with relationship disappointments, they will experience less shame, and splitting will become less necessary.

Tactics that can be helpful for parentified clients learning to cope with relationship disappointments include (a) substituting the 70% Rule (described below) for their all-or-nothing tendencies; (b) learning to recognize love in different forms, and learning to "take it in"; and (c) learning to appreciate parts of themselves that are split off.

Wells and Glickauf-Hughes (1986) introduced the concept of the 70% Rule to help individuals reframe their expectations of self and others, and thereby to cope with relational disappointments. This rule of thumb states that we can reasonably expect understanding and consideration from loved ones (and from ourselves) about 70% of the time. It is intended to help clients begin to see and appreciate the relativity in life and relationships.

Clients with both forms of parentification tend to have a criterion list of behaviors that indicate to them that they are loved. These lists mirror the roles into which they were forced in their families of origin. In particular, clients with the masochistic parentification style tend to believe in reciprocity on demand (e.g., "I show him I love him by buying him presents and cooking his dinner. If he loved me he would surely do these things for me."). In contrast, clients with the narcissistic parentification style tend to look for unconditional positive regard (e.g., "If you loved me you would always love all of me, including my shitty parts. You would love my shit because it was mine and you wouldn't need me to spell things out. You would know me perfectly and love me perfectly.").

When narcissistically parentified clients become disappointed or frustrated in relationships, they often are not able to appreciate what they can get or what is available to them from others, but instead over-focus on how they are being frustrated and then dismiss the other as worthless. Related to this issue, both narcissistically and masochistically parentified clients need to learn that love is expressed in many ways, not just in the ways they define as loving. Through the therapist telling exemplary stories of how different people express love (e.g., other clients, the therapist's friends), clients can learn that appreciating differences, not just similarities, is a measure of maturity, which enriches life by broadening their perspective. It also gets them in less trouble with their partners.

For masochistically parentified clients to come to terms with relationship disappointment, they must learn to accept and actually take in the love and empathy offered to them. Becoming good receivers (as opposed to good givers) who can allow themselves to be vulnerable enough to acknowledge and assimilate empathy is quite a challenge for many masochistically parentified adult clients. Can they tolerate the self-consciousness, shame, and guilt that initially may accompany the act of receiving? Can they tolerate the fear of further loss or disappointment that may be generated if they allow themselves to acknowledge feeling loved? Can they allow their personal identities to evolve from someone who sacrifices for others to someone who enjoys reciprocity in which both parties give and take?

Masochistically parentified clients experience a paradox, in that the more one has that is precious and dear to one's heart, the more one potentially can lose. They believe that if one has opened one's heart to loving empathy, when the other shoe drops and the empathic connection is lost, then the pain will be intolerable, so one had better keep one's heart protected. Teaching masochistically parentified clients how to deal with loss and disappointment without splitting (feeling bad and undeserving) will help them experience more viable options in life and more empathic mutuality in relationships.

Clients exhibiting each form of parentification tend to respond to the inevitable disappointments and irreconcilable differences inherent in intimate relationships in unique ways. Both styles are designed to defensively deny that irreconcilable differences really exist. Clients with masochistic parentification tend to deny feeling a loss in the face of irreconcilable differences by submitting to the other. They rationalize that their own needs must be selfish or that the other person's needs are greater than theirs (e.g., "I'm being selfish to want to buy a house when he has already stretched so much toward my wishes."). In this method, these clients do not honor or respect their own need for something different and usually end up resentful. In other words, they feel compelled or obligated to accommodate to others' wishes, but then often feel secretly resentful that their needs were not met.

Glickauf-Hughes and Wells (1991, 1995, 1997) have articulated in detail the corrective relationship experience needed by masochistic clients. They advise the therapist to (a) be authentic with the client to counteract the manipulativeness and narcissistic exploitativeness of their parents; (b) be consistent to counteract the inconsistency of positive regard in their families of origin; (c) resist sadistic, passive-aggressive, or exploitative pulls; and (d) stay attuned to the client and really listen. All parentified clients need to feel authentically valued for their person rather than their functions.

Like masochistically parentified clients, parentified clients with narcissistic styles also present a characteristic way of responding to disappointment in relationships. The client with narcissistic parentification tends to deny the pain of loss associated with irreconcilable differences in relationships by dismissing the importance or relevance of the significant other's needs and aggrandizing his or her own. When forced to compromise, most individuals feel mild disappointment over the loss of total autonomy. This type of client, instead, is likely to feel righteous indignation. When, ultimately, his or her own wishes do not prevail in a conflict, this client can suffer considerable self-esteem injury, but may defend against this pain by devaluing the other person as too needy, critical, demanding, or unimportant.

Glickauf-Hughes and Wells (1997) describe the corrective relationship experience that may further the therapeutic progress of narcissistic clients. In this model, the therapist emphasizes (a) genuinely acknowledging, validating, and mirroring the client's real self-expressions, while avoiding overt praise or blaming; (b) demonstrating compassion and understanding of the human need for emotional support; and (c) consistently holding on to a balanced perspective and realistic, as opposed to grandiose or catastrophic, meanings of experiences.

good

In other words, it is important for the therapist to be warm and genuine, expecting humanness rather than greatness, and model this expectation by taking responsibility for any empathic failures (e.g., "Sounds like I didn't understand what you were trying to say very well; what's that like for you when someone doesn't fully understand you?"). It is very important during this type of interchange for the therapist not to be overly apologetic, but instead to model self-responsibility without self-shaming. Finally, when working with any client with narcissistic issues, it will be necessary to continue to process resistances to treatment, including favorite child fantasies (i.e., being the therapist's favorite client).

Working Through Projective Identification

Another important treatment goal that applies to both forms of parentification is to recognize and work through projective identifications. Projective identification is a defense in which clients recreate unresolved relational problems from the past that persist within them and between them and others (Scharff & Scharff, 1992). The concept of projective identification can help in understanding how clients recreate, during the treatment hour, the kind of relationship issues with which they most need help, and which they often have a difficult time articulating or discussing directly. In projective identification, a client acts out his or her relational story in a way that offers the therapist an experiential window into the client's inner world, especially into the client's emotional experience.

Specifically, projective identification involves projecting an unwanted or disowned part of the self experience onto the other person and then behaving toward the other in such a way as to induce that cognitive-emotional state. Ogden (1989) believes that the individual using projective identification then unconsciously empathizes with the cognitive-emotional state being induced.

Kernberg, Selzer, Koenigsberg, Carr, and Appelbaum (1989) have clearly outlined their approach to working with projective identifications in borderline clients. We believe a similar format can be used to understand and work through projective identifications common to healthier parentified clients as well as clients experiencing more severe ego/object relations deficits. The biggest difference in these two levels of pathology is that the more disturbed the client is, the more distorted the projection will be, and the more the therapist will feel misunderstood or misrepresented in the client's eyes. We believe that in most projective identifications, there is a grain of truth regarding the therapist's personality (in other words, what the client claims to be experiencing with the therapist may be at least partially true). The more severe the pathology of the client, the more important it may be for the therapist to own (in a realistic and accepting, but not self-shaming, way) his or her own contribution before proceeding into investigating the transference elements of the projective identification (Jordan, 1997).

Our belief is that one possible therapeutic effect of projective identification is to help the therapist empathize experientially with the client's troublesome or even intolerable emotional states. If the therapist is able to recognize the projection, this experience gives the therapist the opportunity to help the client develop a more mature way of processing the emotional state. Thus, when projective identification occurs, the therapist is advised to (a) recognize the feelings created by the client's induction (e.g., shame, inferiority, worthlessness, helplessness, contempt, loathing); (b) contain the feelings by activating a larger perspective that is informed by these feelings but not fueled by them; (c) label the roles or polarities of experience that are formed between client and therapist (e.g., "it seems that we are in a place that we come to often, where there are two roles being played out"); (d) understand these polarities as part of the client's internal struggle (e.g., "it will be important for us to understand how you have experienced both of these roles and the feelings associated with them"); (e) when appropriate, relate the struggle to interpersonal relationships in the client's past or current outside relationships (e.g., "we are playing out roles you and your mother used to play out in your family"); and (f) use the dynamic to inform the treatment regarding what is missing or needed for working through the dilemma or impasse (e.g., "Your parents weren't able to appreciate how you were a strong-willed and naturally exuberant child; it's as if you shut off that part of yourself as unacceptable. This suggests that our challenge will be to help you become more comfortable with being all of you, an active, exuberant, and strong-willed person as well as a very thoughtful mediator who cares about what others feel and think.").

The most common masochistic and narcissistic projective identifications are usually complements or mirror images of one another. Clients, however, can switch roles in their defensive maneuvering to mediate their anxiety (Kernberg et al., 1989) which can be very confusing for the therapist. In this section, we will describe typical types of projective identifications representative of the two types of parentification, as well as how the therapist can address each of these. It is useful to note that these projective identifications prototypically inspire shame (or related feelings of rage or contempt).

Masochistic Projective Identification. The projective identification (PI) that most often occurs during the early phases of treatment with a masochistically parentified adult involves the client's unconscious projection onto the therapist of an unwanted or disowned aspect of the self that feels angry/frustrated/helpless with significant others. These clients often report long-term attachments to someone who is predominantly hostile and rejecting toward them (e.g., a hostile, demeaning, emotionally abusive girlfriend). In PI, the client projects the angry/helpless self experience (which anyone would feel in response to a hostile girlfriend) onto the therapist and then uses tactics to induce these feelings of angry helplessness in the therapist. These tactics may include help-rejecting behaviors (e.g., subtle messages that the therapist is desperately needed but not helping, "yes-butting"), masochistic splitting (e.g., explaining that the self is bad, the girlfriend/boyfriend is good), and masochistic triangulations (e.g., "hate her for me"; see Glickauf-Hughes & Wells, 1995). These tactics often succeed in inducing feelings of urgent need, frustration, and helplessness in the therapist while enabling the client to remain in the relationship, feeling his (or her) positive bond with the erratic and difficult significant other.

The roles induced in this PI drama often fit a victim-persecutor-rescuer paradigm, with the therapist at first thrust into the potential rescuer role, then persecutor and finally victim, rendered helpless while still feeling pressed to save the client. At some point, the therapist probably will want to make explicit just how stuck the two of them can get in the victim, rescuer, and persecutor roles and invite the client's ego to join the therapist in exploring the meaning of these roles. The articulation of this observation is intended, in part, to transform the roles assumed by the therapist and the client, making them partners, or team members, working on a problem together.

The parentified masochist also tends to disown his or her narcissistic shadow or aspects of the self that seem selfish, self-indulgent, or prideful. This client needs to learn what healthy narcissism is and to develop first a tolerance, then an acceptance, and finally an unself-conscious enjoyment of or pleasure in authentic self-activation and expression, self-interest, and genuine pride in self-achievement. The therapist is advised not to argue with the masochistically parentified client on this issue, but first and for a long time to empathize with all the "good stuff" (pride, self-acceptance) the client is barred from experiencing because of the system internalized from childhood. The losses the client suffered then and continue to suffer now are many. If such clients can learn to feel sad for themselves over those losses, or angry that such a system was all they had to rely on, then progress is afoot. The therapist's empathic relationship with the real self of the client who is rightfully sad and mad about his or her predicament is one of the major curative relationship factors. The therapist needs to watch for when clients' internalized shame becomes activated and the clients truncate their anger or sadness and begin defending their parents. This defensive loyalty is activated, as it was in childhood, in order to protect the parent-child bond. The therapist needs to acknowledge the importance of the client's connection with the parents (or the current parent-substitute) while acknowledging the legitimacy of the real self's responses.

Narcissistic Projective Identification. One PI enactment common to the narcissistically parentified client revolves around the client's disregard of the therapist as another separate person in the treatment room. The therapist is treated as a self-object (Kohut, 1971), a set of functions, an extension of self, or an audience for the client, who either ignores or devalues any attempt by the therapist to participate as a separate individual in the client's process. These clients may idealize the therapist, incorporating the therapist into the client's grandiose self-representation. One client described a fantasy in which the therapist would write her next book about the client's course of treatment and the two of them would then go on tour together explaining the success of their collaborative therapeutic work together. At various times in the fantasy, the client was herself, and at other times, she merged with the therapist and they presented to their audience as one. This client helped herself to feel a safe, loving connection in the relationship by making herself the most special client (or favorite child) of the therapist whom she idealized and considered an extension of herself. In this case, the client tended to superficially praise every intervention the therapist made, noting how brilliant it was. In this scenario, the therapist began to feel misrepresented or not accurately seen, just as the client had been misrepresented and not seen by her mother.

Narcissistically parentified clients can also present as arrogant, self-involved, pompous, and/or contemptuous of anyone who does not totally admire and support them. Any intervention by the therapist may be rejected or ignored. The therapist may begin to feel inadequate and ineffectual, superfluous and unimportant. This is the shamed feeling state at the underbelly of narcissism (Morrison, 1989), which is very difficult to tolerate by either client or therapist for any period of time. Bolstering the PI is the client's tendency to employ narcissistic splitting in which the false self of the client is aggrandized and the self of the other is devalued except as it functions to mirror the grandiose false self of the client.

For example, one of the authors worked with a client whose father had required weekly spelling bees at the dinner table. During these episodes, the father praised his children as special and brilliant, while devaluing other children acquainted with the family. In this family, the child's natural talents for leadership and socialization were devalued as mediocre and unimportant. At one point in the treatment, the therapist found herself feeling ineffectual and stupid in ways that were uncommon for her. After multiple instances of the client subtly rejecting the therapist's interventions, yet outwardly praising the therapist for her superior training, the therapist commented on the feeling of inadequacy. She said,

> Sometimes I think you experience what I have to offer as pretty dumb or worthless. You let me know that by sighing or continuing your discourse as if I had never said anything, or by saying something sarcastic, like "Well that was really brilliant." When you do that, it feels as though you are not taking me seriously. I have wondered why you would need to cut me off or not take me seriously. I wonder if it is because you are afraid I could be rejecting or critical of you in some way. Not taking me seriously may protect you from potentially being hurt by me.

The client acknowledged, red-faced and mildly tearful, that he was afraid the therapist would not like him if she really got to know him, that he would not be smart enough or quick enough. The therapist then expressed genuine empathy for the client's fear that he was not good enough.

By acknowledging the feelings of shame and inferiority she had experienced in response to the client's reactions, the therapist was able to speculate on what might be real fears underlying the client's defensive presentation and explore the client's real inner experience. By commenting on the process in this way, the therapist was able to move to an overt empathic stance, which made the PI drama no longer necessary. Of course, in responding to potential projective identifications, the therapist should always take stock of the contribution of his or her own unresolved issues, as they are raised by clients, before intervening.

SUMMARY

We have outlined several core issues in the treatment of adult clients who were pathologically, rigidly parentified as children. The object relations model of therapy perspective adopted in this chapter focuses the treatment on the relationship between the parentified adult client and the therapist. In particular, we have advised the therapist on how to intervene with the prominent clinical issues of specialized splitting, shame-based identity, and projective identification as manifested in two forms of parentification previously described by Jones and Wells (1996). Specifically, we detailed the tailored corrective relationship approach which we have found most effective with masochistically and narcissistically parentified adults in our practice.

As we described, the process of parentification leads to a reliance on the splitting defense and to a tendency to experience feelings of shame when the real self is activated. The ultimate goal with parentified clients is to activate real self experiences that have been buried by a family system that required the child to accommodate to and service the needs of parents. In addition, as parentified adults learn empathy for their shamed identities, these clients can be helped to form relationships with others that do not require submission or self-aggrandizement, but instead are built on a foundation of mutuality, respect, and real love. Parentified clients with masochistic and/or narcissistic styles can learn more realistic expectations for relationships, they can learn to recognize and accept love in different forms, and they can adopt coping strategies to deal with the disappointments that are inevitable in intimate relationships. Through individual therapy designed to heal the relational wounds of parentified clients, the multigenerational process of parentification may be interrupted.

REFERENCES

Fairbairn, W. R. D. (1954). *An object relations theory of personality*. New York: W. W. Norton.

Glickauf-Hughes, C., & Wells, M. (1991). Current conceptualizations of masochism: Generic and object relations. *American Journal of Psychotherapy, 45*(1), 53-68.

Glickauf-Hughes, C., & Wells, M. (1995). *Object relations therapy of the masochistic personality.* New York: Jason Aronson.

Glickauf-Hughes, C., & Wells, M. (1997). *Object relations diagnosis and an individualized and interactional treatment.* New York: Jason Aronson.

Jones, R., & Wells, M. (1996). An empirical study of parentification and personality. *The American Journal of Family Therapy, 24*(2), 145-152.

Jordan, J. (1997). Relational development: Therapeutic implications of empathy and shame. In J. Jordan (Ed.), *Women's growth in diversity: More writings from the Stone Center* (pp. 138-161). New York: Guilford.

Kaufman, G. (1989). *The psychology of shame: Theory and treatment of shame-based syndromes.* New York: Springer.

Kernberg, O., Selzer, M. A., Koenigsberg, H. W., Carr, A. C., & Appelbaum, A. H. (1989). *Psychodynamic psychotherapy of borderline patients.* New York: Basic Books.

Kohut, H. (1971). *The analysis of the self.* New York: International Universities Press.

Meyers, H. (1988). A consideration of treatment techniques in relation to the functions of masochism. In R. Glick & D. Meyers (Eds.), *Masochism—Current psychoanalytic perspectives* (pp. 175-188) Hillsdale, NJ: Analytic Press.

Morrison, A. (1989). *Shame: The underside of narcissism.* Hillsdale, NJ: Analytic Press.

Ogden, T. H. (1989). *Projective identification and psychoanalytic technique.* New York: Jason Aronson.

Scharff, J. S., & Scharff, D. E. (1992). *Projective and introjective identification and the use of the therapist's self.* New York: Jason Aronson.

Wells, M., & Glichauf-Hughes, C. (1986). Techniques to develop object constancy with borderline clients. *Psychotherapy: Theory, Research, & Practice, 23*(3), 460-468.

Wells, M., & Jones, R. (1997). Parentification, splitting and dissociation: An object relations perspective. *American Journal of Family Therapy.*

Wells, M., & Jones, R. (in press). The relationship between childhood parentification and shame-proneness in adults. *American Journal of Family Therapy.*

West, M. L., & Keller, A. E. R. (1991). Parentification of the child: A case study of Bowlby's caregiving attachment pattern. *American Journal of Psychotherapy, 45*(3), 425-431.

CHAPTER 7

Therapeutic Rituals and Rites of Passage

Helping Parentified Children and Their Families

Helen W. Coale

Parentified children frequently develop symptomatic behavior requiring thera-peutic attention. At one level, the symptomatic behavior can be seen as an individual cry for help with problems that tax the child's resources to the breaking point. At another level, the symptomatic behavior can be seen as a cry for help for an entire family system, most specifically for the adults in the system who are unable to provide what the child and/or they themselves need to feel safe and functional in the world. Often, prior to the point of therapeutic intervention, the child's symptomatic behavior also can be understood as an attempt to help the parents cope in some way by giving the parents "practice" in dealing with a situation that makes them anxious and/or in helping the parents avoid the situation that makes them anxious. Thus, the particular nature of the child's symptomatic behavior can have relevance and meaning for the clinician.

Sammy, for example, a 6-year-old Caucasian male, was referred to a child guidance clinic by his teachers because he was "talking crazy" (Coale, 1992a). Sammy, a bright child, had developed his own language, into which he lapsed in any situation that provoked anxiety either for himself or for his parents. The parents did not tell the therapist that they were separated and had decided to file for a divorce until the third session.

When asked to describe the reasons for the divorce, the mother complained that the father acted "crazy." This frightened the mother because there was a long history of mental illness in her family. The father complained that the mother was too anxious. He was the descendant of a long line of show business people and liked to think of himself as a bit wild and "on the edge." The more anxious his wife became with his often outrageous behavior, the more annoyed he was with her anxiety; out of his annoyance, he behaved even more outrageously. In their struggles for power and control, they had abdicated the emotional aspects of their parental roles with Sammy, leaving him frightened about his parents' conflict and about what would happen to him.

It was in the context of this abdication that Sammy developed his "crazy talk," a language only he could understand. The therapist understood his strange language in the following ways: (a) as a message to the parents that both he and they were out of control, (b) as a way of getting help for the family, (c) as a way of detouring the parental fight onto his symptomatic behavior, (d) as a way of talking about the family difficulty without talking about it (as the parents had done until the third session of the therapy), and (e) as an exquisitely balanced metaphor of the parental power struggle. Specifically, Sammy aligned with his father by acting "crazy." In doing so, however, he gave the mother "practice" in dealing with benign "crazy behavior" because it was only talk and because it came from a 6-year-old rather than from an adult.

The therapist immediately began to work with the parents to de-triangulate Sammy from their marital struggles and to help them resume their parental functioning. She helped them discuss with the child all the specific, concrete changes that would occur in his life as the parents moved forward with their divorce, reassure him of their capacities to provide for and protect him, assuage his fears of loss, and so forth. Sammy's anxiety reduced dramatically, but he still "talked crazy," and this continued to frighten his parents and his teachers. The therapist then asked the mother to supervise Sammy in making a dictionary of his "crazy talk" and asked the father to supervise Sammy in telling stories that utilized his "crazy talk." Once the parents connected with the symptom in non-anxious parental ways, the symptom disappeared. The parental connection was a way of both honoring and containing the symptomatic behavior so that Sammy could give it up.

Recognizing and honoring children's attempts to function in parental ways are major themes that inform the following discussion. Standard family therapy maneuvers often solve the problem that the child's symptomatic behavior has attempted to solve, but such maneuvers do not sufficiently address the child's heroic efforts in the family via the symptoms. The parents' resumption of parental functioning makes the child's efforts obsolete. Children often will stubbornly persist in their symptomatic behavior—even with the original problem that spawned it dissolved—because they cannot move on without acknowledgment of their contributions. Moving on without acknowledgment of who they have been and what they have contributed constitutes a kind of loss of self for them.

In addition, there are many situations in which children *must* perform parental functions and will continue to perform them until they are adults. These children fare better when their parental roles are acknowledged and honored; when, in other words, the adults can consistently and congruently name, respect, and honor the adult functions that the children perform for the family. I contend that children get into difficulty not because they perform parentified functions in families, but rather because (a) their parentified functions either go unrecognized, and/or (b) they are incongruent with other expectations for their behavior, and/or (c) they are impossible to perform. These dilemmas are illustrated in the clinical examples described in the following discussion.

PROBLEMS IN THE LACK OF RECOGNITION OF PARENTIFIED ROLES

Developmental shifts in families undergoing transformations in membership via divorce, remarriage, or other changes in family structure often catapult a child into or out of a parentified role in the family (Fishbein, 1982). If the child has functioned as a single parent's chief assistant and co-parent to younger siblings and has received privileges and status for doing so, the fact that the mother remarries and no longer needs the child to perform parental functions does not mean that the child is glad to be relieved of such responsibilities, as the following case examples illustrate.

Remarriage

A stepfamily consulted a therapist because the oldest daughter of the mother was irritating the entire family with her obsessive, nagging behavior (Coale, 1992c). She monitored the family's food intake, compulsively went from room to room turning off lights, and worried aloud about family finances. As the therapist listened to the history of the combined family unit, it became clear that helping the mother safeguard the limited family finances had been an important job for this girl prior to the mother's remarriage, a job for which she had been appreciated. Now, the same job was irritating the mother—and the rest of the family. The therapist guided the family in a discussion honoring the girl's historical contributions in the single-parent family and gradually spreading the job of "family worrier" around so that each of the five children in the combined family unit would perform the job one day a week, with the two adults performing it on the weekends. This would free the girl to enjoy other things. With this kind of recognition, the girl stopped her annoying behavior.

Divorce

Following a conflicted, vicious divorce, Sara, age 9, took care of her mother in both physical and emotional ways throughout the mother's 3-year post-divorce depression. She nagged her mother to keep the house clean, comforted her when she cried, encouraged the mother to go out with friends, and, in various other ways, took care of her. When Sara was 12, the mother's depression lifted, and she started expecting Sara to act more like a child. Sara rebelled, and it was her rebellion that brought the family to a therapist. The therapist facilitated a conversation with mother and daughter about Sara's "job description" as mother's "therapist" for 3 years. Sara was animated and involved in this conversation, obviously relieved to have her "rebellion" understood in a positive light. The mother, after initial expressions of guilt about her 3-year abdication of parenting, ultimately was relieved to have a clear way of honoring Sara for her past parentified functioning. After this conversation, Sara's mother gave Sara an "awards ceremony" over dinner in a restaurant. Sara stopped rebelling in unmanageable ways.

Adoption and Foster Care

It can be assumed that children who are transplanted through foster care or adoption have had to assume parentified roles in some way in their families. Recognizing and honoring their performance in these roles can facilitate their transition to other roles in their adoptive or foster families.

Sandra, age 9, and her 6-year-old sister were adopted from a South American orphanage into an American home. Shortly after the adoption, the family presented for help because Sandra was totally unmanageable. She resisted any efforts on the part of the parents to nurture her or to manage her behavior in any way. She also interfered in the parents' attempts to parent her younger sister. The therapist, in listening to the history, focused on an inquiry into Sandra's functioning prior to the adoption. It became clear that Sandra had been her sister's mother in the orphanage, even to the extent of protecting her from some sexual abuse by taking it herself. As the parents listened to Sandra's halting description of her history in the orphanage, they cried. The therapist suggested that Sandra should be honored in some way for having been her sister's mother and also suggested that Sandra might always need to retain some co-parenting functions for her sister.

After this session, the adoptive parents sat down with Sandra and composed job descriptions of parental functions in the family, allowing Sandra to choose some parental functions that she would like to continue for her sister. They also went to a trophy shop and bought a trophy inscribed with a very moving tribute to Sandra for her mothering role with her sister. After this, Sandra was able to begin receiving some parenting from her new parents.

PROBLEMS OF INCONGRUENCE
IN ROLE EXPECTATIONS

—practical ritual that acknowledges reality

Parentification is a phenomenon that, in and of itself, creates incongruences in role expectations (Coale, 1989a). How can a child be both a child and an adult at the same time? The answer is, of course, that he or she cannot. A person can be a child performing some clearly circumscribed adult functions for which he or she is recognized, or can function in some contexts as a child and in other contexts as an adult, but cannot be both a child and an adult at the same time.

Expectations that he or she will do so lead to problems. The following examples illustrate the dilemmas of children with confused, incongruent adult/child expectations and some clinical ideas for therapeutic intervention.

Making Role Incongruences Explicit

Five-year-old Tommy's mother infantilized him and, at the same time, expected him to be the "man of the house" during a nasty divorce from Tommy's father. Tommy attempted to comply with both sets of expectations. He developed all kinds of somaticized complaints that drew his mother's attention to his dependence and frailty. At the same time, he was the one to call the police during episodes of violence between his mother and father. He and his mother presented for therapy when Tommy's symptoms had escalated to a refusal to go to school. The therapist understood the basis for Tommy's school refusal as an escalation of both role expectations, helpless child and mother's protector. The therapist's primary intervention was to make both roles explicit and, in very concrete ways, to delineate boundaries around each role by helping mother and Tommy define when he was in one role and when he was in another. Together, they defined things that Tommy *could* do as "man of the house" and ways in which, as "child of the house," he still needed his mother to take care of him (Coale, 1994a).

In this conversation, some of the emotionally debilitating "man of the house" responsibilities were blocked via concretizing them physically. For example, the therapist asked "How big are you, Tommy? How big does a boy have to be to be the one who telephones the police? How big do *you* think he should be, Mom, before he is the one who telephones the police?" Similarly, the "child of the house" role was concretized. "How little were you, in comparison to your size now, when you still needed your mother to dress you? Wash your face? Brush your teeth? What are the things that you used to be too little to do for yourself that you can now do for yourself? What are the things that you cannot do for yourself now *because you are too little* that, next year, you will be able to do for yourself?"

Prescribing a Role Incongruence

Some parents and children cannot change a role incongruence simply by being more aware of it. In some situations, therefore, more strategic interventions are in order. Madanes (1984), for example, has developed an intervention in which she prescribes that children be responsible in some way for parental happiness, thus pushing the entire system more into this mode of functioning, but in a way that is manageable for the children. In making the implicit role expectation explicit and prescribing it, the children's parentified functioning is made explicit *in a way that they can fulfill* because it is hypothetical. "*If* you were supervising your parents to be happier, what would you tell them to do? *If* you were in charge of your parents' happiness, what would you do?"

Children also can be given very specific tasks that will make their parents happy, tasks of a *personal* nature that do something nurturing for the parents (as compared with tasks of a *child* nature such as doing their chores or keeping their room clean). In this way, one aspect of the role incongruence is prescribed.

Alternating Role Incongruences

Alternating role incongruences can be another way of making them more explicit and orchestrating the family's experience of them in separate and distinct ways. This is less "crazy making" for the child as he or she *can* perform two mutually contradictory and exclusive roles sequentially rather than simultaneously. Asking the child to perform parental functions on odd days and child functions on even days, for example, is a way of defining and "boundarying" each role (Palazzoli, Boscolo, Cecchin, & Prata, 1977).

Framing Role Incongruences in Ways That Are Toxic

Many times, adults who have grown up as parentified children are shocked to discover that they are expecting parentified things from their own children but find themselves helpless to stop it. Toxic (and empathic) re-framing of the incongruent expectations they have of their own children *in the context of their own family of origin experiences* can be helpful. Examples are "It is impossible to be both parent to your parent and parent to your children. This would make you grandparent *and* parent to your children, child *and* parent to your own parents," and "How can you truly be a parent to your children without feeling like you are abandoning your own parents/children?"

Sometimes, parents, in their attempts to do the *opposite* of their own parents, end up doing the same. In attempting not to expect parentified things of their children, they indulge, spoil, and infantilize them. The children, by acting younger than they are, are actually taking care of their parents. Because they do not seem to be assuming adult role functions, their parentification can be overlooked by therapists. The following case example illustrates how a child's immature behavior actually was a way of taking care of his mother.

Twelve-year-old Danny, an only child of older parents, came to therapy with the presenting complaint of constant combativeness and conflict with his mother. In listening to the family's story, the therapist heard a pattern of indulgence and infantilization by the mother and passive tolerance by the father. As the boy entered adolescence, he began finally trying to fight his way out of his mother's smothering protectiveness, silently but powerfully cheered on by the father, who vicariously enjoyed the son's battle with his wife. The mother, determined to give Danny all the spoiling that she had never had as a child (and frustrated with the emotional emptiness of her marriage), clung to the son fiercely in spite of his rebellious behavior. She could not make the transition that the son was demanding because she felt that it would be akin to setting him adrift, as she had been set adrift by her own parents. She cognitively knew that she should be able to let him have more freedom, but she was emotionally stuck. She therefore attempted to be both the indulgent, overprotective mother *and* the liberated mother who would support the son's independence. The incongruence of the two roles was demonstrated not only in the mother's behavior but also in the son's, as he swung dramatically from infantile to mature behavior.

The therapist suggested to the father that he organize a retirement dinner for his wife in which he and the son together would give honor to the 12 years of faithful service the mother had performed as Danny's mother and marking her transformation from the mother of a *child* to the mother of an *adolescent*. This would give the family a ritual to help the mother move from one role to the next without trying to do both roles at the same time. Having her functioning validated not only helped the mother get "unstuck" but also gave the family a way of noting the two roles in the future. Now, they could identify behaviors that belonged to the role from which the mother had retired *and* the new role she had recently assumed. The son was freed from his parentified role (Coale, 1992b).

Using Rituals and Tasks to Help Parents
Resume Parental Functioning

Ritualized kinds of enactments can help parents practice specific behaviors that are appropriate parental functioning. Such rituals can be direct, as in the first example, or symbolic, as in the second two examples.

Seven-year-old Joan was involved in every conversation between her separated parents. When her father called her mother, she listened to the conversation and then commiserated with her mother about how mean the man was. After getting the mother's "green light" to work on blocking Joan from such parentified involvement in the adults' conflict, the therapist asked the mother and daughter to act out the scene, coaching the mother on how to block Joan gently from the conversation. After practicing this several times, the mother was able to do it on her own at home.

A mother whose own parents had abdicated parenting wanted to provide her 7-year-old daughter with all the affection and love she herself had never received. She could not bear to tell her daughter "no" (in itself, an abdication of parenting), so her daughter had learned to tyrannize the mother until she got her own way. Direct attempts with the mother to educate her about the role reversal had not worked, so the therapist prescribed a ritual in which the mother and daughter would look through a toy catalog, the daughter would pick toys on every page that she wanted, and the mother would say "It's OK to wish for these things, but the answer is no." In this ritualized, contained way, the mother had a positive, noncatastrophic experience in telling her daughter "no" (Coale, 1989a, 1990).

Another mother whose guilt about a divorce interfered with her ability to discipline her 8-year-old daughter told the therapist that she felt like a "witch" every time she set limits. The therapist suggested that the mother ritualistically preface every limit setting with the words "You may think I'm a witch, but. . . ." The mother added her own twist to the ritual by actually donning a witch's hat (from her daughter's room) when she said "You may think I'm a witch, but . . ." (Coale, 1994b).

PROBLEMS OF PARENTIFIED ROLE EXPECTATIONS
THAT ARE IMPOSSIBLE TO FULFILL

When parentified roles are expected from children, the children usually will do their best to fulfill them *even if they are impossible*, thereby damaging themselves and others in the process. Elsewhere (Coale, 1989b), I have described the case of an "emotionally disturbed pseudo-adult." This 8-year-old boy was referred to a child guidance clinic because he had battered his 3-year-old sister. In unravelling with the family the tumultuous divorce history, it became clear to the therapist that the 8-year-old had been mother's spouse, parent, and co-parent since the divorce. His 8-year-old parenting skills were not sufficient to the task of parenting his sister and, in trying to "discipline" her, he had broken her arm. The mother was furious with the boy and wanted to ship him off to a state hospital. She therefore requested a diagnosis to facilitate his removal from the family.

The therapist told the mother that the boy was an "emotionally disturbed pseudo-adult" who would surely go crazy if he had to continue functioning in his present role in the family. She reassured the mother that the boy was capable of functioning like a normal 8-year-old. She challenged the mother to decide which future for the boy the mother would choose: normalcy or hospitalization. The mother chose normalcy. She and the therapist defined what normal expectations would be for an 8-year-old boy, and the mother agreed to try these for 2 weeks to "prove" to the therapist that she could stick to them before proceeding in the therapy any further. Two weeks later, the boy was acting like a normal child. Therapy continued just long enough to support and reinforce the role shift. Once the child no longer had to function as spouse, parent, co-parent, *and* child, he was able just to be a child.

SUMMARY

The concept of parentification lends itself to creative clinical interventions that can help both children and adults move into more appropriate parent/child roles. Rituals and rites of passage help family members acknowledge what has been (or, often, what needs to continue to be) in a congruent, respectful manner and, in so doing, open the way for other possibilities. Difficulties occur when children's parental functions go unrecognized and/or are incongruent with other expectations for their behavior and/or are impossible to perform.

REFERENCES

Coale, H. W. (1989a). Common dilemmas in relationships. *Journal of Strategic and Systemic Therapies, 8*(2/3), 10-15.

Coale, H. W. (1989b). A family systems approach to child abuse: The mental health professional. In N. Barker (Ed.), *Child abuse and neglect: An interdisciplinary model of treatment* (pp. 101-116). Dubuque, IA: Kendall-Hunt.

Coale, H. W. (1990). Families know best: Empowering people and their families. *Insight, 10*(3), 6-11.

Coale, H. W. (1992a). The constructivist emphasis on language: A critical conversation. *Journal of Strategic and Systemic Therapies, 11*(1), 12-26.

Coale, H. W. (1992b). Costume and pretend identities: A constructivist's use of experiences to co-create meanings with clients in therapy. *Journal of Strategic and Systemic Therapies, 11*(1), 45-55.

Coale, H. (1992c, Winter). Use of humor in stepfamily therapy. *Stepfamilies, 12*(4), 10-11.

Coale, H. W. (1994a). Therapeutic use of rituals with stepfamilies. *The Family Journal: Counseling and Therapy for Couples and Families, 2*(1), 2-10.

Coale, H. W. (1994b). Using cultural and contextual frames to expand possibilities. *Journal of Systemic Therapies, 13*(2), 5-23.

Fishbein, H. (1982). The identified patient and stage of family development. *Journal of Marriage and Family Therapy, 8*(1), 577-561.

Madanes, C. (1984). *Behind the one-way mirror.* San Francisco: Jossey-Bass.

Palazzoli, M. S., Boscolo, L., Cecchin, G., & Prata, G. (1977). Family rituals: A powerful tool in family therapy—odd and even days. *Journal of Family Counseling, 4*(3), 3-9.

CHAPTER 8

Trauma, Invisibility, and Loss
Multiple Metaphors of Parentification

Bruce Lackie

"Rough hands." As I repeated these newly minted words of my client, I began to meet a string of alters, or alternate personalities, ranging from a distressed 5-year-old, to an angry 14-year-old girl, to a hypervigilant 12-year-old boy, an 84-year-old woman, a seductress, and a timeless angelic spirit. Rough hands were the magic words that opened the door to a private world of both accommodating and angry alters.

That the woman who hosted this ensemble earned her living by cleaning made these words a double entendre, triggered by the memory of abuse at the rough hands of her stepfather. Her day-to-day life was also a struggle of rough hands, literally and metaphorically. Could she contain that internal perpetrator so as not to pass on this legacy? She had her own Mr. Hyde inside who was a shadow presence, called "Kicking Spirit." Would she be able to hold, create, protect, and comfort with those hands? She also was an artist who, with her hands, created beautiful works of art. How do the hands of parentified children resemble those of parents?

The basic premise of this chapter is that dissociation plays a key role in parentification. The alters developed by persons with Dissociative Identity Disorder (DID) represent internalized efforts to "parent" themselves; for some, this is in response to the abdication of parenting by abusive actual parents, and for others, it is in response to overwhelming events. It is the role of some of the archetypal alters to attempt parenting/protection of the parents as well, despite the seeming impossibility of that task. This full spectrum of alter "types," reflecting archetypal patterns ranging from helper to internalized protector/persecutor, also reflects the range of actual parenting; that is, there is no one form of parentified child any more than there is one form of parenting. Through the bottle glass window of DID, we see an internal typology of living representations of various parenting principles.

Because much of the parenting process is invisible to the child, the corollary is that much of the internal self-parenting may be invisible to the self in the adult with a history of parentification. It follows that this invisibility of internal self-parenting leads to a split or dissociative framework. When this occurs, the capacity for ambivalence lies dormant. This results in the paradox of an adult who strives more and more for perfect "goodness," yet feels insufficient in the task of trusting self-care to the self. Low self-esteem is a hallmark of the parentified person (Bepko & Krestan, 1990; Lackie, 1983). The true self, under the most extreme of these internal battles, becomes a prisoner of war to the armies of reconciliation and revenge, battling on the plains of ambiguity.

Parentified children develop a parody of parenting principles based on what they observed and experienced, and interpreted; the internal struggle in adulthood may be a reenactment of warring parents or hostile landscapes, but in a form that interprets history as a personal narrative rather than representing an exact restatement of the past. This does not invalidate, but rather illuminates, the unresolved nature of the conflict in the victim/survivor. Reenactment is an attempt at reconciling contradictions; furthermore, the passage from victimhood to survivorship requires forgiveness, not so much of the parents as of the self.

The following is a 1-minute metaphor. One of my clients, who had been abused severely as a child, called to say she was baby-sitting for some little girls. My client, the sister of the "rough hands" woman and also diagnosed with DID, talked about how vulnerable these little girls looked, and asked the question, "How could my mother have abused me when I was so small and frail?" She then said she had the little girls obeying her, perhaps fearing her, by showing them a wooden spoon, similar to the one that had been used to "make the blood come" when she was a child. I suggested that there were other uses for that stick in her hand, that perhaps she could use it to bake. My client exclaimed, "That's right! I could bake the little girls cupcakes!" Cuts into cupcakes; the spoon becomes a mixing metaphor.

The full nature of our family of origin experience, at times, emerges only through our own role as parent. When my daughter had just started walking, we visited my parents in Florida. As my daughter wove and wobbled past a sharp edge in the house, my hand darted out with a newly learned instinctive protectiveness, and there I met the hand of my father, at the edge. Ironically, I asked myself, "Where did he learn that?" At that moment, I learned a lesson about the invisibility of parenting. We come to empathize more fully with what we did receive only through such moments as these. Nothing makes us appreciate vulnerability as much as the role of parent. This chapter applies that lesson to the inner world of persons with DID in particular. Where and how did they learn to parent themselves, in the absence of protective parental hands?

To say that these persons are the ultimate parentified children is to imply that they have achieved the ultimate skill and protectiveness of self-sufficiency, but they have not. Theirs is a failed quest as, in the process of seeking comfort and safety, they breed within themselves a near clone of their external perpetrator. Unfortunately, what results is a figure with a double-edged sword (or wooden spoon), in his or her hand, a "protector/persecutor" (Kalsched, 1996). A new prison of the true self results, self-imposed by the creation of a parodied persecutor, perhaps even more severe than the original prototype, leaving the individual to continue struggling with the pull to identify with the abusive parents. This state of self-abnegation exists as a feature of parentification in general.

I propose, based on clinical experience, that these two concepts, parentification and dissociation, are at least siblings and at times identical twins. One premise is that the parentified child relies on some degree of dissociation as a useful, even necessary, defense, in order to carry out the role of suspending his or her individual needs. Amnesia for the needs of the self serves as an anesthetic, barrier, or firewall for "parts" of the self that hold painful, parentifying experience. Such a feature as altruistic surrender, which implies a partial loss of the self, is a hallmark of clinical caretakers as well (Lackie, 1983).

Although terror generally is not associated with parentification, the fear of displeasing the Other, and near panic, can set in when parentified children fear they have not given enough or have failed to anticipate or recognize (through hypervigilance) the needs of or unspoken agenda of that Other at a critical moment. Parentification, in general, is characterized by less severe amnesiac boundaries than in DID, but the capacity to dissociate is clearly present along a continuum. There is increasing awareness of dissociative processes in children in general as a response to stress (Silberg, 1996).

There is an epidemic of parentified children from divorced families who struggle to manage overwhelming conflicting forces. The implicit expectation that these children will covertly manage their own needs can be seen in the following example. A father brings his 4-year-old boy for a meeting because the boy, living with his mother in New England most of the year, claims to be abused by his mother. Later exploration cannot establish a foundation for physical abuse. As he is engaged in play and talk about his family, his father brings out family pictures. One is of the mother and an infant in arms. I ask who this baby is, and the boy replies, "I don't know, it's not me!" I press him a little on this, saying that maybe he has a little baby in him. He protests, "I have blood and stuff in me, but there's no baby in there." I backpedal a little and suggest that the baby in the picture is small and maybe scared. He tries to hide the picture, almost rips it up, and finally brings out a scary faced, tiny monster (the Inner Monster, an archetypal alter) and tries to scare me away to protect the baby.

Eventually, in a meeting with both his parents, I see him crawl into his mother's lap, but when she cries, out of missing her little boy, he looks at me, hands outstretched with genuine dismay, and the true torment of his situation is evident. He provokes her to gain some distance, but he has begun to be more abusive to the self than any abuse that exists in his outside world. There's a small war inside him. He will not develop DID, but he already is a parentified child who I watch undergo little transformations and even the beginnings of dissociation when it gets to be too much. His preschool behavior already marks him as a conflicted child; there is no room for the alphabet. He already is attuned to another language and is seeking to master it. He feels that survival of all of them depends on it.

It is only an extension, then, from distress to terror, as the stakes rise to abuse and sometimes death in truly abusive situations. Banishment is always an implied threat. "Better thou/ hadst not been born than not to have pleased me/ better" (*King Lear*, act 1, scene 1; quoted from Ferguson, 1962, pp. 235-237), a foolish old king once told his favorite but ruthlessly honest daughter, Cordelia, who found displeasure in her father's eye. *King Lear* is a drama of incest, parentification, and the dissociated self (Lackie, 1991).

What does the drama of parentification and DID illuminate so profoundly? That there is no one "parentified child" any more than there is one form of parenting. Parenting is a complicated role with many visible and invisible challenges. Instrumental and expressive dimensions of parenting demand different skills and capacities, different selves to address different needs. The authoritarian versus permissive dimensions apply equally to the self as they do to parental styles. Ego boundaries and core work in conjunction to parent the self. We can then speak of personal authority and authoritative parenting of the self (i.e., optimal empathy for the self and for others). Our personal authority derives from our capacity to see what is invisible both in ourselves and in the Other. Our later professional authority is seen in the informed use of all we can see, with free choice, optimal distance, and preservation of the self.

That elusively optimal empathic stance is what is needed. If the child assumes a pathologically narcissistic stance of avoidance and is preoccupied with self-regulation, or assumes a pathologically empathic stance, characterized by high tracking of the Other and the loss of self-regulation, he or she misses the potential for optimal empathy in which there is a maximum sufficiency—not seemingly self-sufficient or seemingly insufficient, but with enough attention to the self and to the Other.

In DID, we meet the self-effacing alter (whose role is to make oneself inconspicuous, rub one's face out, make indistinguishable, render unrecognizable). There is the self-sacrificing, pathological empath, available to all without limits—the angelic spirit. Resentful but bound by loyalty, there is the angry, exploited, overburdened part.

Much of what it means to be a parent is to be invisible to the child. Perhaps that contributes to the internal splits, with some parts invisible to other parts, in a kind of internal tyranny of invisibility, a learned ignorance of the unrecognized presence of other parts of the self. To be fully aware of the activities of the parenting parts is to feel further connected, even obligated, constituting an unsafe arrangement. Given that these parenting parts are simultaneously associated with the actual parents, a kind of internal transference neurosis can develop.

Divisions of the self are not unique in DID Parentification, in general, finds the needs of the self shelved, often unknown, and frequently disavowed. Deferring comfort or stealing it as contraband in payment for services rendered to others is often the invisible outcome of a life out of balance.

The truly parentified child negotiates a landscape devoid of protective hands, where the edges rule, rather than what feels safe. A major role of the parent is to smooth the ego state changes, buffering the transitions across internal edges. Where there are discontinuous states as a result of inconsistent buffering, the internal world must accommodate these fractures; the terrain for safe footing shrinks.

The parentified child and the person with DID share a reliance on invisibility for survival. DID represents the ultimate in co-dependency; at its core lies the confused identity of the protector/persecutor, and at its boundary we meet a host of engaging and distracting alters. The challenge for the therapist is getting the "monsters" or protector/persecutors to speak and tolerate becoming visible; tolerating the terror they carry becomes the test of one's courage and the client's faith in our safety, for often they protect us from this demon out of fear of losing us. Knowing that parentified children in general already are not what they seem helps with the recognition process. For the "good" parentified child or adult, showing one's anger is a risk, as it points the way inward toward the vulnerable child. It is as if we get a fix on the position of the more vulnerable parts when we get to meet those at the point position.

We are all familiar with the fear of monsters that is characteristic of early childhood, especially at night in bed, facing sleep. Libraries have been written for such moments, to help children make a secure transition into their dreams. On the threshold of dreams, our imagination is our guide to the invisible world, and that is where we are most likely to meet the least visible monsters.

When my daughter was 5, we lived in western Massachusetts. Her room was high up on the third floor. On one hot summer night in July, I went up to kiss her goodnight. I found her playing with the windows closed tight, and the room very hot. I said, "Johanna, it's too hot in here. I need to open the window." As I went to the windows, not knowing what lurked just outside, she insisted, "No, keep them closed!" Asked why, she told me "because the monsters will get in." I countered, "But Johanna, there are screens on the windows." She replied, "But these are tiny monsters."

At the threshold of the near dreams of a little girl, her tiny monsters would hold her in their tiny grasps for a while. Even accepting the reality of them for her, this father is helpless to seize them into submission, stamp them out, spray them, sanitize them, purge the world of them to protect her. The job may be to help the child with this screen memory and with what lies beyond. I don't remember how we settled the matter of the windows and the tiny monsters, but

I do know that they are as real and as close as our imagination brings them to us. There is always tension in not knowing the effects of near universal limitations in parental empathic attunement in the face of a near universal fear of the dark.

There is also the fear of internal monsters, demons whose presence threatens to reveal us in a new light. The personal reality of those parentified people who rely excessively on dissociation often includes monstrous parental introjects. These are encountered not just in their dreams, but in their daily survival. In some, such as in human-made or natural disasters or other monstrous circumstances, the parents may be too incapable, helpless, or overwhelmed to protect their children from harm. The child is then forced to witness the degradation of parental authority, and with it trust, even though the parent has not actually been destructive.

"Monster" is, at the very least, an evocative word. In the inner world of DID, the perpetrator/demon figure, lurking with its invisibility and as an unannounced protector, suffers from posttraumatic stress disorder in its purest form, characterized by hypervigilance, distrust, outrage, and revenge. Similarly, in parentified children in general, deeply folded away through the magic of dissociation but present nevertheless, is the angry, outraged, distrustful, vigilant, vengeful part. It may be politically incorrect yet psychologically accurate to say that parentified children are not what they seem. "We are not as good as we look, but forgiveness comes when we discover we are not as bad as we feel" (Lackie, 1983, p. 319). Can the internal demon ever afford to forgive the self or others? Perhaps hell for the parentified person with DID is other people in the form of internal alters who refuse to individuate, seeking instead a rigid, fixed solution to the demands of survival. Resilience and rigidity live side by side as siblings, members of a silent, secret service.

Much of the inner world of the parentified child is invisible and rarely seen in its purest forms. The self-effacing empath or the enraged, exploited part rarely speak overtly for fear of retribution. It is terror that titrates dilemmas into recognizable parts. These parts or principles echo the essential dilemma of parentified children—the "PC" or politically correct child. To refuse to serve and sacrifice oneself to the needs of the other is to risk abuse; to defy the other is to let down one's shield and be overrun.

The self-care system of the parentified child is chronically at risk of downsizing as various parts are depleted, disavowed, or dismissed. Dissociative children live in terror and dread (Silberg, 1996). Inside each person lives an historian. "History is a pattern of timeless moments," wrote T. S. Eliot (1950, p. 144). The history of dissociative, parentified children is characterized by dread of those timeless moments, remembered in the body, when nothing was ever enough to pacify, satisfy, allay, or make safe. They are frozen. The chill one encounters in the dissociative person, and often in frantic parentified children, is that freezing in the face of terror. All resources are depleted.

One client with DID, whose rough hands found work in the world running a cleaning service, was raped as an adolescent on the excuse that there were cobwebs in the barn that she was supposed to see and clean. After the rape, she spent a long time fixed and focused on all the cobwebs she could find. In her, later on, was the conviction that if she ceased seeking cobwebs, she'd be punished with another rape. With each invisible cobweb across my face as I walk in the evening, I am reminded of her and how even silken tendrils can serve as shackles.

Terror transforms into a frozen paralysis, an inability to flee or fight. Caretaking of others can become a defensive accommodation to the possibility of being overwhelmed and out of control, as well as a defense against unleashing the narcissistic demon within. It is an attempt to contain the pain. If only one could heal these angry, insatiable beasts, the one outside but also the one inside, the inevitable moment of being overrun could be allayed. Compulsive caretakers live in dread of not being able to manage ambiguous situations. The parentified person swims, and often drowns, in ambiguity, unexpectability, and seeming self-sufficiency. My favorite *New Yorker* cartoon shows a man drowning, yelling, "Self-help! Self-help!"

Parentified children swim in a sea of internal, drowning objects, too many to save easily, yet too precious to be abandoned. To where can the true self swim? Does the true self even deserve to stay afloat, hearing the cries for help, the distress, of the other parts who carry the burden of overwhelming experiences? How can the true self justify accepting help for itself, knowing that these related parts have, at times, served to aid in its very survival, and are equally deserving of rescue? The powerful undertow of loyalty to even those most desperate parts makes the prospect of individuation a terrible dilemma. Psychic life comes to resemble the interminable, hellish waiting for the drowning.

At best, the desperate swimmers may find rest as castaways on an invisible island. To be thus marooned is to abandon themselves intentionally in a forsaken place, lost, with little hope of rescue or escape. Such exile marks the lives of many parentified people. Parentified children are often psychic runaways, metaphorically "missing in action," suffering from metaphor madness, relying heavily on dissociation, on not being there. They invent alternative delegates in place of themselves, living metaphors designed to contain the dilemmas of living. An angry alter is an offended complex, with a life and will of its own, endowed with destructive entitlement.

The pull downward to oblivion is strong in those who struggle with overwhelming obligation. Virginia Woolf captured this in *To The Lighthouse*, where she wrote:

> In pity for him, life being now strong enough to bear her on again, she began all this business, as a sailor not without weariness sees the wind fill his sail and yet hardly wants to be off again and thinks how, had the ship sunk, he would have

whirled round and round and found rest on the floor of the sea. . . . Lily Briscoe watched her drifting into that strange no-man's land where to follow people is impossible and yet their going inflicts such a chill on those who watch them with their eyes as one follows a fading ship until the sails have sunk beneath the horizon. (Woolf, 1927, pp. 126-127)

Like Lily Briscoe, amateur and professional caretakers alike are often called on to watch these powerful dramas, and to bear them, not knowing the fate of those who sail away, unprepared and ill-equipped to make the voyage. Like psychological outfitters of the psyche, we provide anticipatory attention to the needs of voyagers, based on our own experience and the maps of others we have known. We can accompany them to the edge, but the voyage is made by them alone.

The dissociatively parentified person (i.e., one cut off from adequate internal sources of self-care) can be said to suffer all the symptoms of any caretaker dealing with trauma: vicarious traumatization based on empathy for both the host's and the parents' wounds—compassion fatigue. One spent alter of a client wanted to go rest for a week at Disney World with no cares or responsibilities, in a realm where "parental" organization, bordering a bit on totalitarian control, could free the burned out internal protector. Internal alters can also suffer "witness guilt" as they listen to the experience of the other alters; they hear what they were spared experiencing. Survivor shame is also present, shame for what was required to survive. The nature of the work of the alters is intense and intimate.

Is it fair to link parentification with posttraumatic stress disorder (PTSD)? Is being parentified a traumatic process? What are the signs of PTSD in the parentified child? Clearly, reenactment of old trauma in symbolic form through caretaking is a frequent sign. Often the original trauma is not a single event, but a lifestyle of slowly eroding trust with the inevitable introduction of sadness. Sadness erodes trust, even as trauma transforms. Compulsive caretaking is a way of keeping trauma out of consciousness. Caretaking can then serve as a dissociative reprieve from attending to the unmet needs of the self. A continuum might follow a thread of manageable parentification, to the emerging features of PTSD, to increased estrangement from the self in the form of the dissociative disorders.

THE THERAPEUTIC PROCESS

Is it fair to speculate about an opposite force, "vicarious healing," as the client astutely watches the therapist become "infected" with the painful dilemmas, even the terror, brought to bear by the client? In the crisis confronting the emotional immune system of the therapist, a drama plays out in which the client can observe and feel encouraged that, in fact, there may be a way out of the labyrinth, even though it has seemed inconceivable. The therapist, in the best of circumstances, is seen as bearing, containing, neutralizing, and transforming the traumatic material into a plowshare, as fertility returns to the wasteland. In this terrible tenderness, the client has a chance to nurture a latent capacity to bear being seen. Just as poet John Keats coined the term "negative capability" to describe that rare capacity to be in mystery, uncertainty, doubt, and invisibility without a yearning for premature closure, perhaps "positive capability" could suggest the capacity to bear being seen, to trust the safety of being sighted by the surrounding world.

The role of the shaman in spirit cultures is to be the intermediary between the visible world and the invisible spirit world. Perhaps the shaman comes the closest to representing that internal healer who seeks, through masks, totems, and other transformative magic disguises, a restoration of the true self.

The shaman is the master of the autohypnotic trance state in the service of integrating the seen with the unseen. Likewise, the internal healer in someone with DID simulates omnipotent parental functions.

The hazard of visibility lies in the fear that when the precious parts of the self are revealed, the vulnerable parts will not be able to protect themselves and close the gates, or say "enough!" A range of protective alters in various stances—the angry, close-fisted, internalized understudies of the perpetrator—are ready to act. The risk of showing who you are to the Other is that the Other cannot be trusted to be respectful of that information, leaving the self even more vulnerable with more people knowing of the existence and nature of the alters. Most people do not even know or believe in the existence of the alters; if they are given maps or guideposts, outsiders might use them only to exploit. For those adults with less powerful histories of childhood parentification, their loyalty struggle is to arrive at an internal consensus of all the more subtle, unknown, competing parts, "the complete consort dancing together" (Eliot, 1950, p. 144), even as they continue to bear the family secrets.

Parentified children fear visibility because they cannot say "no" or "enough" to what's expected of them, or protect those in their charge. Parentified children who are dissociative are not free agents or safe. The vulnerability of the internal caretaker is like that of the leader of a convoy carrying food to starving people, or rescuing boxcars of broken spirits. Those parts in charge of a psychic convoy bearing vulnerable parts cannot get off the road; they are committed to their charges and to the journey of hazardous development. They cannot leave the children or other wounded parts when dangers present themselves; they have to use all their cunning, skill, and wiles to protect, or die trying. They resort to camouflage, staying low to the ground, as close to invisibility as possible, unless they meet up with safe aid along the road. Their capacity to transfigure the face and the self is in the service of defense and survival. The parentified child can never fully expect to receive acknowledgment for service, especially because it is presented in camouflaged form. To be chameleonic is to be the embodiment of inconstancy, a master of camouflage. As one Auschwitz survivor advised his companions, "Make yourself shorter than you are" (to avoid selection).

My perceptions of parentification have been refracted through sitting and listening to the testimony of survivors of the Holocaust. As they describe their survival skills—hypervigilance, multilinguality, capacity for invisibility, awareness of hazard and harm—I am reminded again of parentification. The extremely parentified are often survivors of little Armageddons, on the scale of a single family. There is no escaping these frightening landscapes. Part of what constitutes the underlying terror is the senseless, random nature of violence, in concentration camps and, increasingly, on our streets, where random holdups kill or terrify, compulsively. A vast trauma literature has emerged to address these experiences.

To live in this climate of uncertainty necessarily creates hypervigilance and panic over never knowing with certainty the proper response—whether to be absolutely still, a deer frozen in the unexpected light, or to take action. This is a central dilemma of the parentified, scrutinizing the face of the potential perpetrator or exploiter to see how survival or escape may be possible.

If the capacity for multilinguality is essential for survival in crazy situations (one camp survivor said it was essential to know German, to decipher the commands of the guards or risk being shot, out of their frustration), then the parentified survivor is one who has mastered the whole range of language, all the subtleties of communication including body language, right down to the pupil size of the Other. Contributing to terror of a situation are the ambiguity of cues and the ambiguity of expectations. This is central to the parentified person's dilemma. Paralyzed by terror, the person is trapped in a psychic iron lung, a psychic body cast, out of control. This is the paradigm of the unexpectable world where the worst is expected.

It may be helpful to imagine an internal "bunker" into which the unsafe self retreats in times of peril. The incredible shyness of the survivor is evocative of the image of the chambered nautilus found in the depths of the sea, one elegant example of a movable bunker, in which the organism has multiple hiding places. A "multiple star" is a variation on this theme: It is a star that which at a distance seems to be a unity, but upon closer examination is seen as made up of many smaller stars, creating an illusion of wholeness.

One shy, dissociative prisoner of war described survival in a Japanese camp as a process involving someone always being farther out on the edge of the group, seeking the invisible center. One can picture such internal jockeying for position within the parentified. Which part will take on the task of defense? Which part will mediate, negotiate? Who will risk being seen? Who will seek to distract? Which part will undergo yet another reenactment, offering itself as a vulnerable target by filling the empty space? Who will seek to provide comfort and buffering for the self and everyone else?

The resolution lies in knowing what is enough to move on. The experience of dissociation derives from being a part-object of the narcissistic other, not seen in one's fullness, but rather as an extension of the other's needs, so that a sense of unrealness, or lack of separateness, is reinforced. It is life on the Other's edge. One calls into question one's own perceptions. One only exists as an extension of the Other's need. Sufficient ego strength to reaffirm one's own identity, apart from the Other, is essential to remaining anchored to reality. Without the strength to stay in reality, the parentified person is constantly looking for better and better ways to finally complete and satisfy the insatiable appetites and needs of the Other. One variation on hell may be this relentless attempt to feed an insatiably hungry parent; ultimately, the hungry stay hungry, and the "good" feel bad.

There needs to be some acceptance within the self that the true self might never be known by the Other, that selfhood will retain ambiguity, but that it is enough for the self truly to know itself. Maturity lies in knowing what is enough. The value of meeting the dissociatively parentified person's alters is that we are used to the public self of the parentified child, the good, compliant, self-effacing, hypervigilant, eager to please part. The less visible, less overt, less tangible parts that feel angry, exploited, and overworked, we are allowed to meet in their pure forms, as alters. Ultimately, we identify with the person's plight and want to liberate him or her from the prison of peculiar attachment and responsibility to the dilemmas of these others inside.

The Erinyes, the Greek furies, were unforgiving, punitive, avenging spirits who echoed the shame of Thebes. They were transmuted into the Amenities, who bore Oedipus safely to the spirit world, in forgiveness. A similar transformation has to occur in the life of the parentified, who live with these furies and need to help them transform in order to become safe in the real world.

DILEMMAS FOR THE THERAPIST

Although the blank slate of the masked therapist can evoke distrust, or even terror, too much self-disclosure by the therapist re-evokes parentification. The role of the therapist is to model both the bearing and the containing of affect, to create a safe container for what is too much. The therapist needs to achieve optimal visibility. By being a listener to the tale and by experiencing it empathically, one knowingly takes on the risk of secondary traumatization knowingly.

Switching parts may be an attempt to see whether this evokes a response, whether the Other even notices that one part is gone and another part has emerged as an attempt to evoke the capacity to differentiate the Other. It requires that attention be paid. That capacity probably was missing in the original parental environment. It is unnerving to realize that one can switch and bedazzle, but the depressed, or narcissistic, or undifferentiating parental figure ignores, or does not even recognize, that a shift has occurred. "I'm on my own," is the child's conclusion. Close attention is essential to the work with the parentified in general as well as with the subgroup of DID.

One way the client attempts to hold on to the therapist, by inventing more and more resourceful alters to delay differentiation and inevitable separation, is to induce an enchantment. The ultimate seduction is not about sex but about swimming in the River Lethe—the river of forgetfulness in the land of interminable dreams—a therapy without end (dashes instead of periods) that reenacts an incestuous fusion. The therapist must have the capacity to detect differentiations of the self, in himself as well as in the client; otherwise, both become lost in a hall of mirrors. The client, caught in the illusion of fusion in which enough variation, enough enchantment, is produced, never has to anticipate the ending of the therapy relationship. This sometimes can lead to crashing on the hazardous shoals of fabrications. The "hook" for the therapist is the challenge of a seemingly inexhaustible supply of needy alters in the client. How can the therapist ever finally prove his or her "goodness" as a parenting figure if there are always more and more alters to heal?

Many therapists are addicted to large caseloads; here in one client is a lifetime of work. Therapy then becomes addictive for the therapist, who risks investing too much identity and worth in the healing of the other; it is a significant occupational hazard for the parentified therapist. Dissociative clients may offer the ultimate hook, as there are so many, needing so much, a complete caseload in one package. They provide an endless labyrinth for those therapists who need, rather than choose, to caretake.

The dilemma for the therapist is the need to achieve an optimal stance between two extremes. One extreme is of no need, of self-sufficiency, a picture that can create panic in the parentified client because what it will take to please this person is intolerably unclear. The other extreme is to be inducted into a shared intimacy, based on the gratifying, overspecialized attention and absorption, for which the parentified parts have spent a lifetime preparing.

The optimal stance is, in a modulated way, to acknowledge the inevitability of woundedness, through appropriate self-disclosure by both client and therapist, and free the parentified child from the role of healer or comforter, or covert parent to the "parent." This creates an inevitable reenactment of a core dilemma, probably for both client and therapist. Because the parentified person is exquisitely attuned to the unspoken needs of the Other, the task is in perturbing this internal arrangement to allow for growth, with the end goal of having the PC parent him- or herself, with those internal hands doing the work of parents "holding" the internal self. The solution is not to walk around in the world, hoping to be discovered by a prince or princess therapist who fashions silver hands to decorate or camouflage an old injury, safely hidden away in an orchard of pear trees like the handless maiden in a Brothers Grimm tale (see Brothers Grimm, 1853). The handless maiden ultimately must grow her own hands, with all the skills implied, from weaving to firmly grasping a flaming sword, to embracing the self.

Arthur Miller captured this magnificently in *After the Fall*:

> Quentin, I think it's a mistake to ever look for hope outside one's self. One day the house smells of fresh bread, the next of smoke and blood. One day you faint

because the gardener cut his finger off, within a week you're climbing over the corpses of children bombed in a subway. What hope can there be if that is so? I tried to die near the end of the war. . . . The same dream returned each night until I dared not go to sleep and grew quite ill. I dreamed I had a child, and even in the dream I saw it was my life, and it was an idiot, and I ran away. But it always crept onto my lap again, clutched at my clothes. Until I thought, if I could kiss it, whatever in it was my own, perhaps I could sleep. And I bent to its broken face, and it was horrible . . . but I kissed it. I think one must finally take one's life in one's arms, Quentin.

Come, they play *The Magic Flute* tonight. You like *The Magic Flute*? (Miller, 1985, p. 109)

If the needs of the therapist are not acknowledged, and simultaneously are contained or taken elsewhere, the reenactment of an old incestuous arrangement, like that of a foolish old king and his favorite daughter, is at risk of being replayed (Lackie, 1991). When we talk about the concept of optimal self-disclosure or optimal visibility on the part of the therapist, we are reminded of the dissociative parody of the blank slate stance, of the still face revealing nothing, an undesirable model to present to the client. We must be able to mirror back the terrified, helpless look of the overwhelmed child. We hope that we can recognize that broken face, because it exists in us as well. At times, there are those moments of perfect balance, of being in the world, in dialogue with the self and the Other, freely, two solitudes in conjunction, safe. Those are the moments, not of enchantment, but of true magic.

REFERENCES

Bepko, C., & Krestan, J. (1990). *Too good for her own good.* New York: Harper & Row.
Brothers Grimm. (1853). The handless maiden. In *The complete illustrated stories of the Brothers Grimm.* London: Routledge & Sons.
Eliot, T. S. (1950). *The complete poems and plays.* Harcourt Brace & Company.
Ferguson, F. (Ed.). (1962). *Shakespeare's tragedies of monarchy: Hamlet, Macbeth, King Lear.* New York: Dell.
Kalsched, D. (1996). *The inner world of trauma.* London: Routledge.
Lackie, B. (1983). The families of origin of social workers. *Clinical Social Work Journal,* Winter.
Lackie, B. (1991). Catch a falling kingdom: A meditation on *King Lear. Metaphor & Symbolic Activity, 6*(4), 309-322.
Miller, A. (1985). *After the fall.* New York: Viking.
Silberg, J. L. (1996). *The dissociative child: Diagnosis, treatment and management.* Baltimore: Sidran.
Woolf, V. (1927). *To the lighthouse.* New York: Harcourt Brace & World.

CHAPTER 9

Parentification in the Context of the African American Family

Louis P. Anderson

During the past decade, psychologists with increasing frequency have begun to challenge the Eurocentric base of knowledge and methods used to describe the families of people of African descent. As a result, many researchers, practitioners, and theoreticians have begun to develop culturally specific frames of references, change their research questions, and revise their methods for providing psychological services to people of African descent. Current theoretical models emphasize a sociocultural or contextual understanding of family patterns.

The movement to emphasize sociocultural factors such as ethnic identity, cultural expectations, socioeconomic and political factors, and values has taken many forms. A major impetus of this movement has come from postmodern Afrocentric theorists trained within a cross-cultural and social constructionist tradition. These theorists have encouraged the development of conceptual frameworks that would allow for a better understanding of the factors and contexts that influence behavior. Postmodern Afrocentrists advance the view that culturally based customs and beliefs regulate the behaviors of members of society and determine which actions are acceptable and which are not (Akbar, 1980; Anderson, Eaddy, & Williams, 1990; Nobles, 1980). Furthermore, they argue that the focus of discourse should be on the social/situational determinants

AUTHOR'S NOTE: The author would like to express his appreciation to Stephanie Thoubou for her assistance in the preparation of this chapter.

of behavior. Moreover, because our society consists of diverse cultural groups, they question the validity of universal psychological concepts.

One of the responsibilities of this movement's advocates is to carefully scrutinize the application of new concepts that may be used to explain the African American family system. Thus, the purpose of this chapter is to reconstruct, albeit to critically analyze, the theoretical application of parentification as it pertains to the African American family. Although I would argue that the knowledge accumulated regarding models of parentification has achieved a critical mass and therefore is appropriate for some groups, I question whether that knowledge provides a reasonable foundation for shaping applications for interventions with people of African descent. I say this, in part, because there is no reference of parentification in the African American family literature. Thus, it seems that the African American professional community has not embraced this concept. In addition, existing theories of parentification do not take into consideration the past or the contemporary experiences of people of African descent. In fact, one would be hard pressed to find a single theory of family functioning that explicates the unique racial, ethnic, cultural, or historical experiences of African Americans. The cultural relevance of a concept or a theory is weakened considerably if the environmental context or the past and contemporary experiences of an ethnocultural group are not addressed.

Thus, in keeping with the postmodern constructionist tradition, my primary task is to examine the values and biases that may underlie the concept of parentification. The plan is to examine African American families in a culturally sensitive manner and to present themes that will be of use to clinicians and researchers in this field. It is not anticipated that all the issues being considered regarding parentification will be resolved in this chapter, but I do expect that by focusing attention on them, clinicians and researchers would be in a better position to make basic decisions that will lead to meaningful outcomes. Admittedly, several theories, notably those of Jurkovic (1997) and Minuchin, Montalvo, Guerney, Rosman, and Schumer (1967), raised notions of culture and class in their formulation of parentification. In this chapter, however, an attempt is made to expand the notions of ethnicity, culture, and race as central themes in understanding parentification while at the same time reifying the belief that parentification is a social construct. As social constructs then, I argue that family patterns, social roles, and child rearing behaviors are determined by social/situational factors and defined in cultural terms.

The first section of this chapter begins with a working definition of parentification. Following this introduction, the importance of culture, ethnicity, and race is discussed. The third section gives consideration to contextual themes and a framework for understanding families of African descent. Finally, a discussion of some culturally based themes and their implications for an understanding of the central issues of parentification is presented.

WHY STUDY PARENTIFICATION?
SOME OBSERVATIONS

Family relationships offer us our initial and arguably our best chance for learning and developing skills necessary to maintain intimate relationships such as those found in marriages, parenthood, and friendships. It is within family relationships that we learn our ethnic identity and values, struggle with role relationships, and risk disclosing our most intimate thoughts. To a large degree, the foundation for the types of relationships formed later in life is based on the experiences learned in our families of origin.

Psychologists are particularly concerned with the consequences that early interactions within our families of origins have for the quality of our future relationships. Because we often share more of our vulnerabilities within our families of origin, these early relationships can be our greatest source of both frustration and joy. Although we prefer not to think of our relationships within our families in terms of scripts, roles, power, sexual feelings, role reversals, independence, and goal-seeking behavior, research suggests that these feelings and behaviors do exist (Garbarino, 1992; Gurman & Kniskern, 1991). It is therefore reasonable to assume that if factors (i.e., interactional patterns, personality factors, emotional states, social roles) can be identified that later put family members at risk in terms of their ability to adjust and to cope effectively with life's challenges, then the family can be encouraged to confront such issues or anticipate the type of adjustment that would be required of them. This perspective is the cornerstone in many theories of family functioning and the emerging theories of parentification.

Most theories of family functioning assume that a norm, an ideal, or a standard for optimal family functioning exists. Thus, parentification or the parentified child can be seen as a deviation from a prescribed societal norm of family functioning. The definitions of parentification raise some interesting conceptual and diagnostic questions. One would think that a concept as basic as parentification would lead to a unified and definitive conceptual system, but this does not appear to be the case. Although changing, the term *parentification* has been applied to a wide array of behaviors and symptoms, such that a search for both universal and specific characteristics for parentification has been a challenge.

As Table 9.1 illustrates, it appears that many attributes that are used to describe parentification are socially defined constructs. In addition, when one reviews these attributes of parentification, it appears that many have little diagnostic or practical value in differentiating parentified familial patterns from other family conditions. The search for universal and specific features of parentification seems to be dependent on the nature of measurement instruments used to identify them (Goglia, Jurkovic, Burt, & Burge-Callaway, 1992) and the profession's need to deal with what it sees as pathology (Boszormenyi-Nagy & Spark, 1973; Lowen, 1985) as well as the theoretical orientation of the

TABLE 9.1 Causes, Symptoms, and Consequences of Parentification

Causes	Symptoms	Long-term Consequences
Parent's need for security (eroticized parent-child interactions) Undifferentiated parents, lack of individuation from own fragile parents Parent's lack of maturity Alcoholism—where family rituals are disrupted and parents do not act like parents Single, overburdened parenthood; financial stress, social isolation Symbolic parent-grandparent replication (in child) pathological to the degree and intensity of relationship being repeated Narcissistic needs of parents Emotional or instrumental expectations beyond a child's ability to understand Parent's insecurity in self; inability to provide adequate "mirroring" and "idealization" Breakdown of communities of support Little supportive involvement with extended family, friends, and organizations	Lack of reciprocity in caretaking functions; "overresponsibility" Lack of individuation and differentiation Dependent behavior on part of parent May show as "gifted child" (to heal intrapsychically wounded, underdeveloped parent) Overburdened with mediating, worrying, caregiving, advising Underdeveloped on a number of personality/individuation dimensions Chronic, nonclinical depression Confusion about dependency needs: covert obligations/overt role assignments; sacrificial roles; rivalry with parent; assumed authority for caretaking of siblings; over-adequate family "burden bearer" and "healer"; "regressive core" leading to a desire to possess a loved one "Infantilization" of child = force of eternal devotion through guilt-laden loyalty = delayed maturation Symptoms may show up only when child is old enough to face identity and intimacy issues	Predisposed to co-dependency; anxiety, guilt, depression, child abuse, psychosomatic symptoms, psychosis, delinquency Sacrifice of one's own age appropriate needs/goals Child identity development distorted by projections and needs of family Positive or advanced ability to maintain mature object relations; positive sense of account-ability; increased capacity to care Impaired development of adult emotional wholeness Potential for neurotic development Possible tendency to be overdemanding Guilt, lifelong compliance Child's development handicapped Child may face impairment in psychological and physical relational development Continued caretaking behavior as adult May choose partner to parentify, reverting to childish needy behavior or choosing one they can care for and parent Interfering with the child's awareness and trust of his or her own experience

SOURCE: S. Toubou (personal communication, October, 1997).

author (see Chapter 1 in this volume, by Chase). The core of all theories of parentification, nevertheless, is the societal expectations of the role of the child, expectations for how children should be reared, and the relationship between the parent and the child. A reasonable working definition for parentification therefore includes at least three conditions:

1. Parentification may result when one or both parents abdicate(s) their prescribed social roles as parents,

2. One or both parents either consciously or unconsciously position(s) an underage child to assume roles or to engage in child-rearing practices that are traditionally reserved for adults, and/or

3. A reversal of roles occurs in which the child takes on adult responsibilities or "parents the parent," which has a profound negative impact on the relative "adjustments" required of parent and child.

Admittedly, the above conditions for parentification can be challenged on several grounds based on their simplicity, the reader's theoretical orientation, or the reader's clinical experiences. For obvious reasons, frameworks developed to understand parentification emphasize societal expectations for child rearing and prescribed social roles of family members. Although the field has emphasized an implicit standard for understanding normal family relations, variation by social class, education level, and racial background are poorly understood (Ogbu, 1981). Some of the variations in family functioning may be a deviation from a cultural script, but other variations may result from social class, sociopolitical, and ethnic factors. It seems that many of our struggles regarding definitions and agreements regarding "family functioning" do not occur until we move outside the Western/American cultural definition of nuclear family role expectations.

Many definitions of parentification do not explicitly mention the role of culture or ethnicity, but the paradox is that our basic definitions of parentification and our conceptual systems for understanding parentification are culturally based. For example, our definitions of parentification appear to be based on prevailing professional opinions about the nature and characteristics of the optimal American, primarily Caucasian, middle-class family structures, which emphasize independence, autonomy, the development of the self, and clear boundaries between parents and children (Katz, 1985). Furthermore, our professional practice of categorizing symptoms, our use of criteria for diagnostic purposes, and our reliance on assessment inventories that are independent of context are all based on an imposed Western/American model of science and clinical practice (Dana, 1993; Fabrega, 1989). In our understanding of parentification within African American families, we first need to consider how ethnicity, culture, and sociopolitical factors influence behavior and the environment in which these families live. These and many other contextual factors should influence our basic understanding of parentification, yet they go unnoticed.

Another key issue in our understanding of the construction of parentification lies in the distinction between the linear trajectory of behavior and the functionality of behavior. This distinction is subtle but relevant. In psychology, the former view assumes an implicit linear standard (i.e., a specific behavioral form will lead to specific consequences). This view is represented by theories or frameworks that strive to predict universals of behavior by identifying what are considered to be the essential characteristics of a phenomenon. Moreover, the understanding and clarification of the phenomenon are considered vital first steps in predicting and eventually treating it (Fabrega, 1989). The latter view appreciates the key role that context plays in shaping our experiences. The social context shapes behaviors; thus, behaviors may vary across settings. Advocates of this position also question the assumptions that underlie the creation of new phenomena. They seek multilevel, culturally relevant explanations for behaviors, including the influence that social institutions and sociopolitical conditions have on the development, the course, and the clinical treatment of human behavior (Mednick, 1989).

As Table 9.1 indicates, a review on parentification uncovered a wide range of causes and symptoms associated with this condition. Moreover, the list of possible predictors of parentification is far reaching. This finding can be interpreted in many ways. It could be that parentification may be an elusive concept that cannot be adequately captured by scientific methodologies alone, or it just might be that we need to do a better job at assessing the social context of behavior. I now turn to a discussion of several key contextual concepts that would help us understand families of African descent.

ETHNICITY, RACE, AND CULTURE

It is important to begin a discussion of the African American or Black family by clarifying the terms *ethnicity*, *race*, and *culture*. Ethnicity refers to a sense of identity based on cultural traditions and racial group membership (Lum, 1992). Culture is a broader term, constituting the values, traditions, and worldviews that maintain and sustain a group. Within each ethnic group are built-in mechanisms for transmitting cultural artifacts, values, and traditions from one generation to another. Although some people have used "race" and "ethnicity" interchangeably, contemporary wisdom considers ethnicity to signify a subcategory of people composing a designated racial group. Race, on the other hand, refers to an inbreeding population of people discernible by physical traits and by geographic location (Zuckerman, 1990).

One ethnic group can be distinguished from other ethnic groups by its shared cultural traditions, racial identity, history, and often country of origin. Typically, we use physical characteristics such as skin color as guides to determine racial group composition, but these physical features can be misleading given the range of variability within races (Jones, 1991; Zuckerman, 1990). In fact, research on most psychological variables has found that there is more variability within than between designated racial groups (Zuckerman, 1990). Such findings raise questions regarding the relevance of race as a categorical or classification variable in research or in clinical contexts. More meaningful information about normative child-rearing practices, familial patterns, worldviews, and attitudes can be assessed by determining ethnicity.

Knowledge of ethnicity and culture is important because African Americans are multicultural, comprising a vast number of ethnic groups. In contemporary American society, people of African descent have migrated from among other places, including Canada, the Caribbean, Africa, Europe, and South America. For example, I identify myself as an African American. At least 10 generations of my family have lived in the United States. My maternal ancestral background can be traced back to Sierra Leone, Africa, and Barbados, West Indies.

A student of mine who assisted with this chapter was born in the United States, but her parents moved here from Trinidad. She also considers herself an African American, but she has very strong Trinidadian cultural roots and traditions. Both of us are of African descent and can be classified racially as Black (or Negroid) because we share similar physical features and have common ancestral roots. What complicates matters is that we both may identify as African Americans, but there are differences in regard to cultural traditions, socialization, and family patterns. One may have more West Indian or Caribbean traditions, the other more African or African American traditions. We may share similar language patterns and customs, but we also differ in many distinct ways. Our self-definitions as African Americans, however, tie us both to a distinct ethnic and racial group and presumably a similar cultural group. To look at each of us and to hear us speak, one would be hard pressed to place us in a racial category other than Black or an ethnic group other than African American, but these categories are meaningless constructions unless the migratory pattern, level of self-reported ethnic identity, and acculturation are taken into consideration. These factors in turn go a long way toward helping us understand cultural patterns of child rearing.

In summary, people of African descent should not be viewed as monolithic. In particular, Americans of African descent should be considered as multiethnic and heterogenous with regard to customs, beliefs, and country of origin. For the most part, people of African descent have distinct cultures and are quite variable in their affinity to Africa, America, and the cultures of both areas. The variability in traditions, level of acculturation, and ties to and affinity to a specific culture has to be assessed because of the clinical implications.

DEFINING THE CONTEXT

A successful examination of the nature of the Black family should be characterized by at least two features. More than 25 years ago, C. C. Clark (1972) made a statement that is relevant to this discussion. Clark (1972) said that the scientific study of African American families has to be based on the "black reality." By "black reality," Clark is referring to the acknowledgment of the uniqueness of the historical and contemporary experiences of people of African descent. These experiences include the African culture, the middle passage from Africa, and the experiences of slavery and oppression in contemporary times. This "black reality" is an important consideration in the study of the African American family because these experiences differentiate families of African descent from other ethnic, cultural, and immigrant groups. Moreover, this reality provides a context that allows us to understand how African Americans made sense of their life experiences. Implicit in the notion of the Black reality is the rejection of traditional assumptions that American groups (i.e., African, Asian, European, and Latino) share a common set of cultural values and migratory experiences (Nobles, 1978). If we concede that migratory experiences and cultures set people of African descent apart from other immigrant groups, then it should follow that our conceptual and diagnostic systems regarding these groups should reflect such differences. The cultural and historical experiences of African Americans move us toward a culturally relevant understanding of behavior and thus away from an emphasis on an imposed universal perspective.

The second consideration concerns the heterogeneity of the Black family. Assimilation, religious background, socioeconomic class, sociopolitical factors, language, and migratory patterns all have influenced the pattern of acculturation for families of African descent. Thus, there is a range of diversity among families of African descent. Although there is variability in cultural practices among African Africans and there is no single or unitary set of concepts that definitively describe the "African American family," there are modal cultural values and beliefs found in many American families of African descent that may serve as a useful framework in an understanding of African family functioning.

Pinderhughes (1982, 1989) sees families of African descent as operating out of three different and often conflicting value systems. According to Pinderhughes, these value systems reflect modal European/American values, modal African values, and a set of values resulting from oppression and survival. A system of values, called the Anglo-American, emphasizes individualism, differentiation, autonomy, independence, mastery, and future. Within this system of values, independence and self-actualization are important; the individual is socialized to strive to actively control the environment and maximize his or her self-interest in the form of power and the accumulation of material wealth (Dana, 1993). In general, within Western cultures, family systems are hierarchical, sex roles are rigidly defined, and the nuclear family unit is judged to be optimal for family functioning (Katz, 1985). Assimilated African American families adopt traditional Western/American values. Many of the modal family patterns presented in Table 9.2 are *not* seen in assimilated African American families.

TABLE 9.2 Modal African American Family Patterns Uncovered in the Literature

1. In general, family structures are extended to include multigenerational members and relatives. Insular families may be at risk, or such a pattern may suggest assimilation.

2. Family life is oriented around children, and flexible family roles are practiced.

3. Grandmothers are actively involved in child rearing. It is not uncommon for three generations to live within households, for families to live in a grandparent's home, or for families to live in close proximity.

4. Support systems are multidimensional. Reciprocity generally is expected, and as children prosper, they are expected to contribute financially to the family.

5. Mothers are primarily responsible for child care duties and household maintenance.

6. Children are expected to be independent, to move quickly through early developmental stages, and to participate in child care as soon as possible. Girls are socialized to be independent, self-sufficient, and capable of caring for themselves.

7. Parents are more likely to engage in physical means of disciplining the child than in guilt or emotional withdrawal.

8. The composition of the Black family is fluid.

A second system of values, the traditional African, emphasizes affiliation, collectivity, obedience to authority, belief in spirituality, acceptance of fate, and respect for the past as expressed in reverence for the elderly and ancestor worship. It is likely that most, if not all, of the modal family patterns presented in Table 9.2 are seen in families that have retained many traditional African-centered values. Within traditional African-centered families, ethnic and racial identity formation is practiced by its members.

The third system identified by Pinderhughes (1982) is the victims' system. This system emphasizes strategies to combat powerlessness and interdependence among family members to counteract disorganizing environmental forces. The interaction of these three independent (not mutually exclusive) and often conflicting value systems generates a survival response as the African American family structures adapt to meet life challenges. Families that reconcile these three value systems cope and adapt more effectively with the environment. In contrast, those African American families that have abandoned their cultural values often are not able to cope with disorganizing environmental forces and thus are at risk for engaging in the socially defined parentification practices of (a) abdicating the prescribed social roles of parenting, (b) allowing underage children to engage in culturally inappropriate child-rearing practices, and (c) family dysfunction.

Contextual Factors

Institutional racism is the most significant contextual factor that has shaped the structure, stability, and adaptability of families of African descent. In fact, I would argue that the starting point for assessing the question of what is the "Black reality" is the question "How did the generations of African descendant families cope with racism and oppression?" Some have argued that poverty is the most significant external factor (see Moynihan, 1965; Wilson, 1986), but it is the past and current institutional practice of racism in the form of limited access of African Americans to major social institutions (i.e. housing, educational, employment) that lead to upward mobility that created the conditions for poverty. Intentional or otherwise, institutional racism ensures an imbalance in resources needed to effectively manage the conditions of living (Anderson, 1991; Pettigrew, 1975). Tremendous pressures are placed on the family without adequate resources. Moreover, conflicts often occur when attempts are made by family members to assimilate, to acquire material wealth, and to achieve success and status in this society.

In response to racism, supreme value was placed on the African cultural tradition of collective survival or the survival of the family or tribe (i.e., the African notion of family translates to mean the extended unit or tribe). To cope effectively, resiliency, flexibility in family roles, and spirituality were considered optimal values (Akbar, 1980). Typically, in many families of African descent social roles and family patterns are fluid. In comparison to Western/American families, African descendant families encourage interdependence and believe that a strong extended family unit ensures individual success (Anderson et al., 1990; Nobles, 1980). Contemplative talk, discretion in voicing opinions and feelings to parents and to the elderly, and indirect verbal interactions are qualities present in traditional African-oriented families.

Although these aforementioned features of African descendant families represent cultural norms or modal patterns of behavior, these patterns may be misunderstood by someone who unwittingly imposes a Western/American standard for understanding family functioning. For example, interdependence may be seen as a sign of enmeshment or co-dependency, and flexible family roles may raise concerns about boundary definition.

Factors that necessitate family or collective survival are meaningful in understanding the functionality of behavior of African descendant families. For example, sharing residence with extended family members helps African American families manage resources necessary for successful child rearing (Wilson, 1986). Moreover, when the need arises, older children are asked to be responsible for their younger siblings. Before taking on this position of responsibility, a child undergoes an apprenticeship in which basic child care tasks are taught. Furthermore, in well-functioning African American families, children placed in child-rearing roles are given explicit instructions regarding their roles within the family. Typically, these children are not elevated to the executive structure of the household.

The reality of families of African descent encompasses a worldview that is rooted in a deep spirituality that is based on the belief that everything in the universe is interconnected and endowed with the same Supreme Force (Nobles, 1978). If we believe that an ethnic group's worldview provides an understanding of how that group makes sense out of its life experiences, then the African-centered spiritual nature would mean that the group would value human equality and value a deep sense of family.

In summary, the core of the worldview of people of African descent is collectivism, survival of the group, interdependence, and spirituality. The functionality of behavior, flexibility in role, permeable boundaries, and the influence of sociopolitical factors are very important scientific and clinical issues to consider in assessing the African American family. Although people of African descent share many common values and experiences, migratory patterns, country of origin, acculturation, and racial identity contribute to the variability to which African Americans exhibit these values.

The Buffering Role of Ethnic Identity

To cope adequately, the African American family and individuals within it have had to learn to adapt to the challenges posed by the stigma of race, slavery, and the early constitutional laws that defined the African as 3/5 human. To be of African descent in this country is to contend with power and status differentials, social position, prejudices, cultural pluralism, and conformity (Boykin, 1986). Ogbu (1981) provides convincing data in his arguments that in this country, African Americans are relegated to a caste-like minority status. Unlike class systems, within caste-like societies race or skin color predetermines one's social status and social roles for life. Ogbu (1981) posits that low school achievement and dysfunction among some African American children are linked to their attributions regarding their caste-like minority status and their internalization of our society's low expectations of them. Thus, to be of African descent is to struggle with the cumulative effects of institutional racism. I would argue that dysfunction for the African American is, in part, due to the family's inability to deal with racism and to provide its members a sense of belonging and ethnic identity. Salient features of dysfunctional African American families includes a movement away from culturally based African-centered values and social marginality. These conditions may place the family at increasing risk for parentifying practices.

Ethnic identity and cultural traditions serve two broad buffering functions. According to Phinney (1996), ethnic identity attempts to ensure a deep emotional bond and a mechanism for self-definition, a way of defining self based on cultural beliefs that ensures survival and psychological resilience in relation to the negative influences of the dominant group. As part of child rearing,

African American families, via cultural values, have had to affirm themselves and to teach children ways of learning to interact effectively with the environment (Stevenson, 1995). Cultural traditions provide an anchor that enables the group to determine for itself which realties to accept and which to neglect. The modeling and teaching of cultural pride have been shown to be an effective means to increase self-concept (Crocker, Luhtanen, Blaine, & Broadnax, 1994), educational achievement (Bowman & Howard, 1985), psychological adjustment (Taylor, Casten, & Flickinger, 1993), and interests in the African American community (Stevenson, Cameron, & Herrero-Taylor, in press).

RECONSTRUCTING PARENTIFICATION

An assumption that I make in this chapter is that culture structures our reality. Lakoff (1989) contends that in accordance with socially accepted value systems, all humans impose categories or schema to structure their understanding of nature. Moreover, the roles of linguistic systems and metaphors in determining culturally relevant domains are well documented (Lakoff & Johnson, 1980). Sampson (1993) has taken issue with the field of psychology because of our tendency to apply an implicit standard that emphasizes Euro-American values as an implicit universal norm. For example, Sampson (1993) would contend that if we describe a child as parentified, then we are making a relational judgment that implicitly assumes a cultural standard. That is, calling a behavior "parentified" is but an inference based on the outcome of a comparative process made against an implicit and imposed standard. At work is an epistemological bias grounded in culturally determined Western/American beliefs about child development, family relations, and social roles. If the implicit standard is ignored in making relational judgments in evaluating families of African descent, then the field may be prone to value biases that I consider to be Type I, or errors in saying that there is a problem when one does not exist.

Type I errors are evident when clinical cases lead to early terminations, increased resistances, anger among family members, and suspicion of mental health professionals within the African American community. Moreover, Type I errors also may surface when broad, imprecise terms serve as proxies for political objectives for labeling ethnic minority families as dysfunctional (see Moynihan, 1965).

Categorization or the diagnosis of a phenomenon like parentification should be based on culturally specific empirical research. It should be founded, at least, on quantified data and a culturally based theory. At present, such a database and theory do not exist. Moreover, there is no mention of parentification in the African American family literature. This may not necessarily mean that within African American families the behaviors that we have labeled parentification are not culturally valid. It does mean, though, that within African American families, we must proceed with great care in defining families as parentified.

TABLE 9.3 Clinical Interview

---

1. Using Pinderhughes's framework, determine which values are important to the family. Assess which culture the family identifies with. Determine which African-centered value the family retained.

2. Determine the family's worldview of healthy family functioning. In the assessment, determine if there is congruence between the worldviews of the family and the ethnic group that the family belongs to. Try to gauge the potential cultural contributions to symptoms and behaviors.

3. Try to determine if the family pattern has functional value by examining the meaning of the behavior to the family and to others in the environment.

4. Assess each family member's attitudes, attributions, and expectations about ethnic identity, family roles, child-rearing practices, household arrangements, and community and religious practices.

5. Investigate how socioeconomic and political factors influenced the psychosocial development of family members.

6. Ask questions regarding reactions to racial oppression and racism.

Thus, the clinical assessment of families of African descent should proceed with caution.

Clinical and Assessment Issues

An assessment of African American family functioning should include multiple levels of both behavioral and phenomenological data. The sole reliance on assessment instruments and test data will place the clinician at risk for committing a Type I error; thus, the use of cultural informants, behavioral observations, and conceptual systems that assess a family's competence in *interacting* and *adapting* to the environment are recommended. As Dana (1993) recommends, clients should play an active role in the assessment process. They should be relied on to explicate their worldviews, cultural values, and interpretation of the behavior that is in question. As Table 9.3 illustrates, the clinician should rely on open-ended questions that would allow for an understanding of the conceptual world of the family.

A systems view, in the broadest of terms, is recommended. A professional standard to determine the appropriateness of the relationship between a child and the parent may be just one standard to assess parentification. The behavioral pattern between child and parent should be juxtaposed with questions such as "Is the behavioral pattern a cultural norm?" and "Is the behavioral pattern acceptable and beneficial to the family?" The way in which child-rearing practices and family patterns are developed, experienced, and understood by all members of the family unit as well as their cultural group must be evaluated. The aim of the assessment should be on determining the functionality of behavior or why this pattern exists. As such, the clinician should be mindful that interdependence within families, flexible family roles, grandmothers' involvement in child rearing, and in some families the rapid movement of children through early developmental milestones is purposeful and reflects common practices within African American families.

The assessment of parentification should include behavioral observations and conceptual systems that measure a family's competence in interacting and adapting to the environment. Such an approach gives considerable attention to factors external to the relationship that affect healthy functioning. How environmental conditions, racism, acculturation, and economic status are experienced and understood and coped with should be assessed and taken into consideration. At the core of the evaluation is the question concerning the parent-child relationship. Is the relationship really the factor that causes the most concern?

This perspective, although not the ideal, is much less susceptible to Type I errors. Even so, it is still difficult for someone outside the culture or a professional trained within a linear universalist tradition to define what a cultural group determines to be appropriate. For example, "How do we understand a cultural norm?" "Should we determine for the family and child what is acceptable and what is inappropriate?" "What is the appropriate definition for a person whose family functioning differs from the acceptable professional standard?" Indeed, there may be a real concern when a family manifests characteristics of parentification, but the real challenge for the professional is how to understand these behavioral and emotional patterns in the light of both the cultural understandings of the group and society's role in how these patterns are developed.

As professionals, we are trained to work competently within a Western model. Many scholars have written extensively about how the field of psychology in general and our notions of mental health in particular are rooted in Western European traditions (Lutz, 1985; Nobles, 1980). We are versed in the understanding of the fundamentals of human behavior, but moving outside our frameworks to understand how cultures derive meaning from their experiences present challenges for us. An understanding of the worldview of a cultural group and what members of ethnocultural groups constitute as their conceptual system would prepare us to become more effective agents of change.

To understand culture requires efforts to assimilate within the world of cultural groups and to accommodate the other group's knowledge of how external events influence ethnic identity and self, as well as "how" and "why" concepts, categories, and schema are created. It could be that family structures, family patterns, and child-rearing practices differ primarily in the contexts in which they are manifested. Thus, it is important to understand our biases and, as much as possible, refrain from hastily imposing our own conceptual systems and values on phenomena across cultures. Instead, we should pay closer attention to cultural and historical interpretations within the stories that families reveal to us. These stories may tell us what factors influence behavior, but more important, these stories may lead us to more effective understandings. African Americans have relied on an oral tradition in the form of "The Old Negro Spirituals" to tell their stories. These spirituals are at the core of the African's spirituality. Spirituals tell many important stories that have been passed on for generations. Listening to and examining these spirituals will provide a health provider with an understanding of the values, worldviews, and strengths of African Americans.

CONCLUSIONS

This discussion of parentification underlines the importance of developing models that allow for a sociocultural or contextual understanding of family functioning. The arguments presented suggest that as a social construct, parentified family patterns are determined by social and situational factors and defined in cultural terms. I question theories that search for the essence or universalities of behavior. Human behavior should be understood within its social context.

An implication of this chapter is that cultural beliefs and values have an important impact on the development of theories to understand family patterns. As theoreticians, practitioners, or researchers, our cultural values shape our motives, experiences, and intentions. Understanding the assumptions and values that underlie the development of new phenomena such as parentification is just as important as the understanding of the phenomena themselves. In some regards, this process of questioning the underpinnings of the construct of parentification is a push to move us away from universalistic assumptions to a more contextually grounded view of African American families.

Among the most important cultural values for African Americans are spirituality, interdependence, collectivism, and survival of the group. Accurate interpretation of family patterns of African Americans are contingent on an understanding of what values are applicable and how to interpret them within a given context. Moreover, the unit of observation, assessment, and intervention should include not only the primary social group (i.e., the family) but also the influence of social institutions and sociopolitical factors. An adequate understanding of families of African descent would require an appreciation and an assessment of the impact of cultural, sociopolitical, and historical experiences that are unique to that group as well as the interpretations and the cultural meanings that are ascribed to these behaviors and experiences.

Although the understanding of cultural values and the impact of sociocultural influences is important, these factors have not been researched extensively. In part, this is because we are wedded to a tradition that de-emphasizes the sociocultural context in which behavior occurs. The utility of the construct of parentification for understanding the family patterns of people of African descent is contingent on the advance of research and theory that is grounded in an African epistemology and the Black reality.

REFERENCES

Akbar, N. (1980). The evolution of human psychology for African Americans. In R. Jones (Ed.), *Black psychology* (pp. 99-122). New York: Harper & Row.

Anderson, L. P. (1991). Acculturative stress: A theory of relevance for black Americans. *Clinical Psychology Review, 11*, 685-702.

Anderson, L. P., Eaddy, C. L., & Williams, E. A. (1990). Psychosocial competence: Toward a theory of understanding positive mental health among Black Americans. In D. Ruiz (Ed.), *Handbook of mental health and mental disorder among black Americans* (pp. 253-272). Westport, CT: Greenwood.

Boszormenyi-Nagy, I., & Spark, G. (1973). *Invisible loyalties: Reciprocity in generational family therapy.* New York: Harper & Row.

Bowman, P., & Howard, C. (1985). Race related socialization, motivation, and academic achievement: A study of Black youths in three-generational families. *Journal of the American Academy of Child Psychiatry, 24*, 131-141.

Boykin, A. W. (1986). The triple quandary and the schooling of Afro American children. In U. Neisser (Ed.), *The school achievement of minority children* (pp. 57-92). Hillsdale, NJ: Erlbaum.

Clark, C. (1972). Black studies or the study of black people? In R. Jones (Ed.), *Black psychology* (1st ed., pp. 45-59). New York: Harper & Row.

Crocker, J., Luhtanen, R., Blaine, B., & Broadnax, S. (1994). Collective self-esteem and psychological well-being among White, Black, and Asian college students. *Personality and Social Psychology Bulletin, 20*, 503-513.

Dana, R. H. (1993). *Multicultural assessment perspectives for professional psychology.* Needham Heights, MA: Allyn & Bacon.

Fabrega, H. (1989). Cultural relativism and psychiatric illness. *The Journal of Nervous and Mental Disorder, 177*, 415-425.

Garbarino, J. (1992). *Children and families in the social environment.* New York: Aldine de Gruyter.

Goglia, L. R., Jurkovic, G., Burt, A., & Burge-Callaway, K. (1992). Generational boundary distortions by adult children of alcoholics: Child as parent and child as mate. *The American Journal of Family Therapy, 20*, 291-299.

Gurman, A. S., & Kniskern, D. P. (1991). *Handbook of family therapy.* New York: Brunner/Mazel.

Jones, J. (1991). Psychological models of race: What have they been and what should they be? In J. Goodchilds (Ed.), *Psychological perspectives on human diversity in America* (pp. 3-46). Washington, DC: American Psychological Association.

Jurkovic, G. J. (1997). *Lost childhoods: The plight of the parentified child.* New York: Brunner/Mazel.

Katz, J. H. (1985). The sociopolitical nature of counseling. *The Counseling Psychologist, 13*, 615-624.

Lakoff, G. (1989). *Women, fire, and dangerous things.* Chicago: University of Chicago Press.

Lakoff, G., & Johnson, M. (1980). *Metaphors we live by.* Chicago: University of Chicago Press.

Lowen, A. (1985). *Narcissism: Denial of the true self.* New York: Macmillan.

Lum, D. (1992). *Social work practice and people: A process-stage approach.* Pacific Grove, CA: Brooks/Cole.

Lutz, C. (1985). Ethnopsychology compared to what? Explaining behavior and consciousness among the Ifaluk. In G. M. White & J. Kirkpatrick (Eds.), *Person, self and experience: Exploring Pacific ethnopsychologies* (pp. 735-769). Berkeley: University of California Press.

Mednick, M. T. (1989). The politics of psychological constructs: Stop the bandwagon, I want to get off. *American Psychologist, 44,* 1118-1123.

Minuchin, S., Montalvo, B., Guerney, B. G., Rosman, B., & Schumer, F. (1967). *Families of the slums.* New York: Basic Books.

Moynihan, D. P. (1965). *The negro family: The case for national action.* Washington, DC: Office of Policy Planning and Research, Department of Labor.

Nobles, W. W. (1978). Toward an empirical and theoretical framework for defining Black families. *Journal of Marriage and the Family, 45,* 679-691.

Nobles, W. W. (1980). African philosophy: Foundations for black psychology. In R. Jones (Ed.), *Black psychology.* (pp. 23-37). New York: Harper & Row.

Ogbu, J. U. (1981). Origins of human competence: A cultural ecological perspective. *Child Development, 52,* 413-429.

Pettigrew, T. (1975). *Racial discrimination in the United States.* New York: Harper & Row.

Phinney, J. S. (1996). When we talk about American ethnic groups, what do we mean. *American Psychologist, 51,* 918-927.

Pinderhughes, E. (1982). Afro-American families and the victim system. In M. McGoldrick, J. K. Pearce, & J. Giordano (Eds.), *Ethnicity and family therapy* (pp. 108-122). New York: Guilford.

Pinderhughes, E. (1989). *Understanding race, ethnicity and power: The key to efficacy in clinical practice.* New York: Free Press.

Sampson, E. E. (1993). Identity politics: Challenges to psychology's understanding. *American Psychologist, 48,* 1219-1230.

Stevenson, H. C. (1995). The relationship of racial socialization and racial identity in African American adolescents. *Journal of Black Psychology, 2,* 29-70.

Stevenson, H. C., Cameron., R., & Herrero-Taylor, T. (in press). Merging the ideal and real: Relationship of racial socialization beliefs and experiences for African American youth. In D. Johnson (Ed.), *Racial socialization research.* Hampton, VA: Cobb & Henry.

Taylor, R. D., Casten, R., & Flickinger, S. M. (1993). Influence of kinship social support on the parenting experiences and psychosocial adjustment of African American adolescents. *Developmental Psychology, 29,* 382-388.

Wilson, M. N. (1986). The Black extended family: An analytical consideration. *Developmental Psychology, 22,* 246-258.

Zuckerman, M. (1990). Some dubious premises in research and theory on racial differences. *American Psychologist, 45,* 1297-1303.

CHAPTER 10

The Archetype of the Parentified Child

A Psychosomatic Presence

Paula M. Reeves

The contextual historical roots and inevitable psychosomatic effect of parentification on adulthood are discussed in this chapter using the metaphors of Athena, Hermes, and Sisyphus, figures from Greek mythology. Athena's utilization of intellectualization contrasts with Hermes' avoidance and denial as metaphoric examples with which to broaden our phenomenological understanding of the development of the child's defenses against the diminishing or loss of a central self identity associated with parentification. With each of these complex interior stances, examples of related body symptoms are included to highlight the indiscriminate effect of a narcissistic wound on mind, body, psyche, and soul and experienced, thus, as an alienation *from embodiment*. The contrast between the metaphors of the Athena and Hermes personae will be used as indicators for discerning two of the somatic coping styles of parentification. Sisyphus is offered as a metaphoric description of the repetitive recapitulation inherent to this type of preverbal wounding. It is not my intention to offer possibilities for intervention, but rather to phenomenologically shift our focus from the personal to the collective and back again, perhaps with clearer eyes.

ARCHETYPAL PATTERNS

Carl Jung (1934/1959) utilized the concept of archetype and archetypal energy to amplify much of his belief about the universally unified structure and development of the human psyche. Although Jung would not describe himself as a family systems therapist, his remarkable use of the genealogy and relational dynamics of the Greek cosmology reinforces what family therapists know so well, that the child's psychological health is deeply affected by the unconscious of the larger system, in this case, the parent. Furthermore, as family medical specialists know so well, that the health of the child is intimately reflective of the health of the family.

The concept of psychic archetypal patterns is not unlike that of a biological pattern of behavior. Universally represented in human nature, an archetype is a descriptor of a prototypical psychosomatic dynamic, a pattern that is recognizable across cultures, genders, and races. Archetypes lend a universally recognizable form into which we can place the varying personal contents unique to each individual and each culture. For example, behind all the personal psychosomatic issues with the personal father stands the universally recognizable archetype of Spirit, while lying behind those related to the personal mother is the archetype of Nature, of Matter.

Archetypal patterns describe the equivalently effective potency of both antidote and poison as cure for the somatopsychic dilemma. Each is equally necessary, one needing the other to make sense. This paradox is psychosomatically catalytic. It is discomfortingly so that uncovering and naming the exquisite pain of abandonment threatens to kill the last remnants of hope. "Maybe, just maybe," the grieving adult will plead, "I, we, have overlooked something and I am mistaken. Maybe Mommy loved me just for myself in ways we have yet to uncover." Yet it is equally true that the wound of abandonment must be delicately reopened, cauterized at its deepest point, if the grievously wounded infant is to recover as fully as possible.

The presence of an archetypal pattern, once brought to consciousness, has a psychological impact on the psyche matched by a parallel affectual impact on the body. This impact has a softening effect, homeostatically providing transitional objects whose stories speak directly to the unconscious, relieving the ego of its resistance to remembering the pain. The commonality of an archetype, its universality, is elegantly affirming. Possibly for the first time, the child ego experiences its personal pain as shared by humans everywhere. Eventually, this insight may create a healing bond of understanding between the client and her narcissistically deprived mother, whose own mother withheld from her because her mother . . . and so on. There is, after all, a genealogical, a social and a spiritual context underlying this complexity we are calling "parentification."

ATHENA

Athena, Greek goddess of wisdom and crafts, is depicted as having sprung fully grown and fully armored from the head of her father, Zeus. Protector, adviser, director, and guardian of heroes, she is reputed to rely primarily on the directives and principles of her father. We are told very little about her mother. What we can surmise from the nature of her birth is an absence of embodiment. Birthed from the *logos*, the intellect, of her father, she relates to her keenly focused mind, not to her diffusely instinctual matter. Cooperative and highly achieving, the rational, willful "Athenian" child manages splendidly as a "little adult" while avoiding the messiness of her emotions at all costs.

In the rich context of Greek mythology, we can find the metaphors and developmental maps that provide a lyrical, though no less profound, description of the complex psychosocial interactions that both enhance and thwart individuation. Athena's story has many parallels with the healthier narcissistic dimensions of the child whose truncated or foreshortened childhood becomes the motivation for a well-developed sense of identity that serves her well. Her sense of self, catalyzed by a capacity to relate to the larger context of relationship informed by rational choice, barely hints at a well-concealed deficit. The Athena child has only limited access to her feelings. She can rationalize her way through most any dilemma. Athena's child lives in her head; logic is her law, and perfection is her nemesis. Athena, an only child and a father's daughter, confident of her intellectual grasp on life, knows what she wants and how to develop the *acceptable* tactics to ensure a successful outcome.

HERMES

By contrast, there is Hermes. Born in the morning, Hermes is reputed to have stepped directly out of his cradle, immediately and ruthlessly relieving a passing turtle of its shell, from which he created and played as a lyre by midday. Continuing, he then addressed himself to family dynamics, stole his brother's inheritance, and was back in his cradle by nightfall. The apparent innocence of this infant's sleep masks his ready capacity to relate through manipulation and guile. Only his father has the authority to approve or disapprove of this favored son's behavior. His mother, Maia, is credited with little save Hermes birth and her shyness. Busy, interactive, and manipulative from birth, Hermes performs antics that match the "cunning deception" that often is the primary defense of the child ego that is co-opted into the adult world too soon, without the developmental experiences that will protect her identity from diminishment or eradication by the stronger narcissistic demands of the adult.

Early Bonding/Boundary Confusion

The pendulum of early bonding sways between symbiosis and alienation. Without a parent who is able to welcome and accept the child just as she is, those first rudimentary boundaries between merger and rapprochement are obscured, unreliable. The subphases of separation-individuation, practicing, and rapprochement are orchestrated to meet the parent's needs. The child, unable to differentiate between instinct and performance, internalizes the dissonance as object *inconstancy* (Mahler, Pine, & Bergman, 1975). Eventually, the psychological defenses against the terror and grief over the loss of a securely internalized love object trigger and are triggered by the physical and emotional somatic defenses our culture calls symptoms. Other cultures might see these symptoms as evidence of *soul loss.*

Prolonged boundary confusion leads to a distorted sense of identity. Archetypically, the myths of Athena and Hermes can function as metaphoric descriptions of some of the protective defenses that a child will develop to cope with the developmental issues of boundary and relationship. When a parent usurps the budding selfhood of the child to replace her own lack of a cohesively internalized identity, she vandalizes the child's birthright of conscious embodiment. This mother, unconscious of her own matter, cannot initiate the soul of the child into taking joyful pleasure in the instinctuality of her own body. This mother can neither recognize nor nurture what is foreign to her. She cannot inspire what she herself has never had. Unconsciously, she siphons away the emerging young spirit of the child in order to feed the desperate yearning lodged deeply within her own psyche. Looking into the clear eyes of her newborn for the first time, she recognizes the trusting receptive soul she herself once was. A wicked bargain is struck. Those clear infant eyes, seeking a mirror to reinforce the goodness of the child, are stolen. In a flash, the deprived self of the mother mobilizes and uses the infant's eye as a mirror in which to find her own lost self. The familiar chant, "Mirror, mirror, on the wall, who's the fairest of them all?" is rescripted. "Mirror, mirror, do not see, any image except of me." Archetypically, the positive unconditional mother is displaced by the less individuated personal narcissism of the adult who is emotionally too deficient to separate her needs from those of the child.

A truly parentified child is a disembodied child. Full of the fierceness and intellectual gifts of spirit, maybe, but without an embodied sense of being in matter, of *mattering.* She is left without an affirmation of substantiality, for herself, or to others.

Although the metaphoric behavior of Athena represents the capacity of the parentified child ego able to develop and maintain a strong sense of self (until thwarted), Hermes' behavior is replete with a metaphoric prescription for the child whose lack of a cohesive sense of self compels him to use others without remorse or reflection. The Athena child will resort to righteous indignation when her well-organized intentions are foiled. If she feels betrayed or that her well-defended sense of intimacy is challenged, she can call upon her alter ego, Medusa, whose scathing opinions will turn the interloper to stone. The security of Athena's child lies in perfectionism. Verbal repartee is this child's hallmark, until she is unmasked, her vulnerability revealed; then, rage is her primary defense. Equally, Hermes' frequent unabashed psychic and social "shape-shifting" is not unlike the wiles and charm some parentified children acquire to ensure psychological survival. Security lies in this child's ability to present the persona that secures the moment, discarding relationships and responsibilities as easily as he changes guises. His quick footwork keeps him one step ahead of the depression that follows him. Spiritually, the insidious destructive nature of blurred identity rapes the soul, captures the spirit, and bruises the body. Who are we ever, if not ourselves? The parentified child's psychosomatic desire for authenticity is thwarted by her ongoing struggle to free herself from her relationship to a parent who can neither suffer allowing her to explore her own dependency needs, nor value any evidence of her independence. Metaphorically, this leads to disembodiment, because nothing that does not *matter* to the parent is allowed to *matter* to the child.

Initially, a metaphor's allure resides in its capacity to tell a lie that describes an undeniable unconscious truth. When a metaphor "hits home," it is remarkably transformative, allowing the potency of the truth embedded in the "lie" into consciousness. The metaphoric "lie" disarmingly befriends the ego defense by defusing most of the toxicity, while retaining all the potency, of the repressed, and therefore unexamined, truth. No child has ever "sprung fully grown" from the head of her father, yet an adult who has no recollection of ever being happily dependent, and blissfully at ease with herself, will instantly understand Athena's birthright. The metaphor's paradoxical nature contains the inherent capacity to simultaneously interest the mind, evoke the imagination, and energize the body, mobilizing a mutually shared psychospiritual bodymind gestalt. It is far less threatening to suggest to a client that the protective strategy that is causing her the most grief is not unlike that used by the shape-shifting Hermes, than to name and highlight the mercurial qualities of the defense or the painful self-deception. For the adult who learned, as a child, to purchase relationship with the devalued coin of the false self, the resonant image of "shape-shifting" can ease open a door to an inner truth that has been resolutely off limits. Therapeutically, metaphoric imagery allows a protective defense to remain intact while introducing the mirror of acceptance withheld in infancy and without mobilizing the reactive affect that serves as a sentinel against a breech of ego security.

SISYPHUS

A brief description of the Corinthian hero Sisyphus will help complete the cast for our discussion of the emotional toll that parentification exacts. Sisyphus is the fellow relegated to roll an unwieldy ball up an incline, only to have it endlessly roll backward, to the starting point. The futility of his actions is made worse by the lack of options or choice. Sisyphus must continue his proscribed task unquestioningly, ceaselessly, throughout eternity. So how does one heroic human so displease the gods (parents) that nothing is left except an unsurmountable summit and a path of futile exertion? We are told that Sisyphus arrived at his fate because he was presumptuous, inasmuch as it is forbidden to a human to assume the power of a god.

Ask any adult who was a parentified child. She will tell you of the terrible fate that awaits the child who is falsely empowered by premature and pseudo adulthood. Sisyphus observed Zeus's malfeasance and attempted to use that knowledge to gain power for himself. His purposes uncovered, he was rebuked, with a punishment designed to match the measure of his deceit (Murray, 1897/1898). It does not take the unseen and unechoed infant long to "observe" with the inner vision of the nervous system and the externalized radar of the skin that malfeasance is afoot, perpetrated by the Other. Privilege for the child, it would seem, lies in her ability to be whatever this Other needs. The infant has little recourse for psychic survival but to fill this role in her desperate desire to be found good enough, to please.

Delving further into the myth of Sisyphus, we find he is king of Corinth (in myth, we must read this as the ruling principle of consciousness). When Sisyphus sought to force one of the minor water gods into providing a spring for his parched land in exchange for knowledge about his missing daughter, he stirred up the entire "family of intrapsychic gods." Deceptively, Sisyphus revealed Zeus's role in the abduction in order to get what he wanted from the lesser entity, Asopus. In the cosmology of our interiority, we cannot isolate our commerce with one god without affecting the entire system. The complex and multidimensional effects of our defenses constantly remind us of this psychic economy. Borrowing libido from one place to shore up a deficit in another while damming up libido to avoid the natural line of flow can and does cause chaos. The infant only wants what Sisyphus wanted—water, a fountain of life. The parentified child, like Sisyphus, cannot bribe, coerce, or blackmail the god(s) into giving the life-sustaining substance away except at her peril. To collude with the parent's desire to be parented, the child must psychosomatically deceive herself into believing her role is a "good enough" substitute for what she, herself, needs and is not receiving. This deception insidiously affects every aspect of her evolving selfhood.

Because a deception by its very nature is covert, imbued with the contagious qualities of the occult, one can never predict who or what will be infected by the deceit. Nor can its relentless attraction to further deceptions be slowed once it is set in motion, except by equally relentless pursuit and confrontation. Sisyphus, it would seem, was not naive. Aware of the absolute power and monarchy of Zeus, he challenged that power, lost, and thereby earned his fate. He aspired to a power not his. He is relegated to reenact the exquisite humiliation of powerlessness for eternity.

The parentified child suffers a comparable fate, but with a graphic difference: He does not earn his fate, he inherits it. The deceit that wreaks havoc on the self of the parentified child does not originate with him. The deception begins with the narcissistically deficient parent, and in all likelihood with her parent before her. This deception is thrust on the child in a bargain whose terms are not unlike those earned by the fated Sisyphus. The child, too psychologically unformed to protect herself, is made to believe that she must provide the parent with the narcissistic supplies denied the parent during her own formative years. Furthering the deceit, the child is psychically blackmailed into believing that the parent is too weak, inadequate, entitled, and so on, to be challenged or denied. Instinctually, the child knows that noncompliance guarantees psychic abandonment. The child inherits the "weight" of the parent's neediness and deceptive manipulation, which then must be pushed up the impossible incline of attempting to parent one's own parent. Ultimately, this child is doubly bound. Comply and lose your self; resist, and lose the only mirror available that holds the key to your self. Whether the resolve for psychological survival is Athenian or Hermetic, the task remains Sisyphian.

SYMPTOM AS METAPHOR

The parentified adult who enters psychotherapy in the hope that he will find some relief from the angst that colors life seldom enters with the intention of excoriating the parent (Miller, 1981). The parentified child, especially, reaches adulthood protesting that there was no excessive cost exacted by the loss of childhood. Seldom does she question her family status as the reliable child, "a grownup since birth." Neurotic depression masks the intrapsychic loneliness, abandonment, and emotional deprivation that are the inevitable inheritance of the adult whose childhood was usurped by the psychic betrayal of parenting by an infant in adult's clothing. When our psychic gods are evicted, we feel this loss as a loss of soul. We are left with only the residue of their presence. We call this residue "symptoms." These symptoms matter, with a weight and substance all their own. The body, a shared repository for the affectual story of one's life, symptomatically speaks volumes, sharing the "weight" of a psychic burden in such a way that it can become more manageable.

Poignantly, a client reports

I had an interesting childhood. My mother was delicate so I had to learn to do a lot for myself, and her, since her health was so unreliable. Fortunately I was born grown up. Mother used to tell me it was my job to take care of things just the way she would if she were able. She used to say, "Be my big girl and do everything right. If you don't, I have eyes in the back of my head and I'll know, so no short cuts." I believed her, so I'd work and work to please her. To this day I still feel she is overseeing my every move. My migraines worry me. When I am struck down I can't seem to do anything very thoroughly, except to have these terrible attacks of pain.

There is a lacuna in the psychological literature about the stewardship of sweetness that the body exhibits toward the psyche. Whatever the psyche cannot bear, the body will carry. Whatever the psyche cannot express, the body will demonstrate. In my work, applied psychoneuroimmunology, I have found that every symptom has a psychospiritual message, just as every thought has a somatic (limbic system) response and every psychological defense has some form of physiologic armoring. The migraine that wreaks havoc on the Athena woman's "thoroughness" is painfully embodying the crux of her psychic dilemma. Performance for an introjected and long-since-absent "overseer" goes against her grain. Her symptoms intensify her psychological conundrum to the point of matching her psychical immobility with a physical one. She approaches life by controlling what is manageable while attempting to avoid what is not. Her credo is not to do it, but to do it the absolute best she can in order not to disappoint the absent parent.

The metaphor *going against my grain* is manifest in her physical distress. As a dutiful daughter, she knows only too well how to buck up, tough it out, get a handle on the problem, and do her level best. For the Athena child, keeping one's head is crucial. She copes rationally, cleanly, and neatly. Her body carries any "messiness" as digestive, respiratory, skin, and tension disorders. Migraines, menstrual cramps, and stiff necks are her sad relief. Compliance, adaptation, rebellion, avoidance, intellectualization, and denial, developed for use in the service of parenting the parent, denies the instinctual affects of the child. This denial can be detrimental to recovery when the parentified adult is faced with an illness by undermining hope and a desire to survive.

Coping skills—the ability to utilize a combination of intrapsychic defenses and interpersonal responses in an intrapersonally homeostatic manner—both express and contribute to an individual's sense of self-competency. As the field of psychoneuroimmunology matures, there is a growing body of well-researched documentation linking physical symptoms with repressed and/or unexpressed psychospiritual issues. Our physical body carries the affect of our kinesthetic-psychological interactions from conception onward (Chamberlain, 1988). Each psychically perceived acceptance or rejection, every psychologically perceived satisfaction or dissatisfaction, has a somatic correlate, affecting health and well-being.

When the parentified adult's perception of her capacity to effectively maintain the coping skills of her childhood is challenged, she is at risk to develop a higher level of stress, with a strong probability for concurrent somatic distress. Her identity depends on maintaining the tension between cooperating with (yielding her needs to) an authority figure, such as a doctor, while concealing the growing panic over the perceived loss of control. When an adult parentified child becomes a patient, this tension adds exponentially to the stress of the illness.

In the case of the woman with migraines, the metaphoric description of her debilitating pain stabilized her eroding sense of control by providing a nonthreatening way she could talk about the roots of her pain. She was able to describe how her mother's dependency went against her *grain* as a child. Expanding the metaphor, a *wrinkle* in a relationship can become a *pleat*, skewing the *grain*, making "things" messy, *uneven*. Most parentified children do not give much credence to body signals. The keenly honed sensorium that alerts them to the needs of others is seldom used in their own behalf until the affect becomes acute (Miller, 1981). Once the defense is breached by physical or emotional pain, particularly if the veneer of the false self is pierced, as with a life-threatening disease or prolonged chronicity, the lacuna developed in infancy takes over. Adults with histories of parentification are especially prone to struggle against trusting their body. Parentification prepares their child ego for the exigencies of a loss of power, of defeat, because they never can get the "ball" to the top of the hill. Nor do they dare rest between tries. The consistent ambivalence about the terms of their embodied (mattering) status in the family makes any imminent threat of somatic defeat terrifying. Psychologically, the dependency needs stimulated by somatic vulnerability are synonymous with psychic annihilation because such a person perceives himself as having no one to rely on but *myself.*

EMPATHY AS "GOOD ENOUGH" PARENT

The parentified child is keenly sensitive to the needs of others but doesn't *feel* their need. Instead, he *intuits* or *anticipates* it. The Geiger counter with which he measures the emotional fault lines in another is rigorously governed by his psyche, with stringent guards against any overt participation by his body. I believe that empathy is for the adult what mirroring is to the child. The loss of mirroring in childhood is so painful that it blunts the self-reflective (empathic) sensitivity needed in order to identify, differentiate, and somatically experience personal feelings. One man describes it thus: "I didn't dare let myself feel the real depth of my feelings because every time I tried I was overwhelmed with such a powerful wave of loneliness I felt out of control. I imagined my feelings like a great hole where I could be sucked away, so I refused to let the full impact ever surface and tip me in." The refusal, while essentially self-protective, also blunts genuine affect, causing an inability to relate empathically to self or others in an authentically experiential way. Many therapists, parentified children themselves, listen many hours a day to the sorrow-filled reports of a childhood they personally know only too well. They too have learned not to feel this particular loss, so they re-parent the infant before them intellectually and behaviorally, but not experientially. Many a therapist has at his ready disposal the creative logic and fortitude of Athena, the soulful guardianship of Hermes, when working with the miseries of the disembodied child before him, until he becomes countertransferred; then, Medusa freezes all empathy, or the Trickster colludes with the original deception, much to the therapist's dismay. He quickly learns that his own narcissistic deficits must be listened to and embodied if he is not to sicken himself or the client by ignoring his child ego's need for empathy while creating a recapitulation of the earlier parenting.

The parentified child usually grows into adulthood psychologically groomed for a life of service to others. Voyeuristically, the emotional lives of others become the catalyst for alleviating the intrapersonal suffering that has been denied emotional expression. When another's overt expression of emotional energy cathects a parentified adult's covert feeling, she is susceptible to infection by the cause, complaint, or celebration. With no practiced authentic emotional voice of her own, she is at risk for inserting her own unarticulated affectual energies into someone else's articulated emotional charge, whether or not it reflects her true feelings. Parentified therapists are especially at risk for capture by this dynamic.

Hermes is a splendid example of the persona of the chameleon, whose role-shifting deflects true feelings while maintaining a counterfeit affectual identity. As a youngster, Hermes was charming and quick to steal whatever he lacked. His capacity for protective mimicry, coupled with an ability to reverse his persona at will, merits his designation as the trickster god. Conversely, his adroit footwork, coupled with lightning quick moves, qualifies him as the god of communication, able to maintain the inevitable ambivalence fostered by competing possibilities until a decision is made. He survives his brief childhood by artfully bartering for power. To his advantage, the Hermes child develops an ability to anticipate what he has that others want. Sadly, his penchant for immediate emotional gratification leaves him susceptible to ill-conceived relationships. Having learned that each psychic barter of exchange can only be finessed via manipulation, the anticipated relief of his acquisition is experienced as ingenuine, an ill-gotten gain. Thus, he frequently lies to protect his marginal powers, to avoid exposure. Oddly enough, in adulthood the Hermes child often exhibits the god's finer qualities as messenger-diplomat, as guardian of the crossroads, or as guide to the soul on its journey to the underworld (Bolen, 1989).

How can this be, that a liar, thief, and manipulator is also psychopomp of souls? Any child bereft of access to a true identity knows instinctually, and experientially, the distractions he must maintain to avoid exposing the impostor he fears he is. Of course he will resort to trickery to regain what is, by all rights, his to begin with. Given the tiniest opportunity, the same willfully deceptive child, identifying with another's pain, will respond with acts of tenderness that astonish the parent. Later, his means of coping compromised by his tenderness, the adult parentified child will behave in ways that are so oppositional to the false persona of deceptiveness as to create intrapersonal psychospiritual dissonance. Often, this dissonance precipitates therapy.

HISTORICAL CONTEXT

Concern and interest in the dynamic of parentified children are modern phenomena. Until recent history, children were regarded as commodities. The Victorians, with their penchant to romanticize the reprehensible abuses inflicted on their children (note the tender poignant tale of the Little Match Girl, who, orphaned and destitute, incidentally freezes to death while attempting to make a living), fluffed and dolled their children up in the literary veneer of protective adoration. Meanwhile, women and children remained the property of a society who primarily found them useful as tools of labor or pleasure. A sense of individuality, of self, was of no consideration.

The industrial age brought a migration from country to town, heralding a redistribution of community as resource, a restructuring of family roles, and a further devaluation of nature, nurture, and ritual. Closely knit multigenerational families, no longer stewards of the land, their legacy of relationship and shared community values breached, suffered most as the depersonalizing motives of power and profit emerged. The village that once reared a child was slowly replaced by the nuclear family, with mother as the primary socializer and caregiver. Tragically, as the role of mothering was increasingly separated from the concerns of the extended family, it too was devalued, reflecting the corollary devaluation of females. Predictably, the values of the feminine incurred a similar devaluation. The historical value of maternal wisdom receded, along with respect for mothering. Suzanne Segal, in her book *Collision With the Infinite* (1996), speaking of the limits on her own psychic availability during her daughter's formative years, says she learned that even the most minimal unconditional "mothering mothers." The key word here is "mothering." Across the last two centuries, nature, nurture, and childhood have diverged, lending a certain quality of irreparable psychospiritual damage to each succeeding generation.

Today, primary caregivers may change monthly as children in earliest infancy are passed from baby-sitter to baby-sitter. Age-old blessings of natural birth—breast-feeding, naming, family beds, and being held, stroked, and rocked in innumerable familiar arms—have fallen by the wayside, victims of modernity. We cannot overemphasize how much the deprivation of touch, echoing, and mirroring in a woman's childhood corrupts her instinct to bond with her baby after she gives birth. Such deprivation leaves an indelible stamp of insecurity etched in the psychosomatic memory of the woman. This loss is experienced psychoneuronally in the body (Rossi, 1986). Unconsciously, she is blocked from freely giving her baby what she never had, nor can she easily bear to see her child get such supplies at what appears to be the mother's expense. Alice Miller (1981) says these parents are "looking for what their own parents could not give them at the correct time—the presence of a person who is completely aware of them and takes them seriously, who admires and follows them" (p. 7). They find such a person in the infant who cannot take her eyes off the mother.

TREATMENT

The myth of Athena and Hermes share a common detail, the significant lack of an active influential mother figure. I believe there has to be a significant absence of mothering if a child is to succumb to parentification. Mothering is not to be confused with parenting. Parenting is what a caregiver *does*, mothering is what a caregiver *is*. Parenting teaches the child socially acceptable standards within the hierarchical relationship of adult and child. Parenting teaches the child how and when to limit his instinctual energies. Parenting provides the child with the necessary conditional impediments to total self-absorption while allowing for practice with self-reflection. The child must learn that her temper tantrums will not rule the world and, furthermore, that her behavior will affect herself. Mothering gives the child the stimuli needed to awaken a sensory context of safe, secure embodiment. Mothering protectively envelops the primary instinctual relationship between neonate and the other, providing an unconditional psychosomatic boundary flexible enough to permit eventual psychological separation. The unconditional yet well-bound flexibility of mothering provides varying degrees of intrapersonal insurance against the risk of an irreparable rupture in the psychosomatic bond during each differentiated stage of separation. Parenting mobilizes the ego; mothering mobilizes the self. Each is needed to organize and socialize the child that will "father the adult" during the prolonged period of human infant and childhood dependency. Both parenting and mothering can be provided by either gender. Erich Neumann (1949/1973) reminds us that the hero, the fully individuated self, is nurtured at the breast of both father and mother. Although these two relational gestalts (parent, mother) are by no means exclusive of each other, neither are they necessarily inclusive. Parenting and mothering each provide psychosocial definition in the differentiation of consciousness. Athena's father can be said to have mothered her to some extent, whereas Zeus barely parented Hermes.

The absence of mothering for the Hermes child distorts his ability to trust being cared for or cared about. This mistrust sends him reeling through life shifting emotional gears and relationships in a misdirected effort to acquire what is missing. The search for self is concretized through the acquisition of *more*, compounded by the affectual experience of *never enough*. More often than not, he will disguise his interior emptiness with the razzle-dazzle of avoidance, masterfully concealed through a screen of projections and rationalizations. Hermes children, when parentified, are skillful at the artifice of reversal. In the consulting room, they often appear to *almost* fit the profile of an as-if personality (Deutsch, 1942). This may be in direct relationship to their inner reality of living as an impostor, in a persona not their own. Once trust is established, however, instead of splitting when approached at a point of deep vulnerability, they will let down their guard and accept brief moments of being seen and echoed as the transference deepens and the bits and fragments of the missing identity are remembered and reclaimed.

The absence of mothering propels the Athena child into an intellectual relationship of reason and inquiry. This child suffers from an urgency to always stay ahead of others. Her drive to compete is often subtly disguised as she manages the last word or designs the best idea. She is reasonable beyond reason. The Athena adult can baffle the therapist with her rational explanations for why therapy is not working or her effusive appreciation for what she designates as "correct." She must have the upper hand even when she is the one going down for the count. The unwary therapist can be sliced by Athena's rapier tongue and paralyzed by her Medusian fury. Once she feels that therapy is not a contest but a mutual effort, though, she will eagerly weave together the stories of her life into a tapestry of tensile strength.

Narcissistic wounds are toxic. Hermes adults often have physical problems related to the lower half of the body. This probably is a function of the somatic response to the incapacity of the ego to reorganize itself against the downward psychosomatic pull of the need to be constantly avoidant, "on the move." The greater the toxicity, the deeper and stronger the wall around the repression, the more the investment in the defenses that secure the anonymity of the protective perimeter. In the quest for the recovery of an authentic sense of self, the Hermes child will be more dysfunctionally affected than the Athena child, who actively and effectively uses her focused intellect to resolve her identity issues. Broader, more self-defeating deficits in identify formation (such as Hermes) are registered especially in the tissue and bone reality of the body. What matters to the infant, tactilely, kinesthetically, nutritionally, and neuronally, is recorded in her matter. The original contact between mother and infant during those first crucial months both inspires and impedes healthy individuation. If nurturance is in short supply, the body develops armor to protect against the loss. The affects of the emotional life are spawned by the limbic system, the human body's liquid mind. The limbic system remembers, the body responds. The psyche cooperates and agrees to forget anything that will compromise the somatic shield. Some losses are too profoundly threatening to allow anywhere near the threshold of conscious remembrance. Those experiences lodge themselves deep within the body's major organs, as an illness or dis-ease of elimination, assimilation, circulation, and sexuality. Those that are more accessible to consciousness often reside closer to the surface, as possibilities we have already discussed for the Athena personality.

CONCLUSION AND SUMMARY

Parentification is not a curse to be endured, it is a profound liability that, with therapy, one may come to understand and deal with. With increasing frequency, therapists are witness to a profound loss of childhood, caused not by the demands and requirements of the narcissistically impaired parent but inflicted on the child because of an external catastrophe of war, famine, poverty, or epidemic. Listening to the heart-wrenching tales of extreme courage or acts of extraordinary sacrifice the child had to perform when thrust into the role of parent to her own injured or deeply depressed parent, one can only weep at the depth of the wound and marvel at the integrity of the self for survival. With this consideration, the scope of our present definition of parentification must be revised in future examinations, to include the dire consequences of social and environmental events that will affect not only the parent-child relationship but entire communities as well, forcing children by the score to spring fully grown from the rubble of the catastrophe.

The scope of healing and the definition of health must be widened to include the bodymind, bridging the gap between psyche as the concern of mental health, and soma as the concern of physical health, in order to recognize and respond to the intimate relationship between the two. With war, poverty, famine, and illness, a profound depersonalization can occur. As healers, it is our responsibility to recognize that the soul has many languages. We must learn the multilinguality of soul's voice lest we inadvertently pathologize the bodymind's attempts toward wholeness.

REFERENCES

Bolen, J. S. (1989). *Gods in everyman.* San Francisco: Harper & Row.

Chamberlain, D. (1988). *Babies remember birth.* New York: Ballantine.

Deutsch, H. (1942). Some forms of emotional disturbance and their relationship to schizophrenia. *Psychoanalytic Quarterly, 11,* 302-321.

Jung, C. (1959). *The archetypes and the collective unconscious* (Collected Works, Vol. 9, Part 1, Bollingen Series XX, R. F. C. Hull, Trans.). Princeton, NJ: Princeton University Press. (Original work published 1934)

Mahler, M., Pine, F., & Bergman, A. (1975). *The psychological birth of the infant.* New York: Basic Books.

Miller, A. (1981). *The drama of the gifted child.* New York: Basic Books.

Murray, A. S. (1898). *Manual of mythology* (Revised by W. H. Klapp). Philadelphia: Henry Altemus. (Original work published 1897)

Neumann, E. (1973). *Origins of consciousness* (Bollingen Series XLII, R. F. C. Hull, Trans.). Princeton, NJ: Princeton University Press. (Original work published in 1949)

Rossi, E. L. (1986). *The psychobiology of mind-body healing.* New York: W. W. Norton.

Segal, S. (1996). *Collision with the infinite: A life beyond the personal self.* San Diego: Blue Dove Press.

Index

185

About the Authors

Louis P. Anderson, Ph.D., is Associate Professor in the Department of Psychology at Georgia State University in Atlanta, Georgia. His research interests focus on developing a culturally based approach to the study of mechanisms of stress and coping among African Americans. His publications deal with advancing an ethnocultural perspective in psychology. He serves on the editorial boards of *The Journal of Black Psychology* and *The Journal of Gender, Culture, and Health*.

Nancy D. Chase, Ph.D., M.S.W., is Associate Professor in the Department of Academic Foundations and the Department of English at Georgia State University in Atlanta, Georgia. She is also a licensed social worker in clinical practice at Atlanta Area Child Guidance Clinic, where she works primarily with adolescents and adults. She has published numerous articles on variables affecting students' adjustment to college, including family alcoholism, literacy tasks and experiences, and reader responses to text. Her work has been published in *Alcoholism Treatment Quarterly*, *The American Journal of Family Therapy*, *Journal of Reading Behavior*, and *The Journal of Developmental Education*.

Helen W. Coale, M.S.W., is a clinical social worker and marriage and family therapist, and is the Director of Atlanta Area Child Guidance Clinic in Atlanta, Georgia. She has been in clinical practice in the Atlanta area since 1969. As a clinical social worker and marriage and family therapist, she speaks and publishes extensively on child and family mental health, divorce, stepfamilies, child abuse, humor in psychotherapy, and cultural, contextual, and ethical aspects of psychotherapy. She has recently published *The Vulnerable Therapist: Practicing Psychotherapy in an Age of Anxiety*.

Deborah Jacobvitz, Ph.D., is Associate Professor at the University of Texas at Austin in the Department of Human Ecology, Child Development, and Family

Relations, and is the current president of the Southwest Society for Research in Human Development. She is well known for her extensive work on boundary disturbances across multiple generations and the development of Attention-Deficit Hyperactivity Disorder in young children. She has published papers on family systems, the intergenerational transmission of attachment, identity development in young adults, and relationship violence. Her research has appeared in *Child Development, Developmental Psychology, Development and Psychopathology, Human Development,* and *The American Academy of Child and Adolescent Psychiatry,* and her work has been featured in *The Atlantic Monthly* and in *Parenting.*

Elizabeth Johnson is a doctoral student in Child Development and Family Relationships at the University of Texas at Austin. She specializes in the study of parenting and marriage. Her dissertation is a study of first-time parents' decision-making about employment and child care. Her research on the development of parental preferences about the division of child care has been published in the *Journal of Marriage and Family.*

Rebecca Jones, Ph.D., is Associate Professor and Director of Practicum Training at the Georgia School of Professional Psychology in Atlanta, Georgia. She leads seminars in psychotherapy and family therapy, teaches introductory family therapy, and writes and conducts workshops in the areas of childhood parentification, adult children of divorce, integrative psychotherapy, and women's issues. She maintains a private psychotherapy practice for adults and couples in Atlanta.

Gregory J. Jurkovic, Ph.D., is Associate Professor in the Department of Psychology at Georgia State University in Atlanta, Georgia. He also has a part-time private practice, is an approved supervisor in the American Association of Marriage and Family Therapy, and is known internationally for his research on parentified children. He is author of *Lost Childhoods: The Plight of the Parentified Child,* and has published extensively in the areas of clinical child and family psychology.

Bruce Lackie, Ph.D., is a psychotherapist in private practice in Philadelphia, Pennsylvania, and a faculty member in the doctoral clinical social work program of Walden University, a distance learning institution (WaldenU@edu). He is known for his extensive study of parentification in the family histories of 1,500 professional social workers.

Suzanne Lamorey, Ph.D., is a faculty member in the Department of Curriculum and Instruction and Early Childhood Education at Arizona State University in Tempe, Arizona. Her expertise and research focus is on special education and children with developmental disabilities.

Richard Morrell, J.D., is Vice President of the Meridian Educational Resource Group, Inc., a nonprofit community-based outreach program for children and families in Atlanta, Georgia. He is also pursuing a doctoral degree in Clinical Psychology at Georgia State University and is currently researching children's responses to interparental conflict.

Paula M. Reeves, Ph.D., is a Jungian psychotherapist in private practice in Atlanta, Georgia. She investigates and writes about the mind-body connection in the psychotherapeutic process, and is the author of the forthcoming *Women's Intuition: Unlocking the Wisdom of the Body.*

Shelley Riggs, M.A., is a doctoral student in Counseling Psychology in the Department of Educational Psychology at the University of Texas at Austin. She has conducted research in the areas of gifted and talented education, family systems, and sibling relationships. She is currently exploring the clinical implications of adult attachment, and loss and trauma.

Bryan E. Robinson, Ph.D., is Professor of Counseling, Special Education, and Child Development in the College of Education at the University of North Carolina at Charlotte. He also maintains a private psychotherapy practice in Charlotte, North Carolina, and has authored numerous books and research publications on family functioning. He is distinguished for his ground-breaking research on work addiction and its impact on the family. His latest book is *Chained to the Desk: A Guidebook for Workaholics, Their Partners and Children, and the Clinicians Who Treat Them.*

Alison Thirkield, M.A., a doctoral candidate in Clinical Psychology at Georgia State University, is currently completing her predoctoral internship at the Center for Preventive Psychiatry, White Plains, New York. Her research has focused on designing and evaluating measures of child and adult parentification.

Marolyn Wells, Ph.D., is Director of Training and an Associate Professor at Georgia State University's Counseling Center. She holds a joint appointment with the Department of Counseling and Psychological Services at Georgia State University. In addition, she maintains a part-time private psychotherapy practice in Atlanta, Georgia, and has published more than 20 articles and two books, including *Object Relations Therapy: An Interactive and Individualized Approach to Diagnosis and Treatment.*

Printed in the United Kingdom
by Lightning Source UK Ltd.
125200UK00002B/43-51/A